The Congress at York

Joe Farrell • Lawrence Knorr • Joe Farley

Mechanicsburg, PA USA

Published by Sunbury Press, Inc.
Mechanicsburg, PA USA

www.sunburypress.com

Copyright © 2025 by Joe Farrell, Joe Farley, and Lawrence Knorr.
Cover Copyright © 2025 by Sunbury Press, Inc.

Sunbury Press supports copyright. Copyright fuels creativity, encourages diverse voices, promotes free speech, and creates a vibrant culture. Thank you for buying an authorized edition of this book and for complying with copyright laws. Except for the quotation of short passages for the purpose of criticism and review, no part of this publication may be reproduced, scanned, or distributed in any form without permission. You are supporting writers and allowing Sunbury Press to continue to publish books for every reader. For information contact Sunbury Press, Inc., Subsidiary Rights Dept., PO Box 548, Boiling Springs, PA 17007 USA or legal@sunburypress.com.

For information about special discounts for bulk purchases, please contact Sunbury Press Orders Dept. at (855) 338-8359 or orders@sunburypress.com.

To request one of our authors for speaking engagements or book signings, please contact Sunbury Press Publicity Dept. at publicity@sunburypress.com.

FIRST SUNBURY PRESS EDITION: July 2025

Set in Adobe Garamond Pro | Interior design by Crystal Devine | Cover by Lawrence Knorr | Edited by Lawrence Knorr.

Publisher's Cataloging-in-Publication Data
Names: Farrell, Joe, author | Farley, Joe, author | Knorr, Lawrence, author.
Title: The Congress at York / Joe Farrell Lawrence Knorr Joe Farley.
Description: First trade paperback edition. | Mechanicsburg, PA : Sunbury Press, 2025.
Summary: The participants in the Continental Congress, when exiled to York, Pennsylvania, during 1777 and 1778, are covered in detail.
Identifiers: ISBN : 979-8-88819-405-8(paperback).
Subjects: HISTORY / United States / Revolutionary Period (1775-1800) | BIOGRAPHY & AUTOBIOGRAPHY / Political.

Designed in the USA
0 1 1 2 3 5 8 13 21 34 55

For the Love of Books!

Contents

Introduction... vii

The Presidents

John Hancock The Signature... 3
Henry Laurens First President of the Recognized USA 9

The Secretary

Charles Thomson Secretary of the Continental Congress 17

The Delegates

Eliphalet Dyer "... an honest, worthy man ..." 25
William Williams Puritan Patriot 29
Nathan Brownson Physician, Congressman, Governor 35
George Walton The Orphaned Founder................................... 38
Charles Carroll of Carrollton The Catholic Signer 42
John Adams Second to George.. 48
Samuel Adams Boston's Radical Revolutionary 53
Elbridge Gerry Founder of Gerrymandering 59
Nathaniel Folsom Merchant Militiaman................................. 65
John Witherspoon President of Princeton.............................. 69
James Duane Conservative Founder..................................... 74
William Duer "The Panic of 1792" 79
Cornelius Harnett Hero of Cape Fear.................................. 84
John Penn The Penn with a Pen.. 87
Robert Morris Revolutionary Financier 90
Daniel Roberdeau Pennsylvania Associator............................. 95
Thomas Heyward Jr. The Last to Sign the Declaration 100
Arthur Middleton Defender of Charleston.............................. 105

Benjamin Harrison V Father and Great-Grandfather of Presidents......... 111
Joseph Jones Uncle of James Monroe, Friend of Washington.............. 118
Francis Lightfoot Lee Virginia Congressman........................ 121
Richard Henry Lee Resolution for Independence..................... 125
Richard Law A Judge Named Law.................................. 131
Samuel Chase First to be Impeached............................... 134
James Lovell Teacher, Orator, Signer, Spy........................... 138
Thomas Burke States' Rights Congressman.......................... 142
Henry Marchant Liberty Lawyer................................... 146
William Smith Merchant Congressman.............................. 151
Jonathan Elmer America's First Doctor............................. 154
John Harvie Friend of Jefferson................................... 158
Benjamin Rumsey Soldier, Congressman, Judge...................... 162
William Clingan Chester County Continental Congressman............. 164
William Ellery Early Abolitionist................................. 168
Edward Langworthy An Orphaned Founder........................ 172
Joseph Wood Pennsylvania Transplant.............................. 175
Francis Lewis "All That Glitters Is Not Gold"....................... 177
George Frost Sea Captain Congressman............................. 183
Abraham Clark House burned, sons tortured........................ 185
James Smith York's Radical Revolutionary.......................... 189
Jonathan Bayard Smith Quaker Educator........................... 193
Francis Dana Congressman at Valley Forge.......................... 196
Thomas McKean The Simultaneous Governor of Delaware and
   Chief Justice of Pennsylvania..................................... 199
Governeur Morris The Penman of the Constitution................... 204
James Forbes Forgotten Congressman............................... 209
John Henry Jr. First Senator...................................... 211
Nathaniel Scudder "The Only Congressman to Die in Battle".......... 214
Samuel Huntington First President of the United States?.............. 218
Oliver Wolcott Connecticut Yankee................................ 222
William Henry Drayton Died in Philadelphia........................ 226
Joseph Reed President of Pennsylvania.............................. 229
Thomas Adams Delegate from Virginia.............................. 233

John Banister The Master of Hatcher's Run 236
George Plater Master of Sotterley 240
John Mathews "The Disagreeable One" 244
Roger Sherman Three-Fifths Compromise 248
Philip Livingston Died in York 252
Richard Hutson First Mayor of Charleston 256
Dr. Josiah Bartlett First Vote for Independence 260
John Wentworth Jr. New Hampshire Scion 266
John Collins Rhode Island Representative 270
Samuel Holten Physician Continental Congressman 274
Titus Hosmer Connecticut Lawyer 278

Appendix A: List of Delegates to York 282
Appenix B: The Articles of Confederation 284
Sources 293
Index 297

Introduction

General William Howe had personally led the assault on the center of American forces at Breed's Hill in 1775, realizing the price that would be paid by attacking the Americans directly. The British lost over 1000 men in that engagement, a Pyrrhic victory. He and his brother, Admiral Richard Howe, then focused their attention on New York City, routing the Americans from Long Island and Manhattan in a massive naval and land assault. By taking New York in 1776, the British had split the colonies and now had America's best harbor. Still, the Continental Army was not defeated, and General Washington harassed Howe with the surprise attack across the Delaware River and the Battles of Trenton and Princeton.

The Howe brothers now plotted their next move. They decided that taking the capital city, Philadelphia, would bring an end to the war. Surely, if they captured the largest city in the Americas, the second largest in the British Empire, they would swiftly achieve their goal. To do this, rather than attacking overland, a distance of only about ninety miles, and rather than sailing up the well-defended Delaware Bay to the harbor of Philadelphia, they opted to swing south, to the entrance of the Chesapeake Bay, and then up the bay to the Head of Elk, on the Elk River, on northern Maryland's east shore. Landing there would position them between Philadelphia and Baltimore, the city where the Continental Congress had briefly met in late 1776 and early 1777, when last threatened.

General Washington was very concerned about the movements of the British army and navy when they packed up and left New York in late July 1777. He assumed Philadelphia was the next target, but did not know how they would approach. In early August, sails were seen at the entrance to the Chesapeake Bay, and Washington moved his army to the west side of Philadelphia. On August 25, 1777, he rode to Head of Elk in a downpour to observe the arrival of the Howes and their forces. He stayed at Jacob Hollingsworth's hotel there, witnessing the approach of over 300 ships carrying over 15,000 soldiers. It was an amazing array of force.

The Congress at York

Washington did not stay. He left in time for the British to begin disembarking, slowed by the storm. Ironically, General William Howe stayed in the same hotel room two days later, on August 27, and was waited on by the same servant. It took a few days to outlast the weather, disembark, get their land legs, and organize. Washington, however, was in a defensive mode, rather than attacking while they landed. The British then began marching towards Philadelphia, heading into northern Delaware, and then into Pennsylvania, approaching Chadds Ford, near the Brandywine Creek.

The Battle of Brandywine on September 11, 1777, was a British victory, and it now put the capital city, Philadelphia, in jeopardy. The Continental Congress had continued to meet there during the battle. On September 14, the Congress resolved that anything of value to the army should be moved from the city. The Liberty Bell and other key papers and records were also moved.

On September 19, at 3 AM, John Adams received a letter from Alexander Hamilton, who was with the army, warning of the imminent arrival of the British Army. The Congress immediately began leaving. John Adams captured the moment in his diary:

> 1777. SEPTR. 19. FRYDAY.
> At 3 this Morning was waked by Mr. Lovell, and told that the Members of Congress were gone, some of them, a little after Midnight. That there was a Letter from Mr. Hamilton Aid de Camp to the General, informing that the Enemy were in Possn. of the Ford and the Boats, and had it in their Power to be in Philadelphia, before Morning, and that if Congress was not removed they had not a Moment to loose.
>
> Mr. Marchant and myself arose, sent for our Horses, and, after collecting our Things, rode off after the others. Breakfasted at Bristol, where were many Members, determined to go the Newtown Road to Reading. We rode to Trenton where We dined. Coll. Harrison, Dr. Witherspoon, all the Delegates from N.Y. and N.E. except Gerry and Lovell. Drank Tea at Mr. Spencers, lodged at Mr. S. Tuckers, at his kind Invitation.

Meanwhile, on September 20, in a surprise bayonet attack led by Major General Charles Grey (later the first Earl Grey), the British routed an American garrison at Paoli. The British then entered Philadelphia on September 27, 1777.

The same day that the British entered Philadelphia, the Continental Congress convened at Lancaster, Pennsylvania, the largest inland city in America. There,

INTRODUCTION

they found the Pennsylvania government meeting and were also concerned about being only 42 miles from Head of Elk, on the east side of the Susquehanna River. They decided to pack up and reconvene at York, Pennsylvania.

Of the 29 delegates who convened in Lancaster, only 23 arrived in York on September 30, 1777. John Witherspoon had bypassed Lancaster, heading straight to York, making it 24. President John Hancock and five others followed the next day.

An American counterattack at Germantown on October 4, 1777, was unsuccessful and, after some skirmishes, Washington and the army settled in at Valley Forge for the winter, positioned to the northwest of Philadelphia, on the road to Reading.

Meanwhile, to the north, at the Battle of Bemis Heights, the second Battle of Saratoga, General Horatio Gates and his forces won decisively on October 7. Now outnumbered, British General Burgoyne surrendered to Gates on October 17, 1777. Had the Howes miscalculated by leaving Burgoyne unsupported while they invaded Philadelphia?

The Continental Congress met at the courthouse in York, Pennsylvania, from September 30, 1777, through June 27, 1778, after the Howes abandoned Philadelphia. During this time, the Congress had several great achievements:

- The Articles of Confederation were debated and adopted on November 15, 1777.
- In honor of General Gates' victory, a national day of Thanksgiving was declared for December 18, 1777.
- On February 6, 1778, the Treaty of Alliance with France was signed.

This book expands on the biographies of the men who met in York, Pennsylvania, as members of the Continental Congress, at what was both the darkest hour of the American Revolution and its turning point. During this period, although Philadelphia was lost for a while, the Congress devised the nation's first constitution and negotiated the key treaty that buttressed the American army for the remainder of the war. Given the key victory of General Gates and General Washington's loss of the capital, the Conway Cabal took root at this time, seeking to replace Washington with Gates. Some of these events also occurred in York during this time. Of course, Washington survived this innuendo while also preserving the army during the bitter winter at Valley Forge.

The leadership of the Continental Congress leads off the book. President of Congress, John Hancock, was in York briefly, until October 29, 1777, when he resigned to return to Massachusetts. South Carolinian Henry Laurens was then elevated to the role for the remainder of the York Congress, and beyond. Secretary Charles Thomson, of course, was present throughout, as he was for the entire period of the Continental Congress.

The delegates then follow, in order of their arrival in York. Sixty-two members of the Continental Congress served at least some portion of their time in exile in York. Most of the original arrivals were replaced at some point with new delegates. Nearly all complained about the rustic character and difficulties of the place, removed from the bustling markets of Philadelphia, New York, Boston, or Charleston. Henry Laurens quipped that making him president at least placed him closer to the woodstove.

The appendices include a list of delegates and their arrival dates and a copy of the text from the Articles of Confederation.

Lawrence Knorr, Ph.D.
July 2025

The Presidents

John Hancock
(1737–1793)

The Signature

Buried at Granary Burial Ground,
Boston, Massachusetts.

Articles of Confederation • Declaration of Independence

John Hancock must have been an unusual and remarkable person. He inherited enormous wealth, was educated, nice looking, popular, living a wonderful life, and yet he was willing to risk it all in the cause of the American Revolution. He contributed immensely to our nation's founding in many ways, including serving in the Continental Congress, twice as President of Congress, and as a signer of the Declaration of Independence. His signature on that document was so bold that when people sign their names, they are said to have written their "John Hancock."

John Hancock was born on his family's farm in Braintree, now Quincy, Massachusetts, on January 23, 1737. His father, John, was a minister and died when young John was seven. He was adopted by his uncle Thomas Hancock, one of Boston's wealthiest merchants, and his aunt Lydia (Henchman) Hancock. Young John lived in an elegant mansion on Beacon Hill called Hancock Manor and was sent to the elite Boston Latin School. He graduated in 1750 and enrolled in Harvard. He received his bachelor's degree from Harvard in 1754 at the age of 17. He then entered his uncle's shipping business. In 1760 he moved to England while building relationships with customers and suppliers. He returned in 1761 and soon became a partner in the company, House of Hancock. When Thomas Hancock died of a stroke in August 1764, John inherited the business, Hancock

The Congress at York

John Hancock

Manor, two or three slaves, and thousands of acres of land, becoming one of the colonies' wealthiest men. The slaves were eventually freed through the terms of Thomas's will. John developed a reputation for generosity, but his lavish lifestyle had its critics, including Sam Adams.

In 1765 the British Parliament enacted the Stamp Act tax on the colonies, and it was a catalyst for John Hancock. He became involved in politics protesting regulations like the Stamp Act and Townshend Act. He commandeered public acts of protest and joined in support of a boycott of British goods. To avoid British taxes, Hancock allegedly began smuggling goods aboard his vessels. This made him very popular among the locals, and in 1766 he was elected to the Massachusetts House of Representatives.

Hancock came into direct conflict with the British in 1760, when one of his merchant ships, the *Liberty*, was seized in Boston Harbor by British customs officials who claimed Hancock had illegally unloaded cargo without paying the required taxes. Being a popular figure, the seizure of his ship led to angry protests by residents. He was taken to court and given a huge fine. It was not the first time Hancock had friction with the Customs Board. Many thought they harassed Hancock because of his politics. He hired John Adams to defend him, and eventually, the charges were dropped without explanation. His guilt or innocence is still debated. Hancock became a local hero for standing up to the British authorities. One result of all this was Hancock and Sam Adams emerged as political partners. Adams was a rabble-rousing firebrand who was hated by the British. He and Hancock, along with James Otis, Paul Revere, and others, formed a grassroots group named the Sons of Liberty. Thus, Hancock became increasingly involved in the movement for American independence, and Massachusetts was at the center of the movement. Boston was dubbed the "Cradle of Liberty."

A result of all the unrest in Boston was a show of military might. Four regiments of the British army were sent to Boston to support the royal officials. The tension between the soldiers and civilians led to what became known as the Boston Massacre in March 1770, in which five civilians were killed and six wounded by British troops. Hancock headed a committee that met with Governor Thomas Hutchinson and demanded the removal of British troops from Boston. He claimed that there were 10,000 armed colonists ready to retaliate if the troops did not leave. The troops being in a precarious position were moved to Castle William, and Hancock was celebrated as a hero reflected in his near-unanimous reelection to the House of Representatives.

Boston became a volatile site once again with the passage of the Tea Act of 1773. Although Hancock did not participate in the Boston Tea Party, he was present at the December 16, 1773, meeting preceding the dumping of the tea and approved of the action. On March 5, 1774, Hancock delivered an important speech on the Boston Massacre's fourth anniversary, denouncing British troops' presence in Boston and questioning Britain's authority over the colonists' lives. The speech was published and widely distributed, enhancing Hancock's stature as a leading Patriot.

In May of 1774, Governor Hutchinson was replaced by Thomas Gage. Whereas Hutchinson tried to win over Hancock, believing that he was too influenced by Sam Adams, Gage took a hard line against both men. In December 1774, Hancock was elected president of the Massachusetts Provincial Congress, which declared itself an autonomous government. Later that month, he was chosen as a delegate to the Second Continental Congress, which served as the colonies' governing body.

Hancock was in the middle of several of the most important events of early American history. He was in Lexington, Massachusetts, on April 18, 1775, when Paul Revere rode his horse to warn fellow colonists that the British were on the move toward Boston. Hancock was with Sam Adams when they heard the alarm. Both men were targeted for arrest by the British. The advance warning allowed them to flee and ultimately escape and make their way to Philadelphia to attend the Continental Congress that convened on May 10. On May 24, Hancock was elected as the third President of the Continental Congress.

When the congress adjourned in August, Hancock made his way to Fairfield, Connecticut, where he wed his fiancée, Dorothy (Dolly) Quincy, on August 28. John and Dolly would have two children, Lydia, who died at ten months, and John George Washington Hancock, who died at nine from a head injury while ice skating.

Hancock was President of Congress when the Declaration of Independence was adopted and signed. He was the first person to sign the historical document and did so with a large, flamboyant signature. According to legend, he signed largely and clearly so that King George could read it without his spectacles.

In October 1777, Hancock told the Continental Congress that he would be resigning the presidency and returning to Massachusetts for health reasons. He had fallen out of favor with both Adamses, who disapproved of Hancock's vanity and extravagance. Many doubted he resigned for health reasons. He rejoined Congress in June 1778, and on July 9, joined representatives from seven other states in signing the Articles of Confederation and then returned to Boston.

Hancock had his chance for military glory shortly after when he led nearly six thousand soldiers to recapture Newport, Rhode Island, from the British. It was a complete failure. He suffered some criticism for the failed attempt but emerged with his popularity intact.

After returning to Massachusetts, Hancock desired to stay in the public eye. As the state needed funds to pay soldiers and purchase weaponry, he used his personal funds to assist in these areas. He also handed out food and firewood to the poor at his own expense. According to biographer William Fowler, "John Hancock was a generous man and the people loved him for it. He was their idol."

The new Massachusetts constitution, which Hancock helped frame, went into effect in October 1780. He was the first democratically elected Governor of Massachusetts in a landslide, garnering over ninety percent of the vote. He remained governor until his surprise resignation in 1785. He again cited health reasons, but some critics claim he wanted to avoid a difficult situation. Historian James Truslow Adams wrote that Hancock's "two chief resources were his money and his gout, the first always used to gain popularity and the second

JOHN HANCOCK (1737–1793)

The monument to John Hancock.

to prevent his losing it." The turmoil Hancock avoided was Shay's Rebellion, which his successor, James Bowdoin, had to deal with. In 1786, after nearly two years out of office, Hancock ran again and defeated Bowdoin and pardoned all the rebels. Hancock was reelected to annual terms as governor for the remainder of his life.

He did not attend the 1787 Constitutional Convention but did preside over Massachusetts's 1788 convention to ratify the constitution and gave a speech in favor of it. Even with the support of Hancock and Sam Adams, the convention narrowly ratified it by a vote of 187 to 168.

In his ninth term as governor, he reconciled with his old friend Sam Adams and in his final election as governor, Adams served as his running mate and as lieutenant governor.

In 1789 Hancock was a candidate in the first U.S. Presidential election. He received four electoral votes out of a total of 138 cast. Following a lengthy illness, John Hancock died at his home with his wife at his side on October 8, 1793, at 56 years of age. After a lavish funeral, he was laid to rest in the Old Granary Burying Ground in Boston, where the Boston Massacre victims are also buried. A large obelisk-shaped stone marks his grave.

Henry Laurens
(1724–1792)

First President of the Recognized USA

Buried at Laurens Family Cemetery,
Moncks Corner, Berkeley County, South Carolina.

Articles of Confederation

Henry Laurens was a South Carolina plantation owner, merchant, and partner in the largest slave-trading house in North America. Laurens was active in state and national politics as the Vice President of South Carolina, Continental Congressman, and President of Congress. He signed the Articles of Confederation, presiding over its adoption. He was also the Minister to the Hague during the Revolution but was captured by the British on his return and imprisoned in the Tower of London for fifteen months.

Laurens, born on March 6, 1724, in Charleston, South Carolina, was the eldest son and third child of Jean Samuel Laurens and Hester (née Grasset) Laurens. His father was of French Huguenot descent, arriving with his parents in New York in the late 1600s. About 1715 or 1716, the elder Laurens married a French Huguenot wife from Staten Island; the young couple moved to Charleston, South Carolina, where Henry was born a decade later. Mother Hester Laurens died in 1741, and her husband remarried Elizabeth Wickling. Jean Samuel Laurens then passed in 1747, leaving his estate to his eldest son, Henry.

Laurens was initially educated in Charleston. In 1744, at age 19, he went to England to study business with Richard Oswald, the principal owner of Bunce Island, a slave-trading island base in the Sierra Leone River of Africa. He stayed there until his father's death three years later.

The Congress at York

Henry Laurens

Leveraging his inheritance, Laurens quickly rose as a leader of the merchant class in Charleston, trading with England and the West Indies. His plantation on the Cooper River employed over 300 slaves, and he was an active importer and trader of slaves throughout the colonies.

On June 25, 1750, Laurens married Eleanor Ball, the daughter of a South Carolina rice planter. The couple had thirteen children, most of them dying in childhood. During the 1750s, Laurens held local offices and, in 1757, was elected to the Commons House of Assembly, staying there through the beginning of the Revolution in 1775, except for 1773, when he arranged his sons' education in England.

From 1757 to 1761, Laurens was also a lieutenant colonel in the militia, fighting a campaign against the Cherokee during the French and Indian War. During the spring of 1760, smallpox raged throughout the low country of South Carolina. Lauren's infant daughter, Martha, apparently succumbed to the disease. As was customary, her little body was laid on a bed by an open window. The family then gathered around for a wake for the deceased. Outside, a light rain began to fall, and a cool breeze blew a few droplets on the young girl's head. She began to stir, clearly not dead. The child had narrowly avoided being buried alive! Little Martha recovered, married Dr. David Ramsay, and lived a full life.

HENRY LAURENS (1724–1792)

In 1764 and 1768, Laurens was named to the King's Council of South Carolina but declined. Wife Eleanor died in 1770 of complications from the childbirth of their last child. Laurens left his local offices to care for his children and then, realizing the harsh impacts of British trade policies, traveled to London to attempt to unsuccessfully negotiate a resolution.

In 1772, Laurens joined the American Philosophical Society of Philadelphia and became well-acquainted with the other members. In 1773, on the eve of the Revolution, Laurens took his three sons to England to be educated. John, the oldest, studied law. However, he returned to America in 1776 and served in the Revolution.

Meanwhile, in South Carolina, Laurens, who initially hoped for reconciliation with England, was elected to the Provincial Congress on January 9, 1775. As he became convinced of the need for independence, he became the President of the Committee of Safety and presided over the Congress from June until March 1776. He was then appointed the Vice President of South Carolina through June 27, 1777.

Laurens was elected to the Continental Congress on January 10, 1777, serving until 1780. From November 1, 1777, until December 9, 1778, he was the President of Congress, succeeding John Hancock. During this time, he oversaw the debate and creation of the Articles of Confederation while the Congress was in York, Pennsylvania. Laurens signed the document as President. He then led the transfer of the Congress back to Philadelphia on July 2, 1778.

Congress named Laurens the Minister to the Hague (Netherlands) in the fall of 1779. In early 1780, he traveled to Amsterdam and gained Dutch support for the colonies. However, on his return trip, while aboard the packet *Mercury* off the coast of Newfoundland, Laurens was captured by the HMS *Vestal*. Laurens tossed his dispatches in the water, but they were recovered. Among them was the draft of a treaty with the Dutch that prompted the British to declare war on the Dutch Republic, triggering the Fourth Anglo-Dutch War. Laurens, charged with treason, was examined by British officials. Some of the interrogation by Lord Hillsborough was published in newspapers in England and the colonies:

> "Is your name Henry Laurens?"
> "It is."
> "Are you the same Henry Laurens who was the President of the Congress in America?"
> "I am."
> "We are ordered by the King and Council to examine you and have certain questions to propose."

The Congress at York

"Your Lordships may save yourselves the trouble of an examination, as I think it my place to answer no questions you may put."
"Sir, we are directed to commit you [as a] prisoner to the Tower."
"I am ready to attend."

Thus, former President Henry Laurens became the only American held prisoner in the Tower of London. Fortunately, his former business mentor, Richard Oswald, still thought fondly of him and lobbied for his release. This finally occurred on December 31, 1781, when he was exchanged for General Lord Cornwallis, who was captured at Yorktown. He came home to find his plantation home, Mepkin, had been burned by the British, and the family lived in an outbuilding while they recovered.

Tragically, Colonel John Laurens, Henry's eldest son, was killed in 1782 at the Battle of the Combahee River before the Treaty of Paris ended the war. Father and son had argued over the years about the evils of slavery. John had urged his father to free his slaves and had offered the 40 he was to inherit to the cause, but Laurens did not relent and never manumitted his slaves.

In 1783, Laurens was sent to Paris to assist in negotiating peace with Britain, whose principal negotiator was Richard Oswald. Laurens, though not a signer of the Treaty of Paris, helped to negotiate settlements for the Netherlands and Spain.

Following the Revolution, Laurens retired from public life, declining to continue service in the Continental Congress or the Constitutional Convention. However, he served briefly in the state convention in South Carolina in 1788 for the ratification of the US Constitution.

Laurens died from complications of gout on December 8, 1792, at Mepkin. Due to his fear of being accidentally buried alive, the family waited three days before proceeding with his funeral. Laurens' will ordered the following:

> I come to the disposal of my own person. I solemnly enjoin it on my son (Henry Jr.) as an indispensable duty, that as soon as he conveniently can after my decease, he cause my Body to be wrapped in twelve yards of tow cloth, and burnt until it be entirely and totally consumed. And then collecting my bones, deposit them where ever he shall think proper.

Laurens is believed to be the first Caucasian to be cremated in the United States. However, it did not go well. The pyre was built along the banks of the Cooper River, and his remains were burned as wished. Accounts vary, but due to the amount of fluid in the body, the liquid poured forth and extinguished most of the flames prematurely. Then, the head broke from the corpse, hair aflame, and rolled down the bank into reeds by the water. A slave was sent into the mud to perform the gruesome task of retrieving it. His remaining bones, ashes, and charred head were then buried in the family plot at Moncks Corner, now on the grounds of Mepkin Abbey.

Some in the press did not approve of Laurens' method of disposal. There was a sonnet by someone using the penname Amicus titled "Lines written on reading the singular manner in which Henry Laurens, Esq. ordered his corpse to be disposed of." It read:

> The Pagans oft their funeral piles have made,
> To offer victims, or consume their dead;
> But who in Christian lands, e'er built a fire
> To expatiate their crimes, or burn a Sire!
> Will Christian people dread the worms of earth,
> Since they expect to rise to second birth?
> When Jesus bids the grave its prey resign,
> In his blest likeness they may hope to shine.

The gravestone of Henry Laurens, who was cremated.

The Congress at York

The city and county of Laurens, South Carolina, are named for Laurens. The village of Laurens in New York is also named for him. Laurens County, Georgia, is named for his son John. Fort Laurens in Ohio was named for Henry by his friend, General Lachlan McIntosh. Historian C. James Taylor summarized Laurens as follows:

> In both his public and private life, Henry Laurens' commitment to duty and hard work were recognized and admired. Unfortunately, his impatience and criticism of individuals who did not meet his standards made him appear petty and inflexible. As the strongest political figure in South Carolina during the transition from provincial to state government, he worked to protect the rights of Loyalists and moderate the zeal of the radicals. In Congress, his constancy during the British occupation of Philadelphia and the trying exile at York may have been his most significant contribution to the national cause. The poor health he endured after confinement in the tower and the emotional shock of his son John's death in August 1782 robbed him of the vigor that had marked his career to that time.

Warning of the dangers near the grave of Henry Laurens.

The Secretary

Charles Thomson
(1729–1824)

Secretary of the Continental Congress

Buried at Laurel Hill Cemetery,
Philadelphia, Pennsylvania.

Secretary, Continental Congress

Although few people have heard of Charles Thomson, he was one of America's most significant and influential Founding Fathers. He served as the only Secretary of the Continental Congress for its entire fifteen years. He was a tremendous unifying factor. He kept the minutes of all sessions of Congress, including special minutes of all the secret meetings and deals. His journals and files became the archives of our nation. In all the factional disputes of the Revolutionary period, his judgment was respected. During the rumors and uncertainties of the Revolutionary War, Thomson helped the Continental Congress retain the faith and support of the people by insisting that full and honest reports be issued, under his signature, concerning all battles and engagements whether won or lost. His reputation was such that his reports were in high demand. When a congressional paper appeared containing his signature, the expression was frequently heard, "here comes the truth." Thomson's name was regarded as an emblem of truth.

Charles Thomson was born in 1729 in County Derry, Ireland to Scots-Irish parents. He was one of six children, and his mother died in 1739 during or shortly after the birth of his youngest sibling. Within a few months, his father John set out for Philadelphia with Charles and three of his older brothers. John became violently ill and died within sight of the shore. The ship was just off the capes of Delaware. The children were now left to the mercy of the sea captain,

The Congress at York

Charles Thomson

who embezzled the money which the father had brought with him and landed the boys ashore at New Castle, Delaware.

There Charles was separated from his brothers. He was placed in the care of a blacksmith who intended to make him an indentured servant. Through good fortune, he was admitted to the New London Academy in Chester County, Pennsylvania. While a student there, Thomson made the acquaintance of Benjamin Franklin and frequently sought his advice regarding the prospects of working in Philadelphia. Franklin, being President of the Board of Trustees of the new Academy of Philadelphia (the forerunner of the University of Pennsylvania), secured a position for Thomson at the school. He started as a tutor there on January 7, 1751.

He served as a tutor until 1755 and left to become head of the Latin department at Philadelphia's Friends Public School. In 1758 he married Ruth Mather, a member of a well-to-do Chester family. In 1760 he left teaching to enter into business. He and Ruth separated in 1769. In 1770 tragedy struck when their infant twins and Ruth died.

CHARLES THOMSON (1729–1824)

While at the Friends School, Thomson joined the Quakers in their opposition to the Penn family's Indian policy. He became the secretary for the Delaware Indians in 1756 at a great council held in Easton, Pennsylvania to resolve their differences with the settlers. The tribe adopted him as a son according to an ancient Indian custom. All during this time, he was allied with Ben Franklin, but they parted politically during the Stamp Act crisis in 1765. He then allied himself with John Dickinson. He worked diligently throughout the Revolutionary period to keep English goods out of Philadelphia. By 1773 he was writing fiery handbills against the importation of tea from the East India Company. During this decade Thomson was the colony's most powerful protest organizer. He became known as "the Sam Adams of Philadelphia." He also became a leader in Philadelphia's Sons of Liberty, a secret organization of landowners throughout the colonies formed to protect the rights of colonists and to fight taxation by the British government.

On September 1, 1774, Thomson married Hannah Harrison, the sister of Benjamin Harrison, who would become a signer of the Declaration of Independence. The following Monday, September 5, the First Continental Congress convened in Philadelphia and unanimously selected Thomson as Secretary.

He served over the next fifteen years as secretary to the first and second Continental Congresses and then to the Confederation Congress. Through those fifteen years, Congress saw many delegates come and go, but Thomson's dedication to recording the debates and decisions provided continuity. The Continental Congress was in some respects one of the most remarkable legislative bodies the world has ever seen. Thomson knew better than any other man the secret history of Congress and the motives which influenced its members. He beheld the development of national consciousness, and he was present at the dawn of independence. Thomson's name appeared on the first published version of the Declaration of Independence as the only non-delegate signature. He signed in his capacity as Congressional Secretary.

Among his many accomplishments as Secretary, Thomson designed the Great Seal of the United States. The United States of America continues to use the Great Seal on all of its official documents. It can be easily found on the reverse side of the one-dollar bill.

Thomson's service was not without its critics, however. In 1780 delegate James Searle, a close friend of John Adams, began a cane fight on the floor of Congress, claiming that Thomson misquoted him in the minutes. Both men were slashed in the face. Thomson's recordings of events frequently led to arguments and fights on the floor of Congress.

The Congress at York

Obelisk honoring Charles Thomson

Thomson was keenly aware of the slavery problem. He wrote to Jefferson in 1785: "It grieves me to the soul that there should be such grounds for your apprehensions respecting the irritation that will be produced in the southern states by what you have said of slavery. However, I would not have you discouraged. This is a cancer we must get rid of. It is a blot on our character that must be wiped out. If it cannot be done by religion, reason, and philosophy, confident I am that it will be done one day by blood."

Thomson's last official act as Secretary was to inform George Washington of his election. He traveled to Mt. Vernon on April 1789 to tell him officially that under the new constitution he had been elected the first President. By July,

CHARLES THOMSON (1729–1824)

Thomson was retired, having turned over the Great Seal of the United States to Washington.

As Secretary of Congress, Thomson chose what to include in the official journals of the Continental Congress. He also prepared a work of over 1000 pages that covered the political history of the American Revolution. After leaving office, he chose to destroy this work, stating his desire to avoid "contradicting all the histories of the great events of the Revolution. Let the world admire the supposed wisdom and valor of our great men. Perhaps they may adopt the qualities that have been ascribed to them, and thus good may be done. I shall not undeceive future generations."

Charles Thomson died on August 16, 1824, at the age of 95. He had been residing in Bryn Mawr, Pennsylvania at Harriton House which still stands today and operates as a museum. He was initially buried there, but in 1838 his nephew moved his remains to Laurel Hill Cemetery in Philadelphia. A large handsome monument marks his grave.

The original gravestone for Charles Thomson

The Delegates

Eliphalet Dyer
(1721–1807)

"... an honest, worthy man ..."

Buried at Windham Cemetery,
Windham, Connecticut.

**Continental Congress • Signer of the Continental Association
Militiaman**

Eliphalet Dyer had one of the more unusual names among Continental Congressmen. "Eliphalet" was derived from Hebrew, meaning "God who delivers." Congressman Dyer certainly "delivered" for his constituents in Windham, Connecticut, throughout a long political career. Dyer was variously a lawyer, jurist, and statesman who was a delegate to the Continental Congress and signed the Continental Association.

Dyer was born in Windham, Connecticut, on September 14, 1721, the son of Thomas Dyer and his wife, Lydia (née Backus) Dyer. The elder Dyer was a native of Weymouth, Massachusetts, who moved to Connecticut circa 1715. There, he married Lydia, the daughter of John Backus of Windham. Upon settling in Windham, Thomas served in the Connecticut General Assembly and rose to become a major in the Windham County militia.

Young Eliphalet was taught "preparatory studies" prior to enrolling at Yale College (now Yale University) in New Haven in 1740. Dyer was already a town clerk as a teenager and studied law at Yale. In May 1745, he married Huldah Bowen of Providence, Rhode Island, the daughter of Colonel Jacob Bowen. Upon graduating from Yale, Dyer was admitted to the colonial bar in 1746 and practiced law in Windham.

Eliphalet Dyer

Following in his father's footsteps, Dyer joined the militia and was elected justice of the peace and to the colonial assembly in 1747. He served in sessions in that body in 1747, 1748, 1753, and 1753, and then from 1756 to 1784. During this time, he became directly embroiled in territorial disputes between Connecticut and Pennsylvania. In 1754, the Susquehanna Land Company published in Philadelphia a claim that Connecticut's grant included the lands westward as "far as the South Sea." This happened to carve off the northern tier of William Penn's colony. The Connecticut General Assembly was lobbied to permit Connecticut's citizens to settle the lands, but the outbreak of the French and Indian War distracted from this.

ELIPHALET DYER (1721–1807)

During the war, Dyer was a lieutenant colonel in the Connecticut militia, participating in the capture of Crown Point in 1755. He was promoted to lieutenant and led a regiment in the 1758 attack on Canada.

After the war, in 1763, Dyer traveled to London representing the Susquehanna River land claim but was turned down due to the just-passed Proclamation Line Act, which established set boundaries for the colonies. Unfortunately, this was unsatisfactory for many Connecticut settlers who had invested in land, leading to conflicts known as the Yankee-Pennamite Wars. Three times, hostilities flared between Pennsylvania and Connecticut. Ultimately, after the Revolution, the region was affixed to Pennsylvania by the Continental Congress, and Pennsylvania permitted the Yankees to stay as Pennsylvania citizens.

In September 1765, Dyer was a representative from Connecticut in the Stamp Act Congress. He was then elected a justice on the superior court in 1766, holding the post until 1793. He was chief justice after 1789.

As the American Revolution began to simmer, Dyer was named to Connecticut's Committee of Safety. In July 1774, when the Committee of Correspondence met regarding a delegate to the First Continental Congress, Dyer was selected to represent the colony in Philadelphia. He served in Congress until 1775, then 1777 to 1779, and finally from 1782 to 1783.

On October 20, 1774, Dyer signed the Continental Association, banning certain British imports, including tea. Dyer was not in Congress when it moved to York following the invasion of Philadelphia, but he did return to Philadelphia to hear the final debates about the Articles of Confederation although he was not a signer. In his diary, John Adams described Dyer as "longwinded and roundabout, obscure and cloudy, very talkative and very tedious, yet an honest, worthy man; means and judges well."

After leaving Congress, Yale conferred a Doctor of Divinity degree to Dyer in 1787. He continued to serve as a judge in Connecticut, retiring in 1793 as the chief justice. Dyer died on May 13, 1807, at age 85, and was buried at Windham Cemetery.

The Litchfield Monitor of Connecticut stated, "Died, at Windham, the Hon. ELIPHALET DYER, in the 87th year of his age. He was distinguished for his useful talents and the faithful and honourable discharge of his important duties."

New York's *The Morning Chronicle* said, "He was one of those illustrious patriots (whose name will live in the annals of our nation to all posterity) who signed and assisted in supporting the Declaration of Independence in 1776, which was the keystone to the 'wide arch of our rais'd empire.'"

The Congress at York

Well, contrary to the New York paper declaring so, Dyer never signed the Declaration of Independence and was not in Congress at the time to debate or pass the measure. As Mark Twain once said, "If you don't read the newspaper, you're uninformed. If you read the newspaper, you're misinformed."

Fortunately, you have our series of books to sort out a most accurate account of the accomplishments and contributions of our Founders.

Grave of Eliphalet Dyer

William Williams
(1731–1811)

Puritan Patriot

Buried at Trumbull Cemetery,
Lebanon, Connecticut.

Declaration of Independence

William Williams was a soldier in the French and Indian War, a merchant, local and state government official, and son-in-law of Connecticut royal governor Jonathan Trumbull, the only governor to convert to the patriot cause. Williams was appointed to the Second Continental Congress, where he signed the Declaration of Independence.

William Williams was born March 29, 1731, in Lebanon, Connecticut, to First Congregational Church minister Solomon Williams and his wife Mary (née Porter). After attending local preparatory schools, Williams entered Harvard College at 16, where he studied theology and law, graduating in 1751.

At the age of 21, Williams was elected to the office of town clerk in Lebanon and later town treasurer. He served as town clerk for 44 years. While performing these duties, Williams planned to become a minister and studied with his father. He was ordained a deacon in his father's church. Yale College awarded Williams a bachelor's degree in 1753 for his previous work at Harvard. Williams then completed a master's degree at Harvard in 1754.

On the verge of becoming a minister, Williams heard the call to arms at the outset of the French and Indian War. He served as an aide under his older cousin, Colonel Ephraim Williams, from Massachusetts, who led ten companies of William Johnson's expedition against the French fort at Crown Point, New

William Williams

York. During the expedition, Johnson renamed *Lac du Saint-Sacrement* to Lake George in honor of his king. During the Battle of Lake George on September 8, 1755, Colonel Ephraim Williams was shot in the head and killed by an ambush of French soldiers and allied Indians. This incident became known as the Bloody Morning Scout. The colonel's body was hidden by his regiment to prevent its desecration. He was then buried nearby, and a stone with his initials and year of death stands at Lake George near a monument erected in his honor. The assets of the colonel's estate were subsequently used to establish Williamstown, Massachusetts, and Williams College. In the early 20th century, the colonel's body was disinterred at Lake George and moved to the chapel at Williams College. The alumni also funded the monument at Lake George, marking the site of the ambush.

Though the British ultimately won the battle and erected Fort William Henry on the shores of Lake George, this experience caused William Williams to begin to question his loyalty to them. He did not like how the provincials, including his cousin, were treated as inferiors. He began to think the colonies might do better to govern themselves.

After Lake George, Williams returned to Lebanon and opened a retail store called The Williams, Inc. However, politics soon called, and he was elected to the Connecticut General Assembly in 1757, serving until May 4, 1776, when he was promoted to the upper house known as the Council of Assistants. Having left his business behind, Williams was so passionate about his public service, he never missed a session. In addition to his role in the assembly, Williams was a member of the Sons of Liberty and later served on the Committee of Correspondence and Council of Safety in Connecticut. When British soldiers occupied Boston in 1768, Williams voiced his opposition. When the British implemented the Townshend Acts in 1769, Williams strongly opposed them and was a staunch supporter of the colonials' non-importation agreements. When the British repealed the Townshend Acts in 1770, except for the tax on tea, Williams urged merchants to continue to adhere to the non-importation agreements. However, few listened, including Silas Deane, whom Williams never trusted.

Finally, at the age of 40, Williams set aside his duties to marry Mary Trumbull on Valentine's Day, February 14, 1771. Mary was the daughter of Connecticut Royal Governor Jonathan Trumbull, who had also previously struggled at being a merchant. The couple ultimately produced three children: Solomon, born 1772; Faith, 1774; and William Trumbull, 1777. The marriage forged a strong bond between Williams and his father-in-law, who was also a native of Lebanon, Connecticut.

Following the Boston Tea Party, the British parliament implemented the Coercive Acts in 1774. On July 1 of that year, Williams published a satirical address to the king in the *Connecticut Gazette* under a pseudonym. Wrote Williams:

> We don't complain that your father made our yoke heavy and afflicted us with grievous service. We only ask that you would govern us upon the same constitutional plan, and with the same justice and moderation that he did, and we will serve you forever. And what is the language of your answer . . . ? Ye Rebels and Traitors . . . if ye don't yield implicit obedience to all my commands, just and unjust, ye shall be drag'd in chains across the wide ocean, to answer your insolence, and if a mob arises among you to impede my officers in the execution of my orders, I will punish and involve in common ruin whole cities and colonies, with their ten thousand innocents, and ye shan't be heard in your own defense, but shall be murdered and

butchered by my dragoons into silence and submission. Ye reptiles! ye are scarce intitled [sic] to existence any longer . . . Your lives, liberties, and property are all at the absolute disposal of my parliament.

Williams not only voiced his concerns, he invested over two thousand dollars of his own money in continental currency to support the rebellion. He used his connections as a former merchant to collect blankets and munitions for the cause. He assisted his father-in-law, who was the only royal governor to join the patriots, in preparing to establish the new rebel government in Connecticut. In 1775, Williams was elected speaker of the Connecticut Assembly and then to the Continental Congress to replace Oliver Wolcott on July 11, 1776. That day, word was received of the vote for independence on July 2, nine days prior. Williams hurried to Philadelphia, arriving on July 28. While he was too late to vote for the Declaration of Independence, he signed the document as a representative of Connecticut.

Some have written about Williams's self-righteous attitude. Perhaps he was overly confident as the son-in-law of the governor. In one exchange at a Council of Safety meeting in late 1776, when it looked like the British might prevail, Williams said calmly, "If they succeed, it is pretty evident what will be my fate. I have done much to prosecute the contest, and one thing I have done which the British will never pardon, I have signed the Declaration of Independence." To that, Congressman Benjamin Huntington replied he should be exempt from the gallows because he had not signed the document. Williams retorted, "Then sir, you deserve to be hanged for not having done your duty."

Williams, a man of devout faith, was also somewhat puritanical. In a letter to his father-in-law, the governor, regarding the celebration of the first anniversary of the Declaration of Independence, he wrote:

> Yesterday was, in my opinion, poorly spent in celebrating the anniversary of the Declaration of Independence. But to avoid singularity and Reflection upon my dear colony, I thot my duty to attend the public entertainment; a great expenditure of Liquor, Powder, etc. took up a good part of the Day and of candles thro the City, good part of the night.

After 1777, Williams returned to Connecticut and continued his public service. He was a judge of the Windham County Court from 1776 to 1804 and Windham district probate judge from 1776 to 1808. He became an assistant

WILLIAM WILLIAMS (1731–1811)

councilor in 1780 and served as assistant and as councilor for 24 years. He returned to the state house of representatives from 1780 to 1784 and was the speaker from 1781 to 1783. In 1787, Williams was a member of the ratification convention in Connecticut for the new U.S. Constitution. At the state's constitutional convention in 1788, Williams represented Lebanon. His only objection was a clause banning religious tests for government officials.

The grave of William Williams.

The Congress at York

Under the new constitution, brother-in-law Jonathan Trumbull, Jr. was elected to the first three U.S. congresses from 1789 through 1795. During the Second Congress, he was Speaker of the House, sandwiched between two terms when Frederick Muhlenberg had the role. Trumbull was then governor of Connecticut from 1798 to 1809. Another brother-in-law, John Trumbull, was known as the "painter of the American Revolution."

During his later years, Williams was a pastor at the First Congregational Church in Lebanon and a successful merchant. He spent the last years of his life devoted to reading, meditation, and prayer. On August 2, 1811, he died at Lebanon and was interred in the Trumbull Tomb in the East Cemetery in the town, now known as Trumbull Cemetery. His house still stands and is on the National Registry of Historic Landmarks.

Nathan Brownson
(1742–1796)

Physician, Congressman, Governor

Buried at Midway Cemetery,
Midway, Georgia.

Continental Congress • Governor

Nathan Brownson was a Connecticut physician who moved to Georgia, where he became a state legislator and Continental Congressman. Near the end of the American Revolution, he was the Governor of Georgia.

Brownson was born on May 14, 1742, in Woodbury, near Hartford, Connecticut, the son of Timothy Brownson and his wife, Abigail (née Jenner) Brownson.

Brownson was schooled by private tutors in his youth before attending Yale. He graduated in 1761 with a medical degree and practiced medicine in Woodbury.

On June 29, 1769, Brownson married Abigail Lewis. In 1774, after corresponding with his friend, Dr. James Dunwoody, of St. John's Parish, Georgia, Brownson traveled there. Soon after, he and his wife moved to Riceboro, near the town of Midway, Liberty County, where he worked a 500-acre plantation. Abigail died soon after they moved to Georgia, and Brownson next married Elizabeth Dunham Martin, a widow, on September 2, 1774.

On July 4, 1775, the provincial congress met in Savannah to discuss the issues of the Revolution. Brownson and Lyman Hall were two of eleven delegates from the parish to attend. Back home, Elizabeth died in 1775, likely due to childbirth. Brownson next married Elizabeth McLean in 1776, also a widow, with whom he had two children.

The Congress at York

Nathan Brownson

On October 9, 1776, Brownson joined Lyman Hall as appointees to the Second Continental Congress.

Brownson's service in the Continental Congress lasted from January 4 to May 1, 1777, in Philadelphia, and then from August 23 to October 9, 1777, as the Congress relocated to Lancaster and subsequently to York, Pennsylvania.

As the Revolutionary War progressed, the focus switched to the Southern Theater. After the British were expelled from Augusta in June 1781, there was chaos and factional disputes in Georgia. The Continental Congress sent Brownson to Georgia as a brigadier to assist in bringing order. He was initially made Speaker of the House in the state assembly, but a compromise was arranged whereby John Twiggs became a brigadier general and Brownson became the governor of the state, succeeding Stephen Heard.

Brownson's term lasted only from August 17, 1781, until January 3, 1782. As one of his acts as governor, he congratulated General Nathanael Greene for his efforts to restore the state's government. Brownson put out a call to all men to return to their homes in the state or pay triple the tax that would be due. He also worked to settle the Creek Indians, who had been threatening American soldiers and property. John Martin then succeeded Brownson.

NATHAN BROWNSON (1742–1796)

Next for Brownson was to revisit his medical background. On June 6, 1782, he was appointed as the deputy purveyor for the Southern Hospitals for the Continental Army.

Brownson spent the years after the war as a justice of the peace, a commissioner for a new capital, and a member of the state's Constitutional Convention. In 1788, he was elected to the Georgia House of Representatives and rose to the speaker's chair. He was also appointed to assist in the writing of a new state constitution. When that document was ratified, creating a state senate, Brownson was elected to that body, serving from 1790 to 1791, rising to president of the senate. Around this time, he was also involved as a trustee in the formation of Franklin College, which later became the University of Georgia.

Brownson died at his Riceboro plantation in Liberty County, Georgia, on November 6, 1796, at age 54. He was buried in Midway Cemetery in Midway, Georgia. *The Federal Gazette* of Baltimore, Maryland, announced Brownson's death, then noted that his "various talents as a statesman, philosopher and physician, have placed him in the list of distinguished characters. His expiring moments were marked with that peculiar firmness of mind which attended him through life, and his last words, delivered in whispers, were more sublimely eloquently than all the studied declamation of the pulpit. 'The scene (said he) is now closing, the business of life is nearly over; I have, like the rest of my fellow creatures, been guilty of foibles; but I trust to the mercy of my God to pardon them, and to his justice, and to reward my good deeds.' By his family, by his friends, who knew him, his death will be long lamented."

Historian James F. Cook later wrote: "A friend who was well acquainted with Dr. Brownson and his wife related that Mrs. Brownson, though a good and faithful wife, was not always prompt in responding to the requests of her husband. On occasion, Dr. Brownson playfully said to her: 'Have a care; if you do not acquiesce in my wish, when I am dead, I will come back and plague you.' Years later, after Brownson's death, his widow, when brushing from her nose some vexatious fly or annoying insect, was heard to exclaim, 'Go away, I tell you, Doctor Brownson, and stop bothering me.'"

George Walton
1749?–1804

The Orphaned Founder

Buried at Courthouse Grounds,
Augusta, Georgia.

Declaration of Independence

This founder was orphaned at a young age. Many signers of the Declaration of Independence served in state militias, but few participated in any battles during the Revolutionary War. Not only did this founder see action, but he was wounded, captured, and imprisoned by the British. In addition to serving in the Continental Congress, he would also serve as governor and a United States senator from Georgia. His name was George Walton.

Walton was born in Cumberland County, Virginia. The exact year of his birth is unknown. The *New Georgia Encyclopedia* states that it is believed he was born in 1749; however, some researchers have placed his birth as early as 1740. What is known is that he was orphaned at a young age and adopted by an uncle who apprenticed Walton to a carpenter.

Like the date of his birth, there is confusion about his experience as an apprentice. In their book, *Signing Their Lives Away*, Denise Kiernan and Joseph D'Agnese write that there are two stories about how the carpenter treated him. One describes the carpenter as a mean man who was against Walton seeking to educate himself, so he refused to provide a candle so Walton could read his books. In this version, the resourceful Walton gathers wood chips, which he sets ablaze to provide some light to read by. In another, very different version, the carpenter is a kindly gentleman who lets Walton miss work to attend

GEORGE WALTON 1749?–1804

George Walton

school. The authors conclude that it is difficult to determine which version is accurate, but do note that he was educated enough to study with an attorney when he moved to Savannah, Georgia, in his twenties. He was admitted to the bar in 1774.

Walton became active in supporting the patriots' cause. He was elected secretary of the Georgia Provincial Congress and became president of the Council of Safety. However, his views did not represent those in the majority in Georgia, as evidenced by the fact that Georgia was the only colony that did not send representatives to the First Continental Congress.

It was only when armed conflict between the colonists and the English ensued that the tide turned in Georgia. In 1775, the colony sent delegates to Philadelphia, and in 1776, Walton was elected to join them. Here, he joined Lyman Hall and Button Gwinnett, both considered to be more radical than he was. He would serve honorably and remain in Congress longer than his two colleagues and fellow signers of the Declaration of Independence. If you believe the account of signer Benjamin Rush, Walton was the youngest signer. Rush wrote, "He (Walton) was the youngest member of Congress, not quite being three and twenty when he signed the Declaration of Independence." Thus, Rush added to the possible year of Walton's birth, 1753. However, without additional evidence, the youngest signer must continue to be recognized as Edward Rutledge of South Carolina.

Walton took leave from Congress in 1778 to assume the role of colonel in the militia and fight in the Revolution. During the siege of Savannah, he was shot and fell off his horse. The British quickly captured him. He was not treated harshly and was permitted to seek private medical care to treat the wound in his

Signers Monument in Augusta, Georgia.

GEORGE WALTON 1749?–1804

thigh. Some speculate that the reason for this is that he was a prized prisoner due to his service in Congress and could be used in a prisoner exchange for a high-ranking British officer. He was held prisoner for a year before being exchanged for an English naval captain.

After leaving Congress, Walton continued to serve the people of Georgia as the state's chief justice, governor, and United States senator. He was elected to serve as a delegate to the 1787 Constitutional Convention but declined due to his duties at the state level. In 1789, he served as a presidential elector. He was also the founder and trustee of the Academy of Richmond County in Augusta and of Franklin College, now the University of Georgia in Athens. After serving as governor, he became a judge of the superior court from 1790 until his death.

Walton died in 1804 and was originally buried in Augusta's Rosney Cemetery. His remains were later reinterred in 1848 beneath the signer's monument on the approach to the Augusta municipal building. Lyman Hall is also buried here, and Button Gwinnett is memorialized.

Grave of George Walton

Charles Carroll of Carrollton
(1737–1832)
The Catholic Signer

Buried at Doughoregan Manor Chapel,
Ellicott City, Maryland.

Continental Congress • Declaration of Independence

Though born into one of the wealthiest families in America, this founder had to overcome religious intolerance to take his place among the signers of the document that declared the thirteen colonies independent. Born in Maryland, which was initially founded as a Catholic colony and named after a Catholic queen, by the time this founder entered the world, there were restrictions against Catholics prohibiting those of that faith to practice law, teach or hold public office. Despite these obstacles, this founder, with the aid of the family fortune, received a classical education in France, where he became fluent in that language. A gifted writer, his well-framed arguments against British rule earned him the respect of his fellow patriots. He was instrumental in persuading Maryland to give the colony's delegates to the Continental Convention the instructions to vote for independence. He would later rally the state's support for the Constitution and serve as one of Maryland's first United States senators. When he passed away at the age of 95, he was the last surviving signer of the Declaration of Independence. His name was Charles Carroll, but his signature generally read Charles Carroll of Carrollton.

Carroll was born on September 19, 1737, in the Carroll Mansion located in Annapolis, Maryland. He was the only child of Charles Carroll of Annapolis and Elizabeth Brooke. His father was a wealthy tobacco farmer. Carroll was

CHARLES CARROLL OF CARROLLTON (1737–1832)

Charles Carroll of Carrollton

educated at a Jesuit preparatory school until the age of eleven, when he was sent to France to continue his studies. Among the French schools he attended was the Louis the Great College in Paris, from which he graduated in 1755. For the next decade, he continued his studies in France, becoming fluent in the French language before studying the law in England. He returned to America in 1765 as an intelligent and cultured young gentleman.

Initially, upon returning to the land of his birth, Carroll showed little interest in politics. This lack of interest may have been abetted by a Maryland law passed in 1704 that prohibited Catholics from holding public office to prevent "the growth of Popery in the Province." Also, as detailed by Milton Lomask in his book *Charles Carroll and the American Revolution*, Carroll's father urged him to be cautious in addressing the political issues of the day, especially the increasing tensions between Great Britain and the colonies. He did marry during this period wedding Mary (Molly) Darnell, on June 5, 1768. The couple would have seven children before Mary's death in 1782, but only three would survive infancy.

By 1772 Carroll's reluctance to engage in political debates had vanished. He engaged in what Denise Kieran and Joseph D'Agnese described as "a duel of pens" in their work *Signing Their Lives Away: The Fame and Misfortune of the Men Who Signed the Declaration of Independence*. In this "duel," which began with both participants writing under pseudonyms, Carroll was pitted against a well-known Maryland Attorney and crown loyalist Daniel Dulany the Younger. The subject of their debate was the decision by the proprietary governor to raise taxes so that government officials could receive a pay raise. Dulany supported the governor, while Carroll viewed the move as further taxation without representation. After a series of their arguments were published in a newspaper, word spread as to the true identities of the authors. Dulany began attacking Carroll personally, stressing the fact that he was a Catholic. Carroll's responses to these personal attacks were careful and restrained. He wrote that his opposition had resorted to "virulent and illiberal abuse," adding that "we may fairly presume, that arguments are either wanting, or that ignorance or incapacity know not how to apply them." Dulany's personal attacks backfired, resulting in Carroll being recognized as a strong and leading opponent of British rule.

While Carroll may have risen to patriotic prominence through his pen, he was one of the initial founders who came to believe that the disputes with England would have to be settled by the sword. Legend has it that in a conversation with Samuel Chase, another future signer of the Declaration of Independence, Carroll took the position that it would take more than written arguments if the colonies were to prevail over the British. When Chase asked what else the colonists could resort to, Carroll answered, "The bayonet. Our arguments will only raise the feelings of the people to that pitch when open war will be looked to as the arbiter of the dispute."

On October 19, 1774, Carroll played a prominent role in the event that came to be known as the Annapolis Tea Party. During this time, the colonists were engaged in widespread tea boycotts to protest the British Tea Act of 1773, which permitted only one company, the British East India Company, to sell tea in the colonies without paying tax. These protests had already led to the more famous Boston Tea Party. As a result of the boycotts, most ship captains refused to transport tea. However, in 1774 an English merchant loaded a ton of tea aboard a ship called the *Peggy Stewart*. The ship arrived in Annapolis on October 14, 1774. The co-owner of the ship, Anthony Stewart, was notified of the tax that needed to be paid before any of the ship's cargo could be brought ashore. The cargo included 53 indentured servants who had already endured a harsh crossing and were unlikely to survive a forced return to England. Seeing no other alternative, Stewart guaranteed payment of the tax, got the servants ashore but left the tea on the ship while he met with the local committee that supervised the boycott to resolve the situation.

CHARLES CARROLL OF CARROLLTON (1737–1832)

Stewart met with Carroll, who was chairman of the committee, and an agreement was reached that the tea would be burned and Stewart and his co-owners would publish an apology in the *Maryland Gazette*. On the morning of the 19th, the ship's crew ran her aground. Stewart arrived and, before a large crowd touched a torch to oil-soaked rags in the bow of the *Peggy Stewart*. The ship, tea and all, burned down to the waterline. According to Lomask, after the event, Carroll told his wife, "You must admit that when we hold a tea party here in Annapolis, we do a better job of it than they do in Boston. We do not disguise ourselves as Indians. We do not hide behind war paint and feathers. And we do not lay hands on property that is not ours. We do everything legally and openly - and in a grand manner."

By the time the American Revolution began in 1775, Carroll was one of the colonies' wealthiest men. He inherited enormous agricultural estates, and his personal fortune was 2.1 million pounds sterling, which would amount to over $250 million today. He lived on and ran a ten-thousand-acre estate in Maryland that was worked by approximately 1,000 African slaves.

Carroll became a member of the first Annapolis Committee of Safety in 1775 and served as a delegate to the Annapolis Convention, which ran Maryland's revolutionary government. He was asked to represent his colony in the First Continental Congress but declined, probably believing that his Catholic faith would create problems for the representatives from other colonies. He did accompany Maryland's representatives to Philadelphia as an unofficial member of the delegation.

Though not an official member Congress soon found work for Carroll to do. In 1776 largely due to Benjamin Franklin and Samuel Chase's influence, Carroll was persuaded to head a mission to Canada to convince that country to join the fight against the British. Sending the Catholic French-speaking Carroll to Catholic-heavy Canada seemed a wise choice, but the effort came to naught for several reasons. Most notably, the Americans had invaded Canada less than a year earlier, and in 1774 the British parliament had passed the Quebec Act giving freedom of religion to Canadians and recognizing the Catholic Church. The First Continental Congress, despite Carroll's protests, had criticized the Parliament for passing the act. The Canadians felt they had more to fear from their southern neighbors than from the British crown.

In the summer of 1776, Congress scheduled a vote for July 2 on Richard Henry Lee's resolution calling for American independence. Maryland had yet to advise their delegates on how to vote on the resolution, so Carroll and his old friend Samuel Chase headed back to Maryland to work the Annapolis Convention to support independence. Their arguments proved persuasive, and the convention freed Maryland delegates to support the Lee resolution. On July 4, 1776, Carroll was elected to the Continental Congress, and this time he agreed to serve. He arrived back in Philadelphia too late to vote in favor of independence, but he proudly signed the document that declared the American colonies free of English rule on August 2, 1776. He signed as Charles Carroll of Carrollton. There are stories about this signature, most likely apocryphal. In the 1940s, there was a journalist with a popular syndicated column named John Hix. He wrote in his column "Strange As It Seems" an explanation for Carroll's distinctive signature. Every member of the Continental Congress who signed this document automatically became a criminal, guilty of sedition against King George III. Because of his wealth, Carroll had more to lose than most yet had a very common name. Those signers with common names might hope to avoid being identified by the King. According to Hix's research, when it was Carroll's turn to sign the declaration, he rose, went to John Hancock's desk where the document rested, signed his name "Charles Carroll," and returned to his seat. At this point, another member of the Continental Congress, who was prejudiced against Carroll because of his Catholicism, commented that Carroll risked little in signing the document as there must be many men named Charles Carroll in the colonies so the King would be unlikely to order Carroll's arrest without clear proof that he was the same one who signed. Carroll immediately returned to Hancock's desk, seized the pen again, and added "of Carrollton" to his name. The Society of the Descendants of the Signers of the Declaration of Independence claims that President John Hancock made the comment.

Carroll would represent Maryland in the Continental Congress until 1778. He was a major supporter of George Washington as the two had become friends when the future president made multiple visits to the Carroll estate. He served on the committee that visited Washington and his troops during the harsh winter they spent at Valley Forge. He played a significant role in defeating the Conway Cabal that sought to replace Washington as commander of the new nation's armies. During his final year in Congress, he was asked to serve as President, an honor he declined. He also provided considerable financial support to the Revolutionary War effort throughout these turbulent times.

Carroll returned to Maryland in 1778 to assist in the formation of a state government. Since he had assisted in drafting the state constitution two years prior, he was well prepared for this task. He was elected to the state senate in 1781, where he served for more than a decade. He was elected to represent his state at the Constitutional Convention of 1787 but did not attend the

CHARLES CARROLL OF CARROLLTON (1737–1832)

gathering in Philadelphia. He was active in rallying support for ratification of the historical document produced by that convention. In 1789 he was elected to serve as one of Maryland's first two United States Senators. In 1792 the Maryland legislature passed a law prohibiting anyone from serving in the state and national legislature at the same time. Preferring service in the Maryland Senate, he resigned from the United States Senate in November of 1792.

Like many of the nation's founders, Carroll was a slave owner who wrestled with the question of slavery through much of his life. While he supported the gradual abolition of slavery and said, "It is admitted by all to be a great evil," he did not free any of his slaves. He did introduce a bill calling for the gradual abolition of slavery in the Maryland Senate, but it found little support. In 1828, when he was 91 years old, he served as the president of the Auxiliary State Colonization Society of Maryland. This group supported sending black Americans to lead free lives in African states such as Liberia.

When John Adams and Thomas Jefferson both passed away on July 4, 1826, Carroll became the last surviving founder of those who had courageously signed the Declaration of Independence. He lived his final years with a daughter in Baltimore. His last public act, on July 2, 1828, was the laying of the cornerstone of the B&O's Carrollton Viaduct, named in his honor and still in use today. In May 1832, he was asked to appear at the first-ever Democratic Party Convention but did not attend because of poor health. He passed away at the age of 95 on November 14, 1832. He was laid to rest in his Doughoregan Manor Chapel located in Ellicott City, Maryland.

There are numerous cities and counties named in his honor, and his family manors remain standing. The family still owns Doughoregan Manor, although it is closed to the public. There are numerous memorials to Charles Carroll throughout the eastern United States. Counties in twelve states bear his name, as do elementary and middle schools and a residence hall at the University of Notre Dame. His likeness can be found in many paintings depicting the Signers of the Declaration of Independence, and a statue of him resides in Statuary Hall in the US Capitol.

John Adams
(1735 – 1825)

Second to George

Buried beneath the First Unitarian Church,
Quincy, Massachusetts.

**Continental Association • Declaration of Independence
Diplomat • Thought Leader • First Vice President
Second President**

John Adams was not a real likable guy. His seemingly inborn contentiousness was a constraint in his political career. Yet he would serve in both Continental Congresses, sign the Declaration of Independence after a major role in its writing, serve as the United States' Ambassador to France, Holland, and Great Britain, and become America's first Vice President and second President. He made up for his irritating personality with honesty, competence, and hard work. What he lacked in popularity he made up in respect. Ben Franklin once wrote about Adams "I am persuaded that he means well for his country, is always an honest man, often a wise one, but sometimes, and in some things, absolutely out of his senses."

He was born in Quincy, Massachusetts in 1735, a fifth-generation New Englander. His father was a deacon and a town selectman. He was awarded a Harvard scholarship at age 16 and graduated in 1755 at the age of 20. His father expected him to become a clergyman but John chose law instead. In 1764 he married Abigail Smith. The marriage lasted 54 years and produced six children, one of which (John Quincy Adams) would become the sixth President in 1825. He made his first mark politically with his opposition to the Stamp

JOHN ADAMS (1735–1825)

Portrait of John Adams by Gilbert Stuart, circa 1815.

Act in 1765. He wrote articles in the newspapers and gave speeches claiming the act invalid. He soon after moved to Boston and set up his law practice there.

In 1770, Adams agreed to defend eight British soldiers charged with killing 5 civilians in what became known as the Boston Massacre. He justified taking on the very unpopular clients by claiming "It is more important that innocence be protected than it is that guilt be punished, for guilt and crimes are so frequent in this world that they cannot all be punished. But if innocence itself is brought to the bar and condemned, perhaps to die, then the citizen will say, 'whether I do good or I do evil is immaterial, for innocence itself is no protection,' and if such an idea as that were to take hold in the mind of the citizen that would be the end of security whatsoever." Adams won an acquittal for six of the soldiers and the other two, who had fired into the crowd, were convicted of manslaughter. Ultimately this enhanced his reputation as a courageous and fair man.

Adams was elected to the First Continental Congress in 1774 and then to the Second Continental Congress in 1775. In that year he nominated George

Washington as commander-in-chief of the Continental Army. Publicly, Adams supported "reconciliation if practicable," but privately agreed with Ben Franklin that independence was inevitable. He opposed various attempts, including the Olive Branch Petition, aimed at trying to find peace between the colonies and Great Britain.

On June 7, 1776, Adams seconded Richard Henry Lee's resolution of Independence and backed it strongly until its passage on July 2. Congress appointed Adams, Thomas Jefferson, Benjamin Franklin, Robert Livingston, and Roger Sherman to draft the declaration. This Committee of Five decided at Adams' urging that Jefferson would write the first draft. Adams played an important role in its completion and it passed Congress on July 4.

Adams was soon serving on as many as ninety committees, chairing twenty-five, more than any other Congressman and in 1777 he became head of the Board of War and Ordnance, which oversaw the Continental Army. Late that same year he was named as commissioner to France and in February 1778 he sailed for Europe. He was to negotiate an alliance with the French who were debating whether or not to recognize and aid the United States. In 1779, Adams was one of the American diplomats to negotiate the Treaty of Paris, which brought an end to the Revolutionary War. After the war, he remained in Europe and from 1784 to 1785 he arranged treaties of commerce with several European nations. In 1785 he became the first U.S. minister to England.

In 1788, Adams returned home after nearly ten years in Europe. The following year, he was placed on the ballot for America's first presidential election. Partly because Adams had been out of the country on diplomatic missions, had not participated in the Constitutional Convention, and had not unduly antagonized anyone in America, he received thirty-four electoral votes coming in second to Washington. In accordance with the Constitution at the time, Adams was sworn in as Vice President. The same results occurred in 1792. Adams' two terms as vice president were politically uneventful and he grew increasingly frustrated with the position as he did not have much clout with Washington.

The election of 1796 was the first contested American presidential election. During Washington's two terms, deep philosophical differences had caused a rift and led to the formation of two parties: the Federalists and the Democratic-Republicans. When Washington announced he would not be a candidate for a third term, an intense partisan struggle began. Adams was the Federalist nominee and Jefferson the opponent. Adams won with seventy-one electoral votes to sixty-eight for Jefferson who became vice president. Near the end of his term, he became the first President to occupy the newly constructed White House.

JOHN ADAMS (1735–1825)

During Adams' term as President, the dominant issue was the threat of war with France who were angered over the Jay Treaty with England. France had supported the Americans during the revolution and now they were at war with England and resented our dealing with them. In response, the French navy began attacking American merchant ships. In 1797, President Adams sent diplomats to create a treaty with France. Upon arrival, three French diplomats, nicknamed "X," "Y," and "Z", proceeded to ask for bribes to start negotiations. The story made its way to the American public and over the next two years, the United States carried on an undeclared naval war with France. Although the country's ships fought many battles, war was never formally declared. To silence critics of the war with France, Congress passed the Alien and Sedition Acts in 1798. These acts were created as a way to punish those who criticize the American government with the intent to harm the government's position. These laws proved very unpopular.

In the election of 1800, Adams again faced Jefferson and Aaron Burr in what was a bitter campaign. The results were Jefferson and Burr receiving 73 electoral votes while Adams received 65. The election tie was decided by the House of Representatives and Jefferson declared the winner. Adams left town in the predawn hours of March 4, 1801, and did not attend Jefferson's inauguration.

The Adams crypt beneath the United First Parish Church in Quincy, Massachusetts. John is on the left and Abigail on the right.

The Congress at York

Adams and Jefferson reconciled in 1812 and corresponded with each other for years. Adams got to see his son become America's sixth President. Perhaps fittingly, the two Declaration of Independence signatories both died fifty years to the day of the adoption of the document on July 4, 1826. On his deathbed, the ninety-year-old Adams whispered, "Thomas Jefferson survives." It wasn't the case. Five hours earlier, the eighty-three-year-old Jefferson had died at Monticello.

Adams is buried in a family vault beneath the Unitarian Church in Quincy Massachusetts. Unlike Washington and Jefferson, there is no monument to him in the national capital.

Samuel Adams
(1722–1803)

Boston's Radical Revolutionary

Buried at Granary Burial Ground,
Boston, Massachusetts.

**Continental Association • Declaration of Independence
Articles of Confederation • Governor**

Samuel Adams was an American statesman, political philosopher, and Founding Father, who signed three of the four founding documents. His role in the origins of the American Revolution cannot be overstated. He was a zealot for independence and a thorn in the side of the British. He spoke out against British efforts to tax the colonists and pressured merchants to boycott British products. John Adams, the second President, said of his cousin Sam that he embodied "steadfast integrity" and "universal good character." The Royal Governor of Massachusetts, Thomas Hutchinson, felt differently, saying there existed no "greater incendiary in the King's dominion or a man of greater malignity of heart" . . . as any passionate activist, he was controversial, but for sure, he was an ardent Patriot.

Adams was born in Boston on September 27, 1722. He was one of twelve children born to Samuel Adams Sr. and Mary Adams. Only three of these children lived past the age of three. The parents were devout Puritans, and the family lived on Purchase Street on the south end of colonial Boston. Samuel Sr. was a prosperous merchant, church deacon, and leading figure in Boston politics.

Samuel Jr. attended the Boston Latin School and then entered Harvard College at the age of fourteen in 1736. He supposedly was preparing for the

The Congress at York

Samuel Adams

ministry but exposure at Harvard to the ideas of philosophers like John Locke, who held that certain rights and liberties were inherent to humanity and that government should reflect the truth, shifted his interest toward politics. He graduated in 1740 but continued as a graduate student, earning a master's degree in 1743. In his thesis, he argued that it was lawful to resist the supreme magistrate if the commonwealth could not otherwise be preserved.

After Harvard, Adams decided to go into business. His business ventures were failures, and finally, his father made him a partner in the family's malthouse. His lack of interest and understanding of business led to its shutting down.

In 1748, Adams and some friends established a political newspaper called *The Independent Advertiser*. Sam became a frequent contributor to this newspaper, which became an outlet for his beliefs. His writings argued that people must resist any encroachment on their constitutional rights.

In October 1749, he married Elizabeth Checkley. Over the next seven years, she gave birth to six children, but only two survived to adulthood. In July 1757, Elizabeth died soon after giving birth to a stillborn son. Adams married again in 1764 to Elizabeth Wells but had no children.

SAMUEL ADAMS (1722–1803)

In 1756, he got his first steady job when the Boston Town Meeting elected him tax collector. He often failed to collect taxes and was held liable for the unpaid tax. He often paid with his own funds, and friends often chipped in to bail him out.

The British government was in deep debt after the French and Indian War and passed two measures to tax the colonies. The first, the Sugar Act of 1764, taxed molasses and refined sugar, and Adams was a powerful figure in opposition. He denounced the act, being one of the first to cry out against taxation without representation. Then, in 1765, Parliament passed the Stamp Act, a tax on all legal and commercial documents, newspapers, and court documents. This was like pouring gasoline on a fire and led to the founding of the Sons of Liberty which would play a role throughout the American Revolution. Their motto became "No Taxation without Representation." Adams made frequent use of colonial newspapers and suggested a boycott of British goods. There were frequent riots and violent attacks to intimidate tax collectors. Officials blamed Sam Adams for inciting the violence.

According to the modern scholarly interpretation of Adams, he supported legal methods of resisting parliamentary taxation, such as petitions, boycotts, and nonviolent demonstrations, but opposed mob violence. All the pressure generated by Adams's various activities resulted in the repeal of the Stamp Act in early 1766. The city of Boston rejoiced.

In 1767, Parliament struck again with the Townshend Acts, a series of laws that taxed goods imported to the colonies. The colonists saw the acts as an abuse of power and organized a boycott of British goods. In his letter that became known as the "Massachusetts Circular Letter," Adams urged the other colonies to join in the boycott. In response to protests and boycotts, the British sent troops to occupy Boston and quell the unrest. This resulted in frequent clashes between citizens and troops. In March 1770, after years of agitation, British troops found themselves backed into a corner amid a mob and fired, killing five civilians. Adams called it The Boston Massacre. He wanted the accused soldiers to receive a fair trial, convincing his cousin John Adams to take up their defense. He wanted to demonstrate that Boston was not controlled by a lawless mob. After the defendants were acquitted of murder, however, he wrote a condemnation of the outcome.

In 1772, Adams was behind the formation of the Committees of Correspondence, which connected the town meetings of Massachusetts to one another. Soon similar committees were formed in other colonies as well. In 1773, Parliament passed the Tea Act, which granted the East India Company a monopoly on the tea trade. Sam Adams was a key figure in organizing opposition, resulting in the famous Boston Tea Party in December 1773. His exact role in this event is unsure. Adams never revealed if he went to the wharf or if he was involved in the planning, but he worked to publicize and defend it.

This pain-aggression spiral continued as Parliament responded to the Tea Party by passing a series of four laws in 1774 known as the Coercive Acts or Intolerable Acts. The four acts were intended to punish Massachusetts and send a message to the other colonies. They were the Boston Port Act, Massachusetts Government Act, Administration of Justice Act, and Quartering Act. These oppressive acts sparked strong colonial resistance including the meeting of the First Continental Congress. Adams worked to coordinate resistance to the Coercive Acts, and in June 1774, he proposed the meeting in Philadelphia and was chosen as one of five delegates to represent Philadelphia. Friends bought him new clothes and paid his expenses for his first trip outside Massachusetts.

The Congress met from September 5 to October 26 in Carpenters' Hall with delegates from twelve of the colonies. Georgia did not participate. Sam Adams worked for colonial unity and was a force for the formation of a colonial boycott known as the Continental Association. They agreed to meet again in May. When Adams returned to Massachusetts, he served in the Massachusetts Provincial Congress, which created the first Minuteman companies—militiamen ready for action at a moment's notice. Admiral Montague, the British Governor of Newfoundland and officer in the Royal Navy, upon reading of the events of the Continental Congress, said, "I doubt not but that I shall hear Mr. Samuel Adams is hanged or shot before many months are at end. I hope so, at least."

The Boston Town Meeting selected Adams to attend the Second Continental Congress and added John Hancock to the delegation. Believing rumors that they were to be arrested for treason, Adams and Hancock left Boston in February 1775 and were in Concord on April 19, 1775, when British troops first clashed with local militia, igniting the Revolutionary War. After the battles at Lexington and Concord, General Gage, the commanding officer, issued a proclamation granting a pardon to all who would "lay down their arms and return to duties of peaceable subjects." He, however, excepted Hancock and Adams.

At the Second Continental Congress in Philadelphia, Adams signed the Declaration of Independence. He also nominated George Washington to be Commander in Chief of the Continental Army. His inflammatory rhetoric continued in a speech in Philadelphia where he castigated Americans who sided with the crown. "If ye love wealth better than liberty, the tranquility of servitude than the animating contest of freedom—go from us in peace," he said.

SAMUEL ADAMS (1722–1803)

"We ask not your counsels or arms. Crouch down and lick the hands which feed you. May your chains set lightly upon you, and may posterity forget that ye were our countrymen." Adams served on military committees in Congress and was particularly concerned with punishing loyalists, i.e., Americans who continued to support the British. He was appointed to the Board of War and was the Massachusetts delegate to the committee appointed to draft the Articles of Confederation. The resulting Articles were sent to the states for ratification in November 1777. Adams urged ratification from Philadelphia, and it was ratified by Massachusetts and signed by Adams in 1778, but it took until 1781 for all states to ratify.

Sam Adams took a two-month break from Congress to return home to Boston and move his family to Dedham, Massachusetts. His home on Purchase Street had been destroyed and vandalized, and all the furnishings had been stolen. He returned to Boston in 1781 after retiring from Congress and never left Massachusetts again.

The remainder of Adams's career was devoted to state rather than national politics. In the 1780s, Adams served as President of the Massachusetts Senate. In January 1788, he was elected to the Massachusetts ratifying convention. He was initially opposed to ratification of the Constitution, but he and Hancock listened to the debate carefully and eventually agreed to support it with the

Grave of Samuel Adams

promise that some amendments be added. Even with their support, it barely passed 187 to 168. From 1789 to 1793, he served as Lieutenant Governor under John Hancock. When Hancock died in office, Adams assumed the Governorship. Following that, Adams was elected to three consecutive one-year terms. He retired from politics after his tenure as Governor in 1797. He died at the age of eighty-one on October 2, 1803, and was interred at the Granary Burying Grounds in Boston.

Samuel Adams is a controversial figure in American history. Disagreement about his significance and reputation began before his death and continues to the present. Supporters of the Revolution praised Adams, but Loyalists viewed him as a sinister figure who used propaganda to incite ignorant mobs. Some on each side claim that without him, there would not have been a revolution. For Adams, personal happiness had never been the supreme goal. He preferred virtue. While other men in Congress and the Army found ways to improve their fortunes, Adams returned to Boston in 1781 even poorer than when he left for the first Continental Congress. Some have dubbed his life as a riches to rags story. He wrote no memoir, resisting even calls to assemble his political writings. He was rare for his ability to keep a secret, any number of which he took to the grave, including the backstory of the Boston Tea Party.

Elbridge Gerry
(1744 – 1814)

Founder of Gerrymandering

Buried at Congressional Cemetery,
Washington, D.C.

Declaration of Independence • Articles of Confederation

Elbridge Gerry was a very important Founder of the United States. He signed the Articles of Confederation and the Declaration of Independence. He was a major figure at the Constitutional Convention speaking to the convention 153 times. He served as Governor of Massachusetts and as Vice President under James Madison. He was smart, well educated, hardworking, and tenacious. He was also regarded as annoying and not well-liked. He would, after addressing the convention 153 times and winning many debates and forcing many compromises, be one of only three men who attended the convention to refuse to sign the Constitution. He then went on to oppose ratification. The term "gerrymandering" was coined while he was governor of Massachusetts and approved a controversial redistricting plan that favored Republicans.

Gerry was born in 1744 at Marblehead, Massachusetts. He was the third of eleven children although only five survived to adulthood. The family was wealthy and Gerry was educated by tutors and entered Harvard just before turning fourteen. After receiving a B.A. in 1762 and an M.A. in 1765, he participated in his father's merchant business. He entered the colonial legislature in 1772 where he worked closely with Samuel Adams. He, Adams, and Hancock served on the Council of Safety where Gerry raised troops and dealt with military logistics. On April 18, 1775, Gerry attended a council meeting at an inn

The Congress at York

Portrait of Elbridge Gerry by James Bogle after John Vanderlyn.

between Lexington and Concord and barely escaped the British troops marching on those towns.

In 1774 he was elected to the First Continental Congress but refused to serve because he was grieving the recent loss of his father. In 1776 he served in the Second Continental Congress where he supported and signed the Declaration of Independence and later was a signer of the Articles of Confederation.

Well known for his personal integrity, Gerry felt strongly about and advocated regularly about limiting central government and civilian control of the military. He also opposed the idea of political parties. He felt so strongly about the issue of centralizing too much power that he resigned from the Continental Congress in protest in 1780. He rejoined Congress in 1783 and served until 1785. The next year he married Ann Thompson who was twenty years younger than him. James Monroe was his best man. The couple settled in Cambridge and had ten children between 1787 and 1801.

Gerry played a major role at the U.S. Constitutional Convention held in Philadelphia during the summer of 1787. He arrived in late May several weeks after it had begun. During June he frequently helped check the nationalists by arguing and voting against their motions. He forced them to give up on an absolute veto power for the chief executive and on giving the central government an absolute power to negate state laws.

Gerry advocated indirect elections believing people could be easily misled. He managed to obtain such elections for the Senate whose members were to be elected by state legislatures but was unsuccessful in the case of the House. He made numerous proposals for the indirect election of the chief executive which was somewhat achieved with the Electoral College.

By the end of June, the Convention was on the verge of collapse over the issue of the relationship of the central government to the states. On July 2, after a deadlocked vote on whether the states would be equally represented in the Senate, Gerry told his colleagues that if the Convention failed "we shall not only disappoint America but the rest of the world." A committee was appointed to produce a compromise and Gerry was appointed its chairman. A compromise on the issues was finally achieved which provided for proportional representation in the House and equal representation in the Senate and provided that the House would raise revenue and appropriate money. When Gerry presented the committee report to the full convention for approval he stated: "If we do not come to some agreement among ourselves, some foreign sword will probably do the work for us." On July 15, after ten more days of debate, it was put to a vote. It passed by a 5–4 margin. Gerry had played an important role at a critical juncture in the convention.

Once the convention moved on, Gerry was a strong advocate for issues he believed in. Between July 17 and July 26, he made twenty-nine speeches on the powers to be granted to the central government, the jurisdiction of the judiciary, and the election of the President. He opposed the Congress electing the President instead proposing that the governors select the electors who would elect the President. It was at his urging that the Convention adopted an impeachment provision. He was also successful in proposing that senators of a state vote as individuals rather than cast a single vote on behalf of the state which at that point was the assumption.

During the next six weeks, Gerry made seventy-eight speeches on such issues as limiting the power of the central government, preventing a peacetime standing army, limiting the size of the army, and empowering the President only to make war but not to declare war. He opposed having a Vice President, an office he would one day hold.

Gerry was unhappy about the lack of expression of any sort of individual liberties in the proposed Constitution. On September 17, he addressed the Convention for the one hundred fifty-third and last time stating he could not sign the document. He then watched as thirty-nine men signed it. Two others, Edmund Randolph and George Mason, also refused.

Gerry continued his opposition during the ratification debates that took place after the convention. He published a letter that was widely circulated documenting his objections. He cited the lack of a Bill of Rights as his primary objection. If the people adopted the document as it stood, they were in danger of losing their liberties. But if they rejected it altogether, anarchy may ensue. His opposition cost him a number of close political friends. Massachusetts ratified the Constitution but recommended amendments. Before the Massachusetts

The grave of Elbridge Gerry at Congressional Cemetery in Washington, D.C. (photo by Lawrence Knorr).

ELBRIDGE GERRY (1744–1814)

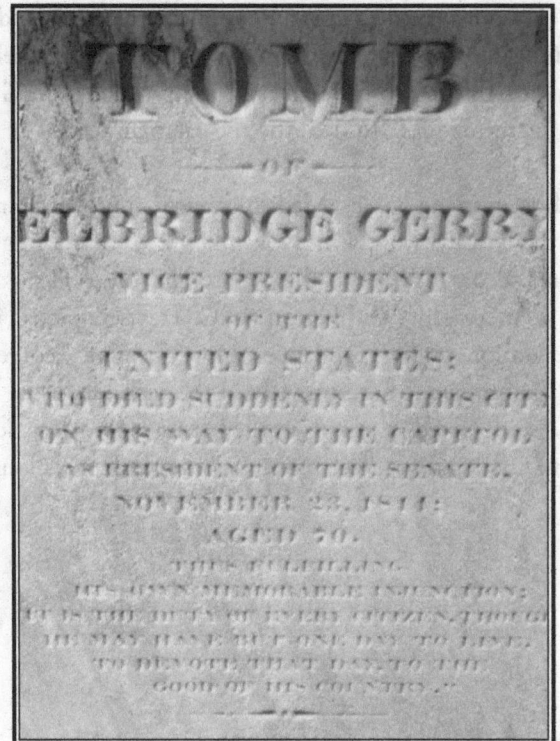

Detail of Gerry's tombstone (photo by Lawrence Knorr).

ratification convention, none of the states had requested amendments. After it, all but one ratified it with proposed amendments.

In 1789, after he announced his intention to support the Constitution, he was elected to the first Congress where he championed federalist policies. He proposed that Congress consider all the proposed constitutional amendments that various states had called for. He successfully lobbied for inclusion of freedom of assembly in the First Amendment and was a leading architect of the Fourth Amendment protections against search and seizure.

In 1793, after two terms in Congress, Gerry did not stand for re-election and returned home. His retirement from public service didn't last long as in 1797 President Adams appointed him to be a member of a special diplomatic commission sent to France to negotiate a reconciliation in hopes of avoiding a war. This episode became known as the XYZ Affair. The mission failed and Gerry's reputation was damaged.

Between 1800 and 1803 Gerry ran four times for the governorship of Massachusetts and lost each time. He tried again in 1810 and won. He repeated a victory in 1811. Both times he ran as a Republican. Near the end of his second term, the Republicans passed a redistricting measure to ensure their domination of the state senate. This led to Federalists heaping ridicule on Gerry and they used the term "gerrymander" to describe the salamander shape of one of the new districts.

He was chosen to be James Madison's vice presidential running mate in 1812 and they easily won. On November 23, 1814, the seventy-year-old Gerry collapsed on his way to the Senate and died. He is buried in the Congressional Cemetery in Washington, D.C. He is depicted in two paintings, the "Declaration of Independence" and "General George Washington Resigning His Commission" both on view in the rotunda of the United States Capitol. He is also depicted in murals in the National Archives near displays of the Articles of Confederation, Declaration of Independence, Constitution, and Bill of Rights.

Nathaniel Folsom
(1726 – 1790)

Merchant Militiaman

Buried at Winter Street Cemetery,
Exeter, New Hampshire.

Continental Association

Nathaniel Folsom was a delegate to the Continental Congress from New Hampshire and the Major General of the New Hampshire Militia. He was also a merchant and holder of several state offices. Folsom signed the Continental Association as a member of the First Continental Congress in 1774.

Nathaniel Folsom was born in Exeter, Rockingham County, New Hampshire, on September 18, 1726, the son of Jonathan Folsom and his wife, Ann (née Ladd) Folsom. Nathaniel was the eighth of twelve children, including siblings Anna, Sarah, Lydia, Elizabeth, Abigail, John, Mary, Jonathan, Samuel, Josiah, and Trueworthy. His ancestors were early settlers in Massachusetts and were related to the Gilmans.

Young Nathaniel attended public schools. When his father died in 1740, when he was thirteen, he took employment with a merchant. As a young man, he invested in timber and opened a sawmill. He married first Dorothy Smith (1726–1776), with whom he had seven children: Nathaniel, Dorothy, Jonathan, Anna, Arthur, Mary, and Deborah. Both Deborah and Mary later married John Taylor Gilman, the Governor of New Hampshire. Nathaniel married second Mary Sprague, with whom he had a daughter Ruth.

With the outbreak of the French and Indian War in 1754, Folsom joined the militia. The next year, he was a captain in Colonel Joseph Blanchard's New

The Congress at York

An imagined Nathaniel Folsom.

Hampshire Provincial Regiment under Sir William Johnson during the Crown Point expedition. At the Battle of Lake George, his company captured the French commander-in-chief, Major General Jean-Armand Baron de Dieskau, the baggage train, and critical supplies. Only six men were lost in his company. Over the rest of the war, Folsom was promoted to major, lieutenant colonel, and then colonel of the Fourth Regiment of the New Hampshire militia.

In 1761, Folsom partnered with his cousins, Joseph and Josiah Gilman, to form the merchant company Folsom, Gilman & Gilman. They operated a general store, a shipbuilding operation, and imported and exported goods. Folsom split from his cousins in 1768 but continued in the timber, lumber, and trade industries. He also became involved in local politics in Exeter, moderating town meetings.

Folsom was a delegate in July 1774, when the revolutionary assembly was convened. They sent him as a delegate to the First Continental Congress in Philadelphia. He attended sessions from September 5, 1774, the Continental Congress's first day, through October 26, 1774. The Continental Association, limiting imports and exports to and from England, was adopted on October 20. Folsom was a signatory.

NATHANIEL FOLSOM (1726–1790)

With the increase in hostilities, Governor Wentworth revoked Folsom's commission as colonel of the militia. This did not deter Folsom from leading his troops to aid in protecting Boston during the British siege. His men safely escorted captured cannons from Portsmouth to Durham. Folsom was given the rank of major general of the New Hampshire militia, numbering about 2000 men. He sent some of his men to aid Fort Ticonderoga.

On April 1, 1777, Folsom was again elected to the Continental Congress. He arrived in Philadelphia on July 20 and began serving the following day. On September 18, word came of the pending invasion of Philadelphia by the British. Whether in haste or as his custom, Folsom hopped on a horse without a saddle and headed out to York. There, he participated in the debates concerning the Articles of Confederation and was against taxation methods being proposed. He felt it unfair to tax property but to exclude slaves in the calculations, as the southern delegates argued. Folsom voted against the Articles of Confederation.

He wrote,

> Inclosed, I send you a copy of the Articles of confederation [*sic*] as far as agreed to by Congress. The 9th article is, 'That the proportion of public expense incurred by the United States for their common defense and general welfare, to be paid by each State into

Nathaniel Folsom's grave marker.

the Treasury, be ascertained by the value of all lands within each state granted to or surveyed for any person, as such land and the buildings and improvements thereon, shall be estimated according to such mode as Congress shall from time to time direct.' This article was opposed by all the New England Delegates and we are yet in hopes of having it re-considered.

Folsom was a member of a delegation of congressmen who visited Valley Forge during the winter of 1777/78. He and the others reported on the terrible conditions to Congress. After his term ended, he returned to New Hampshire, where he was elected Executive Councilor in 1778. This role was essentially the co-governor of New Hampshire.

In 1783, Folsom was a delegate to New Hampshire's constitutional convention, serving as its president. He was then the chief justice on the Court of Common Pleas in Exeter. Folsom died at Exeter on May 26, 1790, and was buried at the Winter Street Cemetery.

John Witherspoon
(1723 – 1794)

President of Princeton

Buried at Princeton Cemetery,
Princeton, New Jersey.

Declaration of Independence • Articles of Confederation

John Witherspoon is a hard man to understand. He was a renowned theologian from Scotland who was invited to be president of the College of New Jersey, now Princeton University. He was extraordinarily successful in that role and went on to embrace the revolutionary cause. He was the only clergyman to sign the Declaration of Independence and the Articles of Confederation. He also served at the convention that ratified the U.S. Constitution in New Jersey. He was a highly active member of the Continental Congress and served in the New Jersey state government. Yet Witherspoon owned slaves and lectured *against* the abolition of slavery.

He was born in Gifford, Scotland, and received the finest education available at that time. He attended the preparatory school in Haddington, Scotland, and obtained a master of arts degree from the University of Edinburgh in 1739. He remained at Edinburgh to study divinity. In 1764 he was awarded an honorary doctoral degree in divinity by the University of St. Andrews. In 1743 he became a Presbyterian Minister at a parish in Beith, Scotland, where he married Elizabeth Montgomery. The couple had ten children, with five surviving to adulthood. He remained in Beith until 1758 and, in that time, authored three notable works on theology. From 1758 to 1768, he was minister of the Laigh Kirk, Paisley, a large growing parish church. There he became very prominent within the church.

The Congress at York

John Witherspoon

Witherspoon was aggressively recruited by the trustees of the College of New Jersey in 1766, who needed a first-rate scholar to serve as its president. He was at first unable to accept due to his wife's great fear of crossing the sea. The trustees persisted, particularly Richard Stockton and Benjamin Rush, who visited the Witherspoons and convinced them to accept. He had a comfortable life and was well respected in the U.K., so it was a big decision. They arrived in Philadelphia in early August of 1768.

He enjoyed great success at the college. He turned it into a remarkably successful institution and was extremely popular as a result. He wrote frequent essays on subjects of interest to the colonies. He taught courses and recruited quality staff and students. Moral Philosophy was a required course as he considered it vital for ministers, lawyers, and those in government. Among his students were five delegates to the U.S. Constitutional Convention, including James Madison. Among his students came 37 judges (3 became Supreme Court Justices), 10 Cabinet officers, 12 members of the Continental Congress, 28 U.S. Senators, and 49 Congressmen.

While Witherspoon first abstained from political concerns, he came to support the revolution, joining the Committee of Correspondence and Safety in early 1774. The British referred to his college as a "seminary of sedition." He was passionate about American independence and the necessity of checks

JOHN WITHERSPOON (1723–1794)

Witherspoon bronze at Princteon.

and balances for an ethical form of government. Following along the traditions of John Locke, he believed that "because of the depravity of human nature, government power needs to be carefully limited and separated among branches and levels . . . to prevent any one level, any one branch, or any one individual in government from becoming too powerful."

In 1776 he was elected to the Continental Congress, where he voted for Richard Henry Lee's famous resolution for independence and the Declaration of Independence. He was one of the most active members of the Congress, serving on an exceptionally large number (Over 120) of committees, was appointed Congressional Chaplain, helped draft the Articles of Confederation, helped organize the executive departments, and drew up the instructions for the Peace Commissioners. Perhaps his most important contribution during the war happened due to his role on the Committee for Foreign Affairs. Fluent in French, he wrote a letter to a French agent introducing Ben Franklin and explaining the necessity of an alliance between the colonies and France, without which the course of the revolutionists might have been lost.

The year 1777 was tough for John Witherspoon. His son Major James Witherspoon was killed at the Battle of Germantown, and as the fighting neared Princeton, he closed and evacuated the college. The main building, Nassau Hall, was severely damaged, and his papers were lost. The school remained closed for several years.

Witherspoon left the Continental Congress in November 1782 to rebuild his beloved Princeton. During the summer of 1783, the Continental Congress met in Nassau Hall, making Princeton the nation's capital for four months. Between 1783 and 1789, he sat for two terms in the New Jersey Legislature and strongly supported the adoption of the Constitution during the ratification debates. In 1789 his wife Elizabeth died. In 1791 the 68-year-old delighted the college community by marrying a 24-year-old widow, Ann Dill, with whom he had two daughters.

The grave of John Witherspoon.

JOHN WITHERSPOON (1723–1794)

Witherspoon's last years were filled with difficulty. He lost one eye on a fundraising trip to Great Britain in 1784 and lost his sight completely in 1792. On November 15, 1794, he died at his farm at the age of 71 and was buried along President's Row in Princeton Cemetery.

An inventory of Witherspoon's possessions taken at his death included two slaves valued at $100 each. This deeply religious man, who required all his students to attend his lectures on moral philosophy, owned slaves and lectured against the abolition of slavery. In 1779 when he moved from the President's House on campus to the newly completed country home called "Tusculum" he purchased two slaves to help him run the 500-acre estate. When helping to draft the Articles of Confederation, Witherspoon sided with Southern states and adamantly opposed the taxation of slaves, comparing slaves to horses as simply another form of property. In 1782 he gave lectures disapproving of the slave trade, yet he owned slaves and retained ownership of them.

For all his discussion about the injustice of holding men in bondage "by no better right than superior power," he ultimately concluded that emancipating them was not necessary, stating, "I do not think there lies any necessity on those who found men in a state of slavery, to make them free to their own ruin."

This conclusion conveniently absolved him and other slaveholders of their moral dilemma. Slavery continued in New Jersey until the end of the Civil War.

James Duane
(1733–1797)

Conservative Founder

Buried beneath the Christ Episcopal Church,
Duanesburg, New York.

**Continental Congress • Continental Association
Articles of Confederation**

This founder's biography, written by the historian Edward Alexander, was titled *A Revolutionary Conservative*. It is true that this patriot sincerely wished for the colonies to find a way to reconcile with England without having to resort to an armed rebellion. However, once that Revolution began, he became a leader of the war effort. He would serve in multiple posts during his lifetime. He represented New York in the Continental Congress, was a New York state senator, the first post-colonial mayor of New York City, and a United States district judge. His name was James Duane.

Duane was born on February 6, 1773, in New York City. His father, Anthony Duane, was an Irish Protestant from County Galway who came to the New World as an officer in the Royal Navy. He left the navy and married Eva Benson, who was the daughter of a local merchant. The couple had two sons Abraham and Cornelius. Anthony Duane grew wealthy through the purchase of land used for rental and development. His wife died, and Duane remarried Althea Ketaltas, who gave birth to the future founder. Ketaltas was the daughter of a wealthy Dutch merchant, and by the time their son was born, his parents were very well-to-do colonial settlers.

Duane's mother passed away in 1736, and his father died in 1747. The fourteen-year-old Duane became the ward of Robert Livingston. He received

JAMES DUANE (1733-1797)

James Duane

his early education at Livingston Manor. By 1754 he demonstrated a thorough command of the law, and he was admitted to the bar. From that year until 1762, he operated a private law practice in the city of his birth. He closed that practice when he became a clerk of the Chancery Court of New York.

Duane married Mary Livingston in 1759. She was the eldest living daughter of his former guardian. The couple had six children. Duane's wife influenced his political thinking. He had been a member of James Delancey's conservative political faction, which opposed British policies and at the same time opposed the use of any violence to protest these measures. Livingston did not share those views, and Duane evolved to the point of becoming a leader among New York's patriots.

In 1767 Duane became the Attorney General for the province of New York. He served as a boundary commissioner within a year, a position he would assume again in 1784. In 1774 he returned to the private practice of law. By this time, his practice was earning him 1,400 pounds a year. He owned a house in Manhattan and an estate close to Schenectady, New York, of 36,000 acres and housed more than 200 tenants. Among his clients was the Trinity Church, who he represented in legal action that resulted when heirs of Anneke Jan's claimed that they were the rightful owners of a majority of lower Manhattan, a tract of land awarded to the church by the British crown.

In 1774, Duane was among New York's representatives to the First Continental Congress meeting in Philadelphia in response to the British blockading Boston Harbor and Parliament's passage of the Intolerable Acts. The American Congress message to England was the Continental Association which Duane supported and signed. The Association took effect on December 1, 1774. It called for a trade boycott with the mother country. Congress hoped that economic sanctions would pressure the English Parliament to repeal the Intolerable Acts. Duane was one of several members of Congress who still hoped for reconciliation with England. He supported the Galloway Plan of Union, which was presented to Congress by Pennsylvania delegate Joseph Galloway. The plan called for creating an American Parliament that would act together with the Parliament of Great Britain. Congress did not accept it though its defeat was a narrow one, losing six to five on October 22, 1774.

After Duane returned to New York, he was named to the Committee of Sixty in 1775. The Committee was responsible for enforcing the boycott brought about by the Continental Association. In April of that year, he was again elected to represent his state in the Second Continental Congress. He would serve in this Congress until 1781. On May 15, 1776, Congress published a resolution saying the colonies needed to form new governments. John Adams believed this was "the most important resolution that was ever taken in America" because by forming their own governments, the colonies were in effect declaring their independence. Duane opposed the resolution and wrote to his fellow New Yorker, John Jay, that there was "no reason that our colony should be too precipitate in changing the present form of government." Despite these reservations relative to breaking with the mother country, he supported the Declaration of Independence, but due to his service with the Provincial Congress of New York, he was not present in Philadelphia to sign that document.

In July of 1776, Duane attended the New York Constitutional Convention. Apparently, by this time, he had changed his views on changing the present form of government since the purpose of the gathering was to draft a constitution to replace the colonial charter.

Duane was present in Philadelphia in 1777 when the Articles of Confederation was written. In July of 1778, he was among the signers of the document that initially united the colonies. The Articles were ratified in 1781, and Duane remained a member of the Confederation Congress until 1783.

JAMES DUANE (1733–1797)

Grave of James Duane inside the chapel at Duanesburg.

Duane remained an active public servant after the war ended. He served as the first post-colonial Mayor of New York from 1784 until 1789. During these years, he successfully revived the city after the damage done during the war and by the British occupation. He was unsuccessful in his attempt to keep the capital of the United States in New York.

In the post-war years, Duane also served two terms in the New York State Senate. He was also one of the prominent New Yorkers who met to create the New York Manumission Society to pressure the state to abolish slavery. In 1789, President Washington nominated Duane to a seat on the United States District Court for New York City. He was confirmed by the United States Senate and served until 1794, when he retired due to health problems. On February 1, 1797, he passed away and was laid to rest beneath Christ Church in Duanesburg, New York.

As recently as 1999, there was a debate in the *New York Daily News* relative to Duane's place as a founder. The debate was prompted by then-Mayor Rudy Giuliani's decision to hang Duane's portrait in City Hall's ceremonial Blue Room. Timothy L. Collins writing in opposition to this decision, stated that Duane "was widely accused of loyalist sympathies before and during the Revolution. He was instrumental in appeasing the crown and impeding the cause of American independence." This view was answered in print by a descendant of the founder, John F. Duane, who acknowledged that while his ancestor was a "conciliator who worked to settle the differences between England and the Colonies before the Revolutionary War, he was no loyalist. Once blood was shed at Lexington on April 19, 1775, Duane became a leader in the war effort. As a member of the Committee of One Hundred, the de facto city government at the outbreak of the Revolutionary War, Duane successfully proposed that all inhabitants arm themselves." Duane's descendant went on to point out that he was instrumental in financing the Colonial Army. He was so successful that he became a trusted confidant of General George Washington. In the authors' view, John Duane presented a convincing case that James Duane be remembered as an "honorable and dedicated patriot who truly was one of the Founding Fathers of our great nation."

William Duer
(1743–1799)

"The Panic of 1792"

Buried at Grace Episcopal Churchyard,
Queens, New York.

Articles of Confederation

William Duer was a British-born financier and land speculator from New York City who was elected to the Continental Congress, where he signed the Articles of Confederation on behalf of New York. During the debates concerning the U.S. Constitution, he wrote under the pen name "Philo Publius," backing the Federalist perspective. Near the end of his life, he was caught up in the 1792 financial panic and died in debtors' prison.

Duer, born March 18, 1743, in Devon, Devonshire, England, was the son of John Duer, a wealthy plantation owner, and his wife, Frances (née Frye) Duer, the daughter of Sir Frederick Frye of Antigua. John Duer owned a villa in Devon and plantations in the Caribbean on the islands of Antigua and Dominica, which generated significant income. The couple met in Antigua and were married there.

Duer was taught by private tutors before attending the prestigious boarding school, Eton, in the northwest of London. Though underage in 1762, Duer entered the British army as an ensign, accompanying Robert Clive as his aide-de-camp as he returned to India to be the governor-general of the British East-India Company. Duer did not adjust to the climate and returned to England.

The British government contracted Duer to build masts and rigging for the British Navy in 1764. He traveled to New York to purchase supplies and noted

The Congress at York

William Duer

the potential of the American colonies. Philip Schuyler, one of the wealthiest men in New York, urged Duer to invest in the timber lands near Saratoga on the Hudson, which he did. This area became known as Fort Miller and served as Duer's first residence in New York. He set up sawmills, warehouses, and a store.

Upon his father's death in 1767, Duer inherited his father's estates in the Caribbean. He now supplied lumber from New York to the islands and the British Navy and traded extensively with Schuyler. By the early 1770s, Duer had moved to Fort Miller permanently. In 1773, he made his final trip to England to settle his affairs, sold his properties, and returned to New York.

As an English gentleman with Caribbean plantations, Duer quickly became an influential citizen in New York. He held local positions of influence including jurist of the Charlotte County court and serving on the road commission.

In 1775, Duer was a delegate to the New York Provincial Congress and was appointed as a colonel and deputy adjutant general of the New York militia. In June 1776, he was a delegate to the New York convention to create a new state constitution. He was then elected as a state senator, serving from September 9, 1777, to June 30, 1778.

WILLIAM DUER (1743–1799)

On March 29, 1777, the New York Provincial Congress elected Duer to the Continental Congress, serving until November 16, 1778. During his tenure, he was worried about the financing of the army and weary of the disagreements in Congress. However, he impressed John Adams, Robert Morris, and others with his participation on the finance committee and the "Board of War." He signed the Articles of Confederation in November 1777.

After leaving Congress, Duer returned to his business pursuits in partnership with John Holker, a French commercial agent. Robert Morris arranged contracts to supply the American army, benefitting Duer.

In 1779, Duer married Lady Catherine Alexander, a daughter of Major General William Alexander "Lord Stirling" and Sarah (née Livingston) Alexander. The wedding was at Stirling's elegant country home, "The Buildings," near Basking Ridge, New Jersey. The marriage connected Duer to the powerful Alexander and Livingston families of New York and New Jersey. The couple had eight children:

- William Alexander Duer (1780–1858) was a justice of the New York State Supreme Court and, for many years, the President of Columbia University. He married Hannah Maria Denning (1782–1862), daughter of U.S. Representative William Denning.
- John Duer (1782–1858) was a noted lawyer and jurist of New York. He married Anna Bedford Bunner (1783–1864), sister of U.S. Representative Rudolph Bunner.
- Frances Duer (1786–1869) was married to Beverley Robinson (1779–1857), grandson of merchant Beverley Robinson.
- Sarah Henrietta Duer (b. 1787) married John Witherspoon Smith, son and grandson of Princeton Presidents Samuel Stanhope Smith and John Witherspoon.
- Catherine Alexander Duer (1788–1882).
- Maria Theodora Duer (1789–1837) married Beverly Chew (1773–1851) in 1810.
- Henrietta Elizabeth Duer (1790–1839) married Morris Robinson (1784–1849), brother of Beverley Robinson and founder of the Mutual Life Insurance Company of New York.
- Alexander Duer (1793–1819) married Ann Maria Westcott (1808–1897), daughter of Colonel and New York State Senator David M. Westcott, in 1815.

Duer moved to New York City in 1783 and helped establish the Bank of New York in 1784. In 1786, he was elected to the New York Assembly. As the Constitution was signed and ratified, Duer was well connected to Robert Morris and Alexander Hamilton, Philip Schuyler's son-in-law. Duer entered into the debates about the merits of the Constitution, siding with Hamilton (who used the pen name "Publius") in three articles signed "Philo Publius" (aka Friend of Hamilton). In 1789, Hamilton became the first Secretary of the Treasury, and Duer was the first Assistant Secretary.

Duer then embarked on a scheme to speculate with government bonds involving the Bank of the United States and the Bank of New York. The goal was to buy up American debt at a discount, but the markets fluctuated wildly in early 1792, bankrupting Duer personally and resulting in the loss of significant funds to the federal government in what was known as The Panic of

The grave of William Duer.

1792. Secretary Hamilton, apparently not involved, requested the resignation of Duer, who refused. On March 23, 1792, Duer was arrested and thrown in debtor's prison. Historians still debate whether Duer's actions were deliberate or due to incompetence. Certainly, there was poor oversight.

While imprisoned, Duer managed to provide resources to his family via his lands in Vermont and Maine, not subject to confiscation. The end of his life was confusing, as there were contrary reports about his death. On April 17, 1799, *The Times* of Alexandria, Virginia, reported that the proceedings of the case of *United States vs. William Duer* in the District Court of the United States in Washington, D.C., was halted due to the "death of the Defendant." Other newspapers reported he was still alive. Another Alexandria paper reported Duer's death, having died in debtors' prison, on April 18, 1799. Reported the *Connecticut Gazette* of New London, "Died, in [a] New-York prison, Col. WILLIAM DUER, aged 54, of speculating memory."

Duer was initially interred at St. Thomas Church in Floral Park, New York, in the Duer family vault. He was later exhumed and moved to Grace Episcopal Churchyard in Queens, New York.

Mrs. Duer remarried William Nelson on September 15, 1801.

Duer's noteworthy descendants include:

- Denning Duer, a grandson.
- William Duer (1805–1879), who served in the U.S. Congress representing New York, a grandson.
- James Gore King Duer, a great-grandson.
- Alice Duer Miller (1874–1942), the feminist poet and writer, a great-great-granddaughter.

Cornelius Harnett
(1723 – 1781)

Hero of Cape Fear

Buried at St. James' Churchyard,
Wilmington, North Carolina.

Articles of Confederation

Cornelius Harnett was a wealthy plantation owner and merchant from Wilmington, North Carolina, who was also a Continental Congressman. He was a signer of the Articles of Confederation and died soon after being captured and tortured by the British.

Harnett was born in Edenton, Chowan County, North Carolina, on April 20, 1723. He was the son Cornelius Harnett, Senior, and his wife Elizabeth. The elder Harnett, a native of Ireland, was a colonial official and planter. In 1726, when young Cornelius was three, the family moved to Brunswick Town near what is now Cape Fear, close to the city of Wilmington, North Carolina. In that city, the younger Harnett grew to become a merchant and operated distilleries, businesses, and a schooner in the Cape Fear area. With the proceeds, he purchased a plantation called "Poplar Grove" nearby.

Meanwhile, Brunswick Town had become the busiest port in North Carolina, shipping goods to and from Europe and the British West Indies. When Spanish privateers attacked the first week of September 1748, the townspeople fled to the woods and their homes were looted. A local captain, William Dry, rallied 67 men to expel the invaders. Among them was Cornelius Harnett, Jr. The counterattack was successful. Only one local was killed while ten privateers were killed and thirty captured. One of their two ships exploded, killing

CORNELIUS HARNETT (1723–1781)

Etching of "Poplar Grove," the home of Cornelius Harnett near Wilmington, North Carolina.

most aboard. The second ship was captured and the goods and slaves recovered. The contraband that was captured was subsequently sold to fund St. Philip's Church in Brunswick Town and St. James' Church in Wilmington.

In 1750, Harnett was elected as a member of the Wilmington city commission and appointed as a justice of the peace, where he served until 1777. In 1754, Harnett was elected to a seat in the North Carolina General Assembly. He took a leading role in that body following the passage of the Stamp Act by the British Parliament. Harnett joined in the march in Brunswick Town in February 1766 to openly protest the act. He became a leading voice against the royal governor, William Tryon, and became chairman of the local Sons of Liberty. In June 1770, Harnett led the resistance to the Townshend Acts, effectively boycotting British imports.

In December 1773, following the Boston Tea Party, Harnett joined the first Committee of Correspondence in North Carolina. He subsequently joined the North Carolina Council of Safety in 1776 as war with Britain was underway. Harnett was unanimously elected the group's president, becoming North Carolina's first (unelected) chief executive as an independent state. In this role, Harnett corresponded with political and military leaders. He also personally took up arms against the British, marching with General John Ashe to sack the British encampment at Fort Johnson. This drew the attention of the British who put a bounty on his head.

The Congress at York

In 1776, Harnett served in the North Carolina provincial congresses in Halifax, North Carolina, and was chairman of the committee that drafted the state constitution. Under his direction, the group sent a document to the Continental Congress, now known as the "Halifax Resolves," calling for a declaration of independence from England. This was the first official action by a colony that called for separation from England.

Harnett was elected to the Continental Congress in May of 1777, just in time for Congress to abandon Philadelphia after the British occupation. Later that year, Harnett participated in the formulation of the Articles of Confederation to which he was a signer. Harnett returned to North Carolina at great risk at a time when the British were reasserting control throughout the south.

In January 1781, the British took Wilmington, North Carolina. Harnett, who was suffering from gout, was recuperating at a friend's house thirty miles away. He was found and captured by British Major James Craig's marauders. His hands and feet were tied and he was tossed across a horse "like a sack of meal." Harnett was carried back to town where he was thrown in a blockhouse that had no roof. Exposed to the elements, Cornelius succumbed on April 18, 1781.

Harnett was laid to rest in St. James' Churchyard in Wilmington, North Carolina. He has a nondescript stone stating an incorrect date of death. Harnett County, North Carolina, is named in his honor. Harnett had married Mary Holt, but the couple had no children. She died in 1792.

Grave of Cornelius Harnett at St. James Churchyard Cemetery in Wilmington, North Carolina (photo by Lawrence Knorr).

John Penn
(1741–1788)

The Penn with a Pen

Buried at Guilford Courthouse National Military Park,
Greensboro, North Carolina.

Declaration of Independence • Articles of Confederation

Though born and raised in Virginia this Founder represented North Carolina in the Continental Congress. His chief contribution to the cause of American independence was affixing his name to the document that declared it. A skilled attorney he was noted for his oratorical gifts in his practice before judges and juries. He also reasoned his way out of a duel with the President of Congress as they were on their way to the dueling ground. His name was John Penn.

Penn was born on May 17, 1741, just outside of Fredericksburg, Virginia. His father was a farmer and his mother the daughter of a county judge. It appears that Penn's father did not value education as his son only attended school for a couple of years. By the time he reached the age of 18, Penn had different ideas regarding how to make his way in the world. His cousin, Edmund Pendleton, was an attorney and Penn began borrowing books from his library which he used to teach himself to read and write. Next, he studied law under Pendleton and earned his license to practice when he was 21.

Penn would practice the law for over a decade in Virginia. During that time he married Susan Lyme and the couple would welcome three children into the world. In 1774 the Penns moved to North Carolina where he not only resumed his law practice but also developed an interest in the patriot cause. He certainly impressed the people in his adopted state as in 1775 he was elected as a representative to the second Continental Congress.

The Congress at York

Portrait of John Penn etched by H B Hall from a drawing in the collection of Dr. F A Emmet, 1871.

It would seem that as a member of Congress, Penn was a strong supporter of American independence. Early in 1776, he wrote to Thomas Person, a brigadier general in the North Carolina militia. Penn urged Person to "encourage our people, animate them to dare to even die for their country. Our struggle I hope will not continue long, may unanimity and success crown your endeavours."

On July 2, 1776, Penn and the other North Carolina representative Joseph Hewes voted in favor of American independence. The duo along with a third representative from North Carolina, William Hooper, who had been absent the day of the vote, signed the Declaration on August 2nd.

In 1778 Penn added his signature to the Articles of Confederation. It was during this time period that Penn found himself in multiple political arguments with Henry Laurens from South Carolina who had succeeded John Hancock as the President of Congress. Their battles reached a boiling point, at least for Laurens, and he challenged Penn to a duel to settle their differences.

The two would-be duelists lived in the same boarding house. The morning they were to meet on the field of honor, they sat together to eat their breakfast. Upon completing their meal, they walked together to the site chosen for the duel. Along the way, they came to a large muddy spot they needed to cross.

JOHN PENN (1741–1788)

Penn, being the younger man, proceeded to help Laurens across. During the crossing, Penn offered to let the whole matter drop and Laurens quickly agreed. They exchanged apologies and canceled the duel.

Penn left Congress in 1780 and the Governor of North Carolina, Abner Nash, promptly appointed him to his state's Board of War. Penn was an active member of the board and worked to supply war materials to Nathanael Greene's Continentals and Francis Marion's guerrillas. When the Revolution ended, he served for a short period of time as North Carolina's receiver of taxes for the Confederation government. He resigned this post because, in his view, he had not been given the authority he required to collect the taxes. He then returned to the practice of law.

Penn passed away on September 14, 1788, at the age of 47. He was laid to rest on the grounds of his home. In 1894 Penn's unmarked grave was located in a pasture marked by two large sassafras trees. According to *The Wilmington Messenger* authorities were able to find Penn's skull as well as many pieces of the walnut coffin. As reported by that paper these "sacred remains" were placed in a copper box and buried on the Guilford Battle Ground beneath a monument erected to honor North Carolina's signers. That spot marks John Penn's final resting place.

Grave of John Penn at Guilford Courthouse National Military Park in Greensboro, North Carolina (photo by Lawrence Knorr).

Robert Morris
(1734 – 1806)

Revolutionary Financier

Buried at Christ Episcopal Church and Churchyard,
Philadelphia, Pennsylvania.

**Declaration of Independence • Articles of Confederation
U.S. Constitution • Finance**

This Founder was once considered the wealthiest man in the country. He gave of his wealth willingly for the Revolution he helped bring about during his service in the Continental Congress. His signature can be found on the Declaration of Independence, the Articles of Confederation, and the United States Constitution. Along with George Washington and Benjamin Franklin, he is still widely viewed as one of the three men who made American Independence possible. He is also regarded as one of the founders of the financial system of the United States. For three years he served as the Superintendent of Finance, a time during which he was the central civilian in the government and considered by many to be, next to George Washington, the most powerful man in the country. He represented Pennsylvania in the United States Senate. Despite his widely successful career in business he spent over three years in debtor's prison and passed away in poverty. His name was Robert Morris.

Morris was born in Liverpool, England on January 20, 1734. His father was an ironmonger in Liverpool prior to emigrating to America to establish a tobacco shipping company in Oxford, Maryland. This business proved successful and when Morris reached the age of 13 he joined his father in America. In 1750 the elder Morris took a small boat in order to board a ship called the

ROBERT MORRIS (1734-1806)

Oil on canvas painting of Robert Morris by Robert Edge Pine, circa 1785.

Liverpool Merchant to follow the custom of welcoming the captain to America. That task completed, he climbed back into the little boat to return to shore. The captain, also following the custom at the time, readied the ship's cannon to fire a salute. An insect, possibly a fly, landed on the captain's nose and he raised his arm to chase it away. The crew viewed this action as a signal to fire the cannon which they did prematurely. Morris, Sr., who was only 20 yards away, was struck by wadding which broke his right arm. The wound developed an infection and he died six days later leaving his considerable fortune to his son.

The suddenly wealthy Morris had been educated in Philadelphia where he became an apprentice to a merchant and mayor of the city, Charles Willing. The mayor died in 1854 and his son made Morris a partner in the firm. In 1757 the two young businessmen formed a shipping and banking firm. They would remain partners until 1779.

In 1769 at the age of 35, Morris married the 20-year-old Mary White. The couple would produce seven children; five sons, and two daughters. White came from a well-respected Maryland family. Her brother, William White, was a well known Episcopal Bishop. Morris worshipped at St. Peters Church

The Congress at York

in Philadelphia which was run by his brother in law. When the Continental Congress was in session many of its members also worshipped there.

As a leading merchant in one of America's most important cities, Morris could not escape the political issues of the day. Though he did not believe the time was right for independence, he took the side of the colonies in the struggle with England. In 1774 he signed on to boycott the importation of British goods despite the damage it would do to his business.

In 1775 Morris was appointed to the Continental Congress. Here he put his business experience to work for the American cause. As a member of the committee for commerce, he worked to supply the Continental Army with supplies by paying for them with shipments of American goods. Still, as of July 1, 1776, he wasn't ready to vote for American independence. On that day he cast a preliminary vote opposing separating from England.

On July 2, 1776, when the official vote was taken he abstained so that Pennsylvania would not be the only colony that failed to support the measure. Once the measure was passed, he became an ardent supporter of American independence and on August 2, 1776, he signed the Declaration of Independence. Regarding this act, he said, "I am not one of those politicians that run testy when my own plans are not adopted. I think it is the duty of a good citizen to follow when he cannot lead."

There are numerous examples of the work Morris did that earned him the title "Financer of the Revolution." One of the most important of these occurred after Washington crossed the Delaware on his way to victory in the Battle of Trenton. As General Howe's British and German Hessian troops retreated, the American general was being urged to pursue and strike the enemy in order to capitalize on his recent victory. Washington's problem was that his battle-hardened New England recruits' enlistments were ending and they were due to go home. Washington sent a messenger to Morris asking him to gather enough money to pay each soldier a ten dollar bonus for extending their enlistment for six weeks. Since Washington wanted the funds to return with the messenger, Morris immediately went to work using his own funds and his own credit to fulfill Washington's request. In addition, Morris had heard that the general was also low on wine so in addition to the requested funds he sent along a quarter cask of good vintage. Using the funds Morris provided, Washington was able to keep the New Englanders in the army. It seemed that every time Washington was short on cash, Morris was able to find it. It has been reported that Morris gave one million of his own money to fund the decisive Yorktown campaign.

ROBERT MORRIS (1734–1806)

By the time the Revolution ended, Morris had already signed the Articles of Confederation creating a loose and ineffective union of the thirteen former colonies. In 1781 Congress named him the Superintendent of Finance. Only days after taking this position, Morris proposed the establishment of a national bank. The Bank of North America was the first financial institution chartered by the United States. The funding for the bank came, in part, through a loan from France which Morris had worked to obtain. He served as the Superintendent until 1784.

In 1787 Morris was one of Pennsylvania's representatives at the Constitutional Convention meeting in Philadelphia. On May 13th of that year Morris, now considered the richest man in the country, welcomed his old friend General Washington to Philadelphia and walked with him to his temporary residence where the General settled in comfortably in one of the city's grand mansions. On May 25th it was Morris who nominated Washington to be the President of the Convention. Though he attended the Constitutional Convention regularly, his participation was rare in that he spoke only twice and one of those occasions was nominating Washington. When the convention concluded, he added his name to the Constitution and worked for its ratification.

Some historians say that Washington wanted Morris to be the first Secretary of the Treasury but that the Pennsylvanian declined and recommended Alexander Hamilton who supported many of the policies that Morris had championed as the Superintendent of Finance. Morris was elected to the Senate and served in the first Congress. As a senator, he supported the Federalist agenda and strongly backed Hamilton's financial proposals. When some of his fellow members of that initial Congress expressed their frustration at what they viewed as slowness and inefficiency of the new government in accomplishing tasks, Morris disagreed. Older than many of his peers, Morris stated, "I have so often seen good consequences arise from public debate and discussion that I am not amongst the number of those who complain of the delay."

Morris, like several other Founders, was heavily involved in land speculation schemes. Unfortunately, in his case, a number were unsuccessful and he found himself unable to sell his western properties or pay the taxes on them. Many of those who witnessed the spectacular rise of Morris to the wealthiest man on the continent now watched a fall that was no less spectacular. Hounded by his creditors he was arrested and placed in a Philadelphia debtors' prison from February 1798 to August of 1801. In 1946 the *Harrisburg Evening News* reported that a review of his papers showed that Morris paid $1.25 a week for his board in his cell during his stay there. In 1800 Congress passed the temporary Bankruptcy Act which once enacted resulted in his release. The act was passed, at least in part to get Morris out of prison.

After his release, Morris was in ill health and was cared for by his wife for the rest of his days. He passed away May 8, 1806, and was laid to rest in the family vault of his brother in law Bishop William White in what is now the Christ Episcopal Church and Churchyard in Philadelphia. If you visit you will see a plaque placed by the Pennsylvania Constitution Commemorative Committee that notes his service during the Constitutional Convention. There is clearly far more to the story of this Founder who went from being the richest man in America to a Founder who, according to an April 19, 1939 article in the *Pittsburgh Post Gazette*, submitted "with patience and fortitude" to poverty.

Grave of Robert Morris at Christ Episcopal Church & Churchyard in Philadelphia, Pennsylvania (photo by Joe Farley).

Daniel Roberdeau
(1727 – 1795)

Pennsylvania Associator

Buried at Hebron Cemetery,
Winchester, Virginia.

Articles of Confederation • Military

Daniel Roberdeau was a Philadelphia merchant and brigadier general who led the Pennsylvania Associators, a branch of the militia. He was also a political leader in Philadelphia who was elected to the Second Continental Congress, where he signed the Articles of Confederation as a Pennsylvania delegate.

Roberdeau was born in 1727 on the Island of St. Chrisopher, also known as St. Kitts, in the West Indies, east of Puerto Rico. He was the son of a French Huguenot father, Isaac Roberdeau, and his wife, Mary (née Cunningham) Roberdeau, of Scottish origin. When his father died, the family moved to Philadelphia.

Roberdeau was initially educated in England, but then learned the merchant trade in Philadelphia, where he became a timber merchant, leveraging his connections in the Caribbean.

Circa 1749 to 1754, as an early adherent of Freemasonry in Philadelphia, Roberdeau became established among the leadership of that colonial city, including Benjamin Franklin. He was elected as a city warden in 1756 and served on the hospital board with Franklin. He was then elected to the Pennsylvania Assembly from 1756 to 1760.

On October 3, 1761, Roberdeau married Mary Bostwick of Philadelphia and joined in her Presbyterian faith. The couple ultimately had nine children,

Daniel Roberdeau

and Roberdeau became an elder of the church. He was again elected to the Pennsylvania Assembly, serving from 1766 to 1776, serving on the Committee of Finance and actively engaging the negotiations with the Native Americans.

Despite being involved in importing and exporting goods, Roberdeau was in favor of the non-importation protests of the early 1770s. After railing for the replacement of the current members of the Pennsylvania delegation in the Continental Congress, Roberdeau was appointed to the Pennsylvania Council of Safety in 1775 and chaired a protest against the king in May 1776 in Philadelphia that caught the attention of John Adams, who was attending the Continental Congress. Roberdeau signed as chairman of the committee that declared the King a mortal enemy. Adams wrote to James Warren on May 20, 1776, about the event, noting how orderly it was run. Roberdeau was a staunch supporter of independence and was appointed as a brigadier general in the Pennsylvania Militia, in charge of the Pennsylvania Associators.

Following the fall of New York in the summer of 1776, Roberdeau and his Associators engaged the British in New Jersey. Said Roberdeau to his men in a speech made on August 19, 1776: "As it hath pleased Providence, for the exercise of our patience, and for the defense of that freedom which we inherit from the great Giver of all things, to call us from our families to the field; and as I have the honor of being your General officer, I trust you will take it well in me to endeavor to point out to you whatever appears necessary, either for your own particular good, or the more noble object — the good of all."

Roberdeau's ability to lead and motivate was widely evident. Unfortunately, he became ill and was evacuated to Lancaster, Pennsylvania to recover. Meanwhile, the Pennsylvania Associators disbanded following the Battles of Trenton and Princeton. The colony then formalized the Pennsylvania Militia in March 1777.

Recovered from his illness, Roberdeau was elected to the Continental Congress on February 5, 1777, serving for two years. During the winter of 1777/78, when General Washington was at Valley Forge, Roberdeau set up and commanded what became known as the Flying Camp, an attempt to rally and organize state militias to the cause. Ultimately, the Flying Camp concept gave way to a centralized Continental Army.

In November 1777, Roberdeau was among the Continental Congressman who adopted the Articles of Confederation. Sadly, wife Mary Roberdeau passed away this year.

In April 1778, Roberdeau decided to deal with the shortage of ammunition in the army and left Congress for several months on an expedition into western Pennsylvania at his own expense to discover and establish a lead mine in what is now Blair County. He also built a timber palisade fort to protect it that became known as Fort Roberdeau or "Lead Mine Fort."

Roberdeau married his second wife, Jane Milligan, on December 3, 1778, and the mine produced 1000 pounds of lead. The mine ran into 1780, when production halted, and the fort became a haven for local settlers.

Following the war, in 1783, Roberdeau traveled to England with his son, Isaac, to arrange his education. He then returned to Philadelphia in 1784, but did not stay long. Instead, he moved to Alexandria, Virginia, where he established a wharf and distillery.

As his health began to fail, Roberdeau moved to Winchester, Virginia, to be near his daughter. He died there on January 5, 1795. The *Aurora General Advertiser* of Philadelphia noted, "Died . . . in this town, on Monday last, after a lingering illness, which he bore with great Christian fortitude, and patient resignation to the Divine Will, General Daniel Roberdeau. He formerly resigned in Alexandria, and was a man universally esteemed, not only on account of the meritorious services [that] he rendered this country in a military capacity, but also for his strict integrity, piety, benevolence and philanthropy."

The grave of Daniel Roberdeau

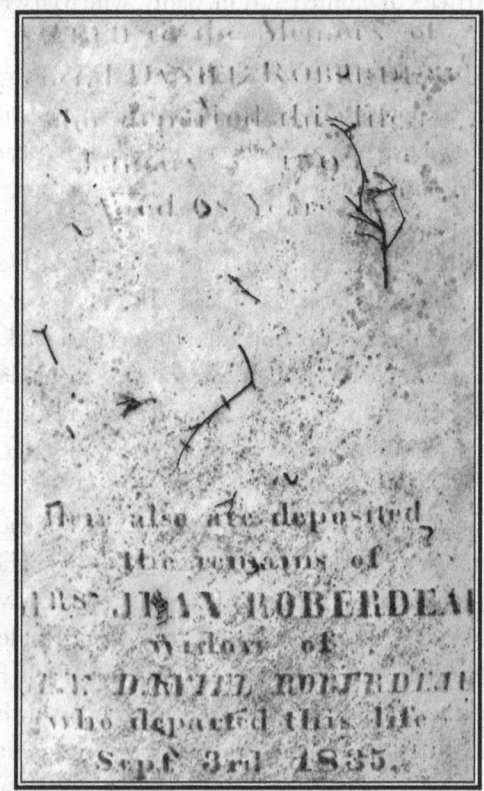

DANIEL ROBERDEAU (1727–1795)

Roberdeau was buried in Mount Hebron Cemetery in Winchester.

Son Isaac Roberdeau was an Army officer and civil engineer who assisted Pierre L'Enfant with the plan for Washington, D.C.

Fort Roberdeau was reconstructed in the 1930s and remains a historic site near Altoona, Pennsylvania.

Thomas Heyward Jr.
(1746–1809)

The Last to Sign the Declaration

Buried at Heyward Family Cemetery,
Old House, South Carolina.

Declaration of Independence • Articles of Confederation • Military

Thomas Heyward Jr. was a wealthy planter from South Carolina who, as a Continental Congressman, signed the Declaration of Independence and the Articles of Confederation. He also fought in the South Carolina militia during the Siege of Charleston.

Heyward was born on July 28, 1746, at the family estate "Old House," near Beaufort, Jasper County, South Carolina, the son of Daniel Heyward and his wife, Mary (née Miles) Heyward. Oddly, the family already had a son named Thomas when Heyward was born, and they liked the name so much that they had another and appended "Junior" to it. The Heyward ancestors were among the first to settle in what was then Carolina in 1670 and became wealthy planters.

In his early years, Heyward was educated at home. Then he decided to study law and traveled to London to attend the Middle Temple, starting on January 10, 1765. He achieved the bar on May 25, 1770.

The following year, now twenty-five, Heyward returned to South Carolina and was admitted to the bar there. He then followed in his father's footsteps as a planter and attorney. Next, the young scion found himself elected to the South Carolina Commons House of Assembly in 1772, where he served for several years.

THOMAS HEYWARD JR. (1746–1809)

Thomas Heyward Jr.

When tensions rose with England, Heyward was a delegate to the South Carolina provincial convention to determine the course of action in the colony. During this time, Heyward married Elizabeth Matthews of Charleston, the sister of John Mathews, a future governor of South Carolina. The couple had two sons.

When the new General Assembly was formed, Heyward was elected to it and appointed to the Council of Safety, serving in 1775 and 1776. On February 16, 1776, the General Assembly elected Heyward to a seat in the Continental Congress. He attended sessions from April 24, 1776, to September 4, 1776. During this time, he signed the Declaration of Independence and was likely the last to do so.

Heyward then returned to South Carolina and served in the General Assembly again. He was reelected to the Continental Congress and served from December 24, 1776, until October 31, 1777. During this time, he escaped with the Congress to York, Pennsylvania, and signed the Articles of Confederation.

Again, Heyward headed home to South Carolina, alternating between his plantation "White Hall" and his home in Charleston. In 1778, Heyward became a judge. At one trial, Heyward presided over a treason trial for several traitors. They were convicted and executed within sight of the British.

The Congress at York

When the British besieged Charleston, Heyward took up arms, fighting with General William Moultrie. He was badly wounded and unable to escape when the British took the city. On August 27, 1780, he was captured, and all 130 of his slaves were taken as booty, and then White Hall was burned. For this loss, he was later described by the press as a "martyr of the revolution."

Heyward and 28 others were taken to a ship in Charleston harbor. On September 4, they were moved to St. Augustine, Florida, where they remained until they were exchanged eleven months later. To pass the time in prison, Heyward rewrote the British song "God Save the King" and to reflect an American version, changing the title to "God Save the Thirteen States."

During his captivity, his wife and children lived in Philadelphia. Unfortunately, while awaiting his release, she died in childbirth in 1782. She was buried in the St. Peter's Episcopal Churchyard in Philadelphia. Although they had six children, only Daniel survived to adulthood.

Following his release, Heyward was elected to the American Philosophical Society in 1784. The following year, he was one of the founders of the South Carolina Agricultural Society and was its first president.

In 1786, he married Elizabeth Savage, with whom he had three children. During these intervening years, he worked as a judge. In 1790, he was a delegate to the convention to draft a state constitution.

Thomas Heyward, Sr., Heyward's older brother, died in October 1795, after a painful illness that he handled with "Christian fortitude." Three years later, Heyward retired as a judge, and citing the pain from his war injuries, withdrew from public life soon after.

Heyward died on April 17, 1809, at the rebuild White Hall, in St. Luke's Parish (now Jasper County), South Carolina. He was buried at the Heyward Family Cemetery at "Old House," the site of the former White Hall. A marker near his tomb reads, "Tomb of Thomas Heyward, Jr. 1746–1809. Member of South Carolina Provincial Congress and Council of Safety and of Continental Congress. Signer of Declaration of Independence and Articles of Confederation and captain of militia at Battle of Port Royal and Siege of Charleston. Prisoner of war 1780–81. Circuit Court Judge 1778–89."

In 1835, several newspapers heralded Heyward:

> He was at that a very young man, not more than twenty-five or thirty . . . he was, perhaps, the wealthiest planter in the Southern country. His estate consisted entirely of land and negroes [sic], a species of property very easily got hold of by the goods, he heard of the Declaration of Independence. To him, it appeared to be an act

THOMAS HEYWARD JR. (1746–1809)

Memorial of Thomas Heyward Jr.

of great indiscretion, and altogether premature. The total conquest of the country, with a confiscation of all of the property belonging to the rebels, was to be, he feared, the sad result of this effort to throw off the yoke of the mother country . . . Thomas Heyward was one of the few Signers of the Declaration of Independence who returned home, and took up arms in defense of that Independence which they had declared . . . in fighting for his country, Thomas Heyward was severely wounded. He had the honor of sealing with his blood the written appeal which he had signed with his hand.

All white Heyward descendants alive today trace their lineage to the three children, Thomas, William, and Elizabeth, descended from the second wife. Thomas E. Miller (1849–1938) was the grandson of Heyward and a slave woman. Miller was one of five African American congressmen from the South in the 1890s.

Descendant DuBose Heyward's (1885–1940) novel *Porgy*, published in 1927, was used by George Gershwin to create *Porgy and Bess* in 1935, which critiqued racism.

It is estimated that Heyward's younger brother Nathaniel was the largest slaveholder in the United States with over 2,000 slaves working over 35,000 acres.

Grave of Thomas Heyward Jr.

Arthur Middleton
(1742–1787)

Defender of Charleston

Buried at the gardens at "Middleton Place,"
Charleston, South Carolina.

Declaration of Independence • Military

Arthur Middleton was a signer of the Declaration of Independence and, along with his father, Henry, was a delegate to the Continental Congress (1776–77 and 1781–82). A wealthy plantation owner, Arthur was also a leading attorney in colonial South Carolina.

Arthur was born at "Middleton Place," his father's expansive estate along the Ashley River west of Charleston, South Carolina, on June 26, 1742. He was the son of Henry Middleton and Mary Baker Williams, both of English descent. Father Henry owned, at one point, 20 plantations comprising approximately 50,000 acres, worked by over 800 slaves.

Young Arthur was first taught by private tutors and schools in the Charleston area before traveling to England to attend Hackney (later Harrow), Westminster School, and Trinity Hall, Cambridge University, where he graduated in 1760 at the age of 18. He then studied law at the Middle Temple in London, before touring Europe for two years, acquiring a taste for music, painting, sculpture, and architecture. He enjoyed a prolonged stay in Rome, appreciating its ancient heritage. He returned home just before Christmas 1763, a well-educated and cultured Renaissance man.

On August 19, 1764, Middleton married Mary Izard, the daughter of his neighbor, Walter Izard, a plantation owner and captain of a Berkeley regiment

The Congress at York

Portrait of Arthur Middleton from the detail from a 1771 family portrait of the Middleton Family. The full portrait depicts Arthur; his wife Mary Izard Middleton, and their infant son Henry. It was painted by Benjamin West.

in 1712 who also served in the Yemassee War. The young couple settled in at "Middleton Place" and produced nine children.

During his 20s, Arthur engaged in planting and became a justice of the peace Berkeley County in 1765 followed by election to the South Carolina House of Commons from 1765 to 1768 and again from 1772 to 1775.

Vehemently anti-Loyalist, Arthur was a member of the American Party in Carolina, a founding member of the Council of Safety in 1775 and 1776 (including its Secret Committee), and a delegate to the South Carolina Congress when it created its state constitution in 1776. Middleton wrote to William Henry Drayton on April 15, 1775:

> You put me in mind of Cicero Parthians after the Surrender of Pindenissum. You may say with him 'take it however as a Certainty, that no one could do more than I have done with such an Army."
> I hope you will do great matters with your great Guns, & I wish

ARTHUR MIDDLETON (1742–1787)

your Second in Command was not quite so sleepy, it is pity you had not roused him with a discharge. If you should not find it hot enough up your way, pray hasten down for in all probability we shall have warm work here 'ere long. It is confidently said Transports & Frigates will be here soon. Col. Laurens writes you & I suppose will acquaint you with our late Transactions. Fort Johnson is in our hands, & garrisoned with 150 men, which will be reinforc'd this night.

Said Benjamin Rush of Middleton, "he was a man of cynical temper but upright intentions towards his country." Others described him, variously, as being middle-sized, well-formed with great muscular strength and fine features expressive of firmness and decision, a celebrated, capricious aristocrat but like his forbears very public-spirited. Middleton had great disdain for Loyalists and assisted in the confiscation of the estates of those who had fled the country. He also participated in the tarring and feathering of those who remained.

Middleton succeeded his father when elected to the Continental Congress from 1776 to 1777 during which he proudly signed the Declaration of Independence. He served again in the Congress from 1781 to 1782. This entire time, from 1776 through 1786, he was also a justice of the peace in South Carolina.

During the Revolution, Middleton served as an officer in the local militia in the defense of Charleston. As the British scoured the countryside, they plundered plantations, grabbing anything that they could carry. The Middletons fled to Charleston ahead of the troops. During this time, the British plundered his estate including over 200 slaves, which were sold in the West Indies. After the city's fall to the British in 1780, he was a prisoner, along with Edward Rutledge and Thomas Heyward, Jr., from May 1780 to July 1781 in St. Augustine, Florida, until exchanged. Wife Mary begged, to no avail, for help from the British to care for her nine children.

During his imprisonment, Arthur was again elected to the Continental Congress. He was reelected on 4 October 4, 1781, and again on January 31, 1782. A note from Daniel of St. Thomas Jenifer to John Hall, July 24, 1781, mentioned the freed patriots, "Ned [sic] Rutledge, Middleton, and Gadsden with many others exchanged are dayly [sic] expected from Augustine."

Middleton left the Congress before his term was out and returned home to "Middleton Place" where he focused on restoring his plantation and South Carolina affairs. Governor John Rutledge, the brother of his cellmate Edward

The Congress at York

The rebuilt "Middleton Place" as it looks today (photo by Lawrence Knorr).

Rutledge, appointed him to the state senate. He was re-elected to the seat in 1782. He was a member of the privy council that year and subsequently a member of the state house of representatives in 1785 and 1786. He was also a member of the board of trustees of Charleston College.

Middleton passed away suddenly on January 1, 1787, at the age of 44 at one of the Middleton plantations, "The Oaks." He was interred in the family mausoleum in the gardens at "Middleton Place," near Charleston, South Carolina, where he rests to this day. The *State Gazette of South Carolina* of January 4, 1787, included a notice about Middleton, describing him as a "tender husband and parent, humane master, steady unshaken patriot, the gentleman, and the scholar." He left behind a wife, eight children, "an untarnished name," and 600 slaves.

Historian Alexander Garden wrote in 1828:

> I know no man, whose exemplary conduct, throughout the whole progress of the Revolution, deserves more gratefully to be remembered, than that of Arthur Middleton. Possessed of ample fortune, and endowed with talents of the highest order, improved by study, and refined by traveling, he devoted himself with decision to the service of his country . . . He, on all occasions, advocated the most vigorous measures, clearly evincing that he was not one of those, who shrunk in times of danger from responsibility. Frank and open to temper, he freely uttered the bold conceptions of his ardent spirit, censuring with indignant pride the cautious policy of

ARTHUR MIDDLETON (1742–1787)

the timid and irresolute, and expressing the highest indignation at the arts of the designing.

Among Middleton's heirs included his son Henry Middleton (1770–1846), who served as Governor of South Carolina (1810–12), in the U.S. House of Representatives (1815–19), and as U.S. minister to Russia (1820–30), and his daughter Emma Philadelphia Middleton (1776–1813), who married U.S. Senator Ralph Izard (1741/42–1804). His grandson, Williams Middleton (1809–1883), signed the Ordinance of Secession that separated South Carolina from the Union and launched the American Civil War in 1861. Arthur Middleton's son-in-law was Congressman Daniel Elliott Huger who was the grandfather-in-law of Confederate General Arthur Middleton Manigault who was also a descendant of Henry Middleton. Arthur Middleton was also an ancestor of actor Charles B. Middleton, who played Ming the Merciless in the Flash Gordon movies of the 1930s.

The plantation passed to Henry, his eldest son, but it was burned and pillaged by Union troops during the Civil War. Today, "Middleton Place" is a historic landmark. A mansion was rebuilt and the grounds, including the Middleton gardens, are open to the public.

The grave of Arthur Middleton in the lovely gardens at "Middleton Place" near Charleston, South Carolina (photo by Lawrence Knorr).

The Congress at York

Arthur Middleton has been remembered in other ways. The United States Navy ship, USS *Arthur Middleton* (AP-55/APA-25), was named for him. Middleton's signature and those of all the signers of the Declaration of Independence are carved on granite rocks in a lagoon near the Washington Monument. The famous Trumbull painting "The Declaration of Independence" hangs in the U.S. Capitol. The figure of Arthur Middleton is shown standing in a group of five delegates on the left side of the painting, on the extreme right of the group, with his head tilted forward.

Benjamin Harrison V
(1726–1791)

Father and Great-Grandfather of Presidents

Buried at Berkeley Plantation,
Charles City, Virginia.

Continental Association • Declaration of Independence

Benjamin Harrison V was a wealthy planter and merchant who served in the colonial Virginia legislature, followed by the Continental Congress, where he signed the Continental Association, Olive Branch Petition, and the Declaration of Independence. He was then governor of Virginia. Harrison's son, William Henry Harrison, became the 9th President of the United States. His great-grandson and namesake became the 23rd President of the United States.

Benjamin Harrison V was born April 5, 1726, in Charles City County, Virginia, to Benjamin Harrison IV and his wife, Anne (née Carter), the oldest of ten children. The family lived on the Berkeley Plantation, built by the elder Harrison. He was a member of the Virginia House of Burgesses, as had been the prior three generations of Benjamin Harrisons going back to the colonist in 1630, only 25 years after Jamestown. The elder Harrison was also a major in the Charles City County militia and the local sheriff. Benjamin's mother was the daughter of Robert "King" Carter, the president and treasurer of the Virginia colonial council, who served as the acting governor of the colony and the rector of the College of William and Mary.

On July 12, 1745, the elder Harrison and daughter Hannah were killed at Berkeley Manor by a lightning strike as they shut an upstairs window during a storm. Now the patriarch of the family at only 19, Benjamin inherited Berkeley

The Congress at York

Benjamin Harrison

and several other plantations in the area in addition to thousands of acres, a fishery, and a grist mill. His siblings split six other plantations.

In 1748, Harrison married Elizabeth Bassett, the daughter of Colonel William Bassett and Elizabeth (Churchill) Bassett. Together they had eight children. The eldest daughter, Lucy Bassett Harrison, married Peyton Randolph. Daughter Anne Bassett Harrison married David Coupland. Benjamin Harrison VI was a successful merchant and member of the Virginia House of Delegates. Carter Bassett Harrison served in the Virginia House of Delegates and the US House of Representatives. Their youngest child, William Henry Harrison, became a popular general known as the Hero of Tippecanoe. He was then a congressional delegate for the Northwest Territory, the Governor of the Indiana Territory, and a US senator. In the 1840 United States presidential election, running under the slogan "Tippecanoe and Tyler Too," William Henry Harrison, the first candidate of the Whig party, defeated Martin Van Buren. He fell ill after his inauguration and died just one month into his presidency.

Benjamin Harrison had attended the College of William and Mary at Williamsburg. He did not graduate. Instead, pursuing a life in politics. His brothers also served their communities. Carter Henry Harrison became a leader in Cumberland County, west of Richmond. Nathaniel Harrison was elected to the House of Burgesses and then the Virginia Senate. Henry Harrison fought in the French and Indian War. Charles became a brigadier general during the American Revolution.

In 1749, Harrison was elected to the Virginia House of Burgesses, serving for over a quarter-century representing Surry and Charles City Counties. In 1768, Harrison was appointed to a committee to draft Virginia's response to the Townsend Acts, protesting the tax on tea and other imports as payment for the French and Indian War. In 1770, he was a signer of the association boycotting British imports. He also sponsored a bill declaring Parliament's laws illegal if they were passed without the consent of the colonial legislature. In 1772, Harrison served as a justice and was one of several gentlemen who purchased a building for the city of Williamsburg to use as its courthouse. Also that year, he and Thomas Jefferson were among a group of six Virginia delegates who prepared and delivered an address to King George calling for an end to the importation of sales from Africa. The King rejected this, and both Harrison and Jefferson continued to own slaves.

On March 12, 1773, Richard Henry Lee, the recipient of a report from Samuel Adams in Massachusetts, offered resolutions to establish a Committee of Correspondence to cooperate with that colony and others. Upon the adoption of Lee's resolutions, the Virginia Assembly appointed the following members to act as a Committee of Correspondence: Peyton Randolph, Robert Carter Nicholas, Richard Bland, Richard Henry Lee, Benjamin Harrison, Edmond Pendleton, Patrick Henry, Dudley Digges, Dabney Carr, Archibald Cary, and Thomas Jefferson.

In December 1773, the colonists of Boston protested the tax on British tea by destroying cargos in the harbor. Harrison initially thought the colonists should reimburse the East India Company for the damages caused by the Boston Tea Party, but the subsequent Intolerable Acts hardened his position against the King and Parliament. On May 24, 1774, he and 88 other Virginia delegates signed an association condemning Parliament and invited other colonies to convene a Continental Congress. Harrison was selected to be one of Virginia's delegates to this new body August 5, 1774, to travel to Philadelphia. Said Edmund Randolph of him, "A favorite of the day was Benjamin Harrison. With strong sense and a temper not disposed to compromise with ministerial power, he scruples not to utter any untruth. During a long service in the House of Burgesses, his frankness, though sometimes tinctured with bitterness, has been the source of considerable attachment."

The Congress at York

Harrison arrived in Philadelphia on September 2, 1774, for the First Continental Congress. John Adams, in his diary of the first days of the Congress, wrote that day of his first meeting with the Virginian:

> 2 [Sept]. Friday. Dined at Mr. Thomas Mifflin's, with Mr. Lynch, Mr. Middleton, and the two Rutledges [Edward and John, both of South Carolina] with their ladies. The two Rutledges are good lawyers. Governor [Stephen] Hopkins and Governor [Samuel] Ward [both of Rhode Island] were in company. Mr. [Thomas] Lynch [of South Carolina] gave us a sentiment: "The brave Dantzickers, who declare they will be free in the face of the greatest monarch in Europe." We were very sociable and happy. After coffee, we went to the tavern, where we were introduced to Peyton Randolph, Esquire, Speaker of Virginia, Colonel Harrison, Richard Henry Lee, Esquire, and Colonel Bland. Randolph is a large, well-looking man; Lee is a tall, spare man; Bland is a learned, bookish man. These gentlemen from Virginia appear to be the most spirited and consistent of any. Harrison said he would have come on foot rather than not come. Bland said he would have gone, upon this occasion, if it had been to Jericho.

On September 6, 1774, recording his observations of some of the early debates in Congress regarding proportional representation, delegate James Duane of New York wrote:

> Col. Harrison from Virginia insisted strongly on the injustice that Virginia should have no greater Weight in the determination than one of the smallest Colonies. That he should be censured by his constituents and unable to excuse his want of attention to their Interest. And that he was very apprehensive that if such a disrespect should be put upon his Country—men we shoud [sic] never see them at another Convention.

Around that time, Silas Deane of Connecticut wrote to his wife about the delegates:

> I gave you the character of the South Carolina delegates, or rather a sketch. I will now pursue the plan I designed. Mr. Randolph, our worthy President, may be rising of sixty, of noble appearance, and presides with dignity. Col. Harrison may be fifty; an uncommonly large man and appears rather rough in his address and speech.

BENJAMIN HARRISON V (1726–1791)

Harrison aligned with John Hancock, while Richard Henry Lee aligned with John Adams. Adams later described Harrison in his diary variously as "another Sir John Falstaff," "obscene," "profane," and "impious." The next month, Harrison was one of the delegates to sign the Continental Association, implementing a trade boycott with Britain.

The following May, when Harrison arrived for the Second Continental Congress, he roomed with his brother-in-law, Peyton Randolph, and George Washington, until he left to take command of the Continental Army in June. On July 5, 1775, Harrison was one of the signers of the Olive Branch Petition, albeit reluctant. The two had a war of words during the debate. Dickinson remarked he disapproved of only one word in the petition, "congress." Replied Harrison, "There is but one word in the paper, Mr. President, of which I do approve, and that is the word 'congress.'" The King rebuffed the chance of reconciliation.

That October, Peyton Randolph died suddenly from a heart attack while dining with Thomas Jefferson. This left Harrison alone in his Philadelphia residence. Harrison now kept busy with military affairs, corresponding with his former roommate. In November, he traveled with Washington, Benjamin Franklin, and Thomas Lynch to Cambridge to inspect the army's condition. Congress now realized the need to increase the number of troops and to increase their pay.

Nearing July 1776, Harrison was chairman of the Committee of the Whole, presiding over the final debates of the Lee Resolution, expressing a desire for independence. Harrison oversaw the amendments of the Declaration of Independence after the Committee of Five presented the draft of the Declaration of Independence. Harrison reported the approved final form of the document on July 4, giving its final reading. Congress then unanimously adopted it. Harrison was one of the signers the next month. At that event, many of the signers were nervous. Benjamin Rush described a "pensive and awful silence" as the delegates believed they were signing their death warrants. He then described how Harrison, known for his sense of humor, lightened the mood. Rush wrote that the corpulent Harrison approached the slender Elbridge Gerry when he was about to sign and said, "I shall have a great advantage over you, Mr. Gerry, when we are all hung for what we are now doing. From the size and weight of my body, I shall die in a few minutes and be with the angels, but from the lightness of your body, you will dance in the air an hour or two before you are dead."

During 1777, Harrison was named to the Committee of Secret Correspondence for the Congress, whose objective was to communicate securely with colonial agents in Britain. He was also named the Chairman of the

The Congress at York

Board of War, overseeing the army's movements and the exchange of prisoners. During this time, he had a spat with Washington over the commission of the Marquis de Lafayette. Harrison insisted the position was only honorary and without pay. He also endorsed a controversial idea that the Quakers had the right not to bear arms based on their religious beliefs.

In September 1777, Congress fled Philadelphia, stopping briefly in Lancaster before heading to York, Pennsylvania. There, they debated the Articles of Confederation. Again, Harrison argued for greater representation for the larger states, like Virginia. Concerned about his properties back home and not making headway with the Articles, Harrison headed back to Virginia in October. There, he returned to the Virginia House and was elected Speaker. There, he focused on providing for the defense and western land interests.

In January 1781, Benedict Arnold, now on the British side, led an invasion of the James River in Virginia. Harrison arranged for his family to flee Berkeley before Arnold arrived and destroyed most of Harrison's possessions and a large portion of his house. Arnold also burned all the family portraits so that no likeness of the family would survive. Fortunately, the Harrisons escaped with their lives. Soon after the British left, the Harrisons returned and began rebuilding. Harrison returned to his duties, helping supply the army.

Following the victory at Yorktown in October 1781, Harrison was elected the fifth Governor of Virginia. During this time, he focused on the financial difficulties the state was facing at that time. This included negotiating with the native tribes rather than warring with them. This did not please George Rogers Clark, who wanted to secure more western territory. Harrison served as governor through 1784, after which he returned to the House of Delegates.

Elizabeth Harrison, Harrison's wife of over forty years, died in September 1787. In June 1788, Harrison was named to the state constitutional convention to ratify the new US Constitution. Harrison spoke against it because it did not clarify the rights for which they had fought. He voted against its ratification, but when it was known that reforms would be included after all the states passed it, Harrison became a supporter.

Harrison, suffering from chronic gout and other ailments, continued in his service in the Virginia House until his death at Berkeley on April 24, 1791, while celebrating his re-election. Harrison was laid to rest in the family burial ground at Berkeley.

As mentioned previously, Harrison's youngest son, William Henry Harrison, became the 9th President of the United States in 1841. He served only one month before he died. In 1846, Harrison's heirs asked the US government to reimburse the family for pay, bounty land, and other expenses incurred by Harrison from the American Revolution to his death. Harrison's great-grandson, Benjamin Harrison, served in the US Senate from Indiana (1881–87) and as the 23rd President of the United States (1889–93). His great-great-grandson, William Henry Harrison (1896–1990), served in the US House of Representatives (1951–55, 1961–65) as a Republican from Wyoming. A residence hall at the College of William and Mary is named for Harrison. Also, a bridge spanning the James River near Hopewell, Virginia, bears his name.

In the foreword of the book *The Harrisons* by Ross F. Lockridge, the author writes, "The Harrison family is justly believed to have given more distinguished men to American history than any other family."

The grave of Benjamin Harrison.

Joseph Jones
(1727 – 1805)

Uncle of James Monroe, Friend of Washington

Buried at unknown location,
Virginia.

Continental Congress

Joseph Jones was a lawyer and militia leader from King George County, Virginia, who was elected to the Continental Congress. He later served as a major general in the Virginia state militia. His nephew, James Monroe, was later President of the United States.

Jones was born in 1727, in King George County, Virginia, the son of James Jones, a merchant and tavern owner, and Hester (née Davis) Lampton Jones, a widow. The Joneses had six children, including three sons and three daughters. Father James's sister, Elizabeth, married Spence Monroe, who had a son named James Monroe.

Jones was educated at local schools and received legal training at the Inner Temple in London in 1749 and the Middle Temple in 1751. Jones returned to Virginia and started practicing law in Fredericksburg, becoming the king's attorney there in 1754.

In 1758, Jones married Mary Taliaferro, the daughter of Colonel John Taliaferro of Spotsylvania County. After Mary's death, he married Elizabeth Brewton. Jones had several children from these marriages, including James Jones, who served in the Continental Army during the American Revolution.

Jones first entered politics in 1772 when he became a member of the Virginia House of Burgesses. However, as the Revolution began, he served on the Virginia Committee of Safety following Lexington and Concord in 1775.

The following year, Jones continued with the Virginia Committee of Safety and was elected to the Fifth Virginia Convention which drafted the Virginia Declaration of Rights.

On May 22, 1777, Jones was appointed to the Continental Congress by the Virginia legislature. He first attended sessions on August 11, 1777, and followed the Congress to Lancaster and then York. While President of the Continental Congress John Hancock left Philadelphia in a luxurious coach, Jones took George Washington's phaeton so it would not be captured. He wrote a letter to his friend, Washington, about the condition of the carriage:

> I have your phaeton here ... the bolt that fastens the pole and part of the long reins were lost, some brass nails also gone, and the lining much dirtied and in some places, torn. I will get these little matters repaired and have the carriage and harness kept clean and in good order as I can, which is the least I can do for the use.

Jones's last attendance at the Congress was on December 20. During his final months in Congress, Jones was out conferring with George Washington for most of the duration and missed the signing of the Articles of Confederation on November 15. He also alerted Washington to the actions of Thomas Mifflin and others, who sought to replace him as commander-in-chief in what became known as the Conway Cabal.

On January 23, 1778, Jones was appointed as a judge on the Virginia General Court, serving until his resignation in October 1779.

Two months later, on December 14, 1779, Jones was again appointed to the Continental Congress. He attended the Congress back in Philadelphia from April 24 to September 7, 1780, and then from January 29 through February 28, 1781. During this time, his focus was on finance and the French alliance. He was also appointed to the committee to resolve the border disputes between Pennsylvania and Connecticut.

During the debates about the new Constitution in 1787, Jones confided with his friend, Thomas Jefferson, about his split with James Madison, noting his many objections. Jones insisted that a declaration of rights should be included.

At the Virginia Ratifying Convention the following year, Jones joined with Patrick Henry, George Mason, and others in proposing amendments. Jones voted against ratification, believing Madison had betrayed the rights of Virginians.

Jones was reappointed to the Virginia General Court on November 19, 1789. He now also served in the Virginia militia as a major general during the

1790s. During the administrations of Washington and Adams, he remained a loyal friend of Jefferson.

While his nephew was Governor of Virginia during the 1800 election, Jones was appointed as a presidential elector. He was then made the postmaster general of Petersburg.

Jones died in Fredericksburg, Virginia, on October 28, 1805, following a brief illness. His burial place is lost.

Nephew James Monroe became president following the 1816 election and was a consequential two-term executive.

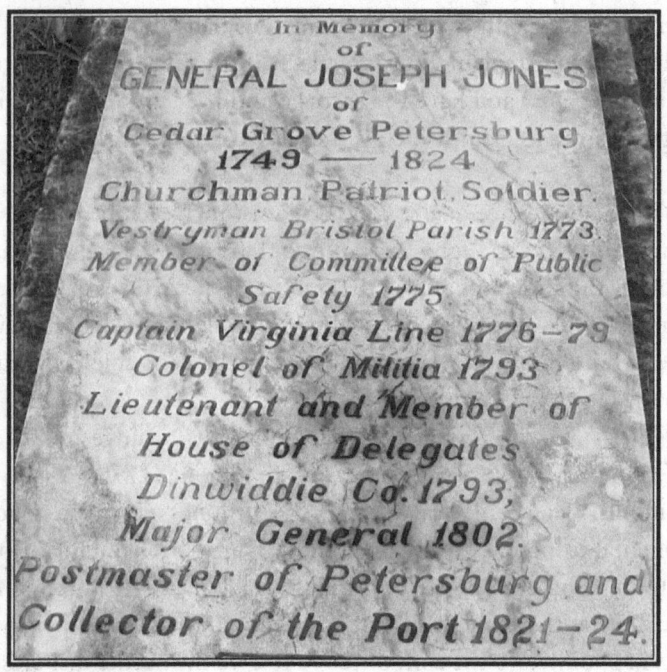

Grave of Joseph Jones

Francis Lightfoot Lee
(1734 – 1797)

Virginia Congressman

Buried at Tayloe Family Burial Ground,
Warsaw, Virginia.

Declaration of Independence • Articles of Confederation

Francis Lightfoot Lee, the brother of Richard Henry Lee and cousin of "Light Horse Harry" Lee, was a Continental Congressman who signed the Declaration of Independence and Articles of Confederation. He was also a member of the Virginia state House of Delegates and the state Senate.

Lee was born October 14, 1734, at "Machadoc," later known as "Burnt House Field," in Hague, Westmoreland County, Virginia. After the completion of "Stratford Hall," in Westmoreland County, Virginia, a few years later, the family moved there. He was the fourth son, and one of eleven children, of Thomas Lee, a planter in Virginia, and his wife Hannah Harrison (née Ludwell) Lee. Thomas Lee was a leading Virginia planter with over 30,000 acres of land prior to his death in 1750.

Francis was taught by private tutors at "Stratford Hall." When his parents died in 1750, the estate was left to the older children, leaving out Francis and his younger siblings. His oldest brother, Phillip Lee, controlled his parents' assets. Francis and the younger children sued in court for a portion but lost. Eventually, Francis reconciled with his brother and was granted one of the family estates in Loudon County.

Lee then got into politics and ran for a seat in the Virginia House of Burgesses in which he served from 1758 to 1768. Lee's first patriotic action was

Portrait of Francis Lightfoot Lee, artist unknown.

his protest of the Stamp Act. He signed the Westmoreland Resolves which was a business protest of the act that played a part in the repeal of the Stamp Act.

In 1769, Lee married his second cousin Rebecca Plater Tayloe and moved from Loudon to Richmond County where his father-in-law had gifted them "Menokin" plantation on which to reside. He was again elected to the House of Burgesses but only served occasionally. From 1770 to 1774, he was a justice of the peace for his new Richmond County. He also served in that position for Loudon County in 1771.

In March 1775, a convention of delegates gathered in Richmond to organize for the Revolution. Lee was one of the delegates from Richmond. In August of that year, Lee was appointed to the Continental Congress and moved to Philadelphia with his wife, staying with his sister and brother-in-law, William Shippen, who himself was later a Continental Congressman. Lee served in the Continental Congress into 1779, but biographers recorded that he rarely spoke, though his opinions were valued.

The Reverend Charles Goodrich wrote in 1842,

> During his attendance upon this body, he seldom took part in the public discussions, but few surpassed him in his warmth of patriotism, and in his zeal to urge forward those measures which

contributed to the success of the American arms, and the independence of the country. To his brother, Richard Henry Lee, the high honor was allotted of bringing forward the momentous question of independence, and to him, and his associates in that distinguished assembly, the not inferior honor was granted of aiding and supporting and finishing this important work.

Robert T. Conrad added in 1846, "Although not gifted with the powers of oratory, his good sense, extensive reading, and sound and discriminating judgment, made him a useful member of the house."

It is believed Francis Lee signed the Declaration of Independence with many others in August 1776. In an 1821 letter to painter John Trumbull in a Washington newspaper, the artist was critiqued for not including Francis Lee in the painting of the signers, though many who were not present on July 4 were included in it.

Lee continued in the Congress until he resigned in April of 1779, having also signed the Articles of Confederation before they were ratified. He returned to Virginia and served in the state senate for a period, but then retired. In 1788, he clashed with his brother, Richard Henry Lee, when he supported ratification of the Constitution.

Francis Lee died of pleurisy at "Menokin" on January 11, 1797, at the age of 62, only four days after his wife passed. *The American Minerva* newspaper of New York City printed an obituary,

"Mount Airy" Plantation where Francis Lightfoot Lee is buried (photo by Lawrence Knorr).

> Died. At his seat in Richmond County, on Wednesday, the 18th ultimo, in the sixty-third year of his age, Francis Lightfoot Lee, Esquire. He was an early, zealous and active friend to the revolution, which established the independence of the United States of America. He was a firm, calm, and enlightened patriot, and a most unequaled social companion.

Lee and his wife were laid to rest at the Tayloe's "Mount Airy" plantation near Warsaw, Virginia. The authors were unable to visit the graves which are on private property posted with a sign threatening gunshots if dust was seen in the driveway.

In 1877, Mark Twain wrote about Lee,

> This man's life-work was so inconspicuous, that his name would now be wholly forgotten, but for one thing—he signed the Declaration of Independence. Yet his life was a most useful and worthy one. It was a good and profitable voyage, though it left no phosphorescent splendors in its wake.

Francis and Rebecca Lee had no children; his namesake Francis Lightfoot Lee II was the son of his brother Richard Henry Lee, and further men of the same name descend from him.

The grave of Francis Lightfoot Lee.

Richard Henry Lee
(1732 – 1794)

Resolution for Independence

Buried at Lee Family Plot,
"Burnt House Field" plantation, Coles Point, Virginia.

**Continental Association • Declaration of Independence
Articles of Confederation • President of Congress**

Richard Henry Lee, the brother of Francis Lightfoot Lee and cousin of "Light Horse Harry" Lee, was a Continental Congressman who signed the Continental Association, Declaration of Independence, and Articles of Confederation. He was also the President of Congress (1784–1785). He is best known for proposing the Lee Resolution, the motion in the Continental Congress calling for independence from Great Britain. He was also a United States Senator from (1789–1792).

Lee was born January 26, 1732, at "Machadoc," later known as "Burnt House Field," in Hague, Westmoreland County, Virginia. He was the fifth son, and one of eleven children, of Thomas Lee, a planter in Virginia, and his wife Hannah Harrison (née Ludwell) Lee. Thomas Lee, the president of the Virginia Colonial Council, was a leading Virginia planter with over 30,000 acres of land prior to his death in 1750. After the completion of "Stratford Hall," in Westmoreland County, Virginia, a few years later, the family moved there.

Richard was taught by private tutors at "Stratford Hall." He was then sent to England to study at Wakefield Academy in Yorkshire. When his parents died in 1750, his oldest brother, Phillip Lee, urged him to return home, but he refused, instead going on a tour of mainland Europe.

The Congress at York

Portrait of Richard Henry Lee by Charles Willson Peale.

Richard returned to the colonies in 1753 and continued his studies. In 1755, during the French and Indian War, he was named the head of a volunteer militia serving under General Edward Braddock. Fortunately for Lee, Braddock did not utilize his unit and he saw no action nor did he play a role in the fateful Braddock Expedition. Lee married Anne Aylett in December 1757, and settled at his plantation, "Chantilly-on-the Potomac," near "Stratford Hall." Richard and Anne had four children—two sons and two daughters. The following year, while hunting, Lee's gun exploded in his hands, taking all but one finger on his left hand. For the remainder of his life, Lee wore a glove to cover up the wound. Later that same year, Anne Lee died of pleurisy.

In 1764, Lee was named to a committee by the House of Burgesses to send a message to the king calling for an end to harmful economic measures being enacted against the colonies. In February 1766, Lee was one of the leading figures behind the establishment of the Westmoreland Association. One surviving draft of that document in Lee's hand stated,

> . . . the Birthright privilege of every British subject (and of the people of Virginia as being such) founded on Reason, Law, and

RICHARD HENRY LEE (1732–1794)

Compact; that he cannot be legally tried but by his peers; and that he cannot be taxed, but by the consent of a Parliament, in which he is represented by persons chosen by the people. The Stamp Act does absolutely direct the property of the people to be taken from them without their consent.

In 1767, Lee was a justice of the peace in Westmoreland County. The following year, he was elected to the Virginia House of Burgesses, taking the seat of his brother Philip. He served until 1775 along with his brothers Thomas Ludwell Lee and Francis Lightfoot Lee. In this body, he railed against slavery wanting to tax it into oblivion. He believed slaves were entitled to equal freedom and liberty. Such views put him at odds with most of the men in that body. In 1769, Lee married Anne Gaskins Packard, a widow, and together the couple would have three daughters and two sons.

In 1773, Richard Lee was a member of the Virginia Committee of Correspondence along with Peyton Randolph, Robert Carter Nicholas, Richard Bland, Benjamin Harrison, Edmund Pendleton, Patrick Henry, Dudley Digges, Dabney Carr, Archibald Cary, and Thomas Jefferson. The following year, Lee was elected to the Continental Congress where he served until May 1779. During

"Burnt House Field," Lee Family Estate, in Coles Point, Virginia (photo by Lawrence Knorr).

this time, Lee was a signer of the Continental Association, the Declaration of Independence, and the Articles of Confederation.

Regarding independence, Lee was an early and ardent proponent. Following Lexington and Concord, he was still in the minority, but as time went by, more and more delegates joined him. On June 7, 1776, Lee put forth a motion for independence,

> Resolved: That these United Colonies are, and of right ought to be, free and independent States, that they are absolved from all allegiance to the British Crown, and that all political connection between them and the State of Great Britain is, and ought to be, totally dissolved.

There was rancorous opposition to the motion, so much so that the President of Congress, John Hancock, had to table it to avoid a fight. Meanwhile, the Committee of Five including Thomas Jefferson, Ben Franklin, John Adams, Roger Sherman, and Robert Livingston set about drafting a formal declaration. Though absent on July 4th, Richard and his brother Francis returned in August to sign the document, being the only brothers to do so.

Soon after, Lee was accused by John Hancock and Robert Morris of conspiring with John and Samuel Adams to remove Washington as commander of the Continental Army. At this time his brother Arthur Lee was serving as a diplomat to France along with Benjamin Franklin and Silas Deane. Arthur informed Richard that Deane was using the position for his own personal gain. Richard took to the floor of the Congress and denounced Deane and moved to recall him from Paris. Deane did so and defended himself before Congress, causing a rift in the body. This forced Henry Laurens to resign as the President of Congress. In retaliation, Deane accused the entire Lee family of corruption. Lee's friend, John Adams, wrote to Samuel Cooper in February 1779 a defense of the Lee family,

> The complaint against the family of Lees is a very extraordinary thing indeed. I am no idolater of that family or any other, but I believe their greatest fault is having more men of merit in it than any other family; and if that family fails the American cause, or grows unpopular among their fellow-citizens, I know not what family or what person will stand the test.

RICHARD HENRY LEE (1732–1794)

Lee soon resigned from his seat in the Congress and returned to Virginia where he continued to serve in the state House of Delegates and as a colonel in the Westmoreland militia.

In 1784, Colonel Arthur Campbell wrote to encourage Lee to reconsider service in the Continental Congress. He did so and was elected in June 1784. At that point, Thomas Mifflin resigned as President of Congress and the position was vacant for several months. In November, Lee agreed to take the position and held it until November 1785 when he was succeeded by John Hancock. During his tenure, the U.S. dollar was established as the currency of the land, tied to the Spanish dollar (piece of eight). The Congress also unsuccessfully worked to sell western lands to cover the war debts.

Lee was a delegate to the Virginia convention to ratify the U.S. Constitution in 1788 and was one of two senators appointed to serve in the first Congress. He did so from March 1789 until he resigned in October 1792 as his health was beginning to fail.

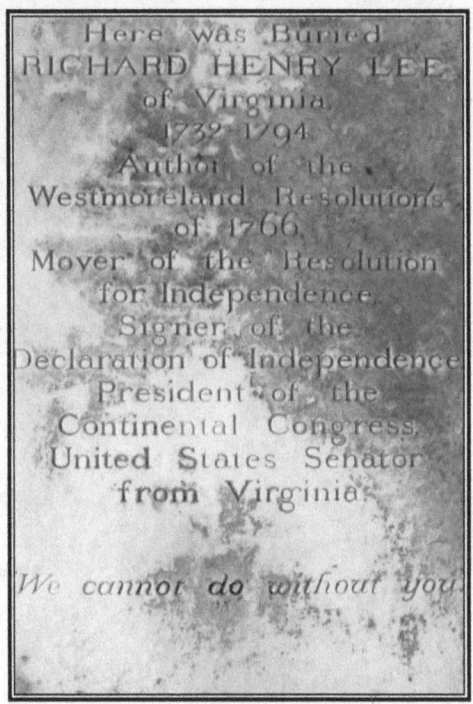

Detail from Richard Henry Lee's gravestone (photo by Lawrence Knorr).

Richard Henry Lee died on June 19, 1794, at the age of 62. Lee was buried at the Lee family estate's graveyard at "Burnt House Field," in Coles Point, Virginia. His gravestone reads,

> Here was buried Richard Henry Lee, of Virginia, 1732–1794. Author of the Westmoreland Resolutions of 1766. Mover of the Resolution for Independence. Signer of the Declaration of Independence. President of the Continental Congress. United States Senator from Virginia.

Many public schools across the nation are named after Lee. In 1941, a liberty ship bore his name.

Richard Law
(1733 – 1806)

A Judge Named Law

Cedar Grove Cemetery
New London, Connecticut

Continental Congress • Judge

Richard Law was the son of a Connecticut governor who was a delegate to the Continental Congress. He was also the mayor of New London, Connecticut, and a US District Judge in Connecticut, appointed by George Washington.

Law was born on March 7, 1733, in Milford, Connecticut, the son of Jonathan Law, an attorney, and his wife, Eunice (née Hall) Law. The elder law had been born in 1674 and was the grandson of Richard Law, the king's attorney in England before emigrating in 1635. Jonathan Law was a Harvard graduate who became the chief judge in the New Haven County court and governor in 1742, serving until his death in 1750.

Law studied the classics before being admitted to Yale College, from which he graduated in 1751. He then studied law under Jared Ingorsoll in New Haven until 1755, when he was admitted to the Connecticut bar. Law opened a private practice in Milford from 1755 to 1757 and then moved to New London, where he continued his practice through 1765.

While in New London, Law married Anne Esther Prentiss on September 21, 1760. Together, they had twelve children, ten of whom lived to adulthood.

In 1765, Law became the Justice of the Peace for New Haven, serving until 1775. He was also elected to a seat in the Connecticut General Assembly, serving until 1776. For the last two years in the assembly, Law was the Clerk. In

The Congress at York

Richard Law

1773, Law was appointed the Chief Judge of the New London County Court, serving until 1784.

As the Revolution was underway, Law sided with the Patriots. He was appointed to the First Continental Congress in 1774, but did not attend. He assisted the Governor's Council of the Connecticut General Assembly from 1776 until 1786. In May 1776, he was appointed to the Connecticut Council of Safety. He was also appointed to the Second Continental Congress on October 10, 1776, but attended from June 25, 1777, through December 3, 1777, during the period when the Congress relocated from Philadelphia to Lancaster and then York, reconvening on September 30.

Later, Law was elected again to the Confederation Congress on May 11, 1780, and reelected on May 9, 1782. He was recorded as attending the Congress from October 22, 1781, until about May 16, 1782.

After his national service, Law was elected Mayor of New London, Connecticut, in 1784, remaining in the role until 1806. Also in that year, he was appointed to Judge of the Connecticut Superior Court in New London from 1784 through 1789. He was the Chief Judge the last three years.

During this time, Law condemned a twelve-year-old Pequot girl, Hannah Ocuish, to death for the murder of a six-year-old child in the community in July 1786. Ocuish had killed the child because she had tattled on her for stealing fruit during the strawberry harvest. Ocuish plotted her revenge and beat and strangled the child when she had the opportunity. When confronted, she accused four boys whom she said were in the area, but the lads could not be found. When confronted again, Ocuish confessed. Judge Law was the presiding judge for the case and was brought to tears multiple times during the trial. The court found Ocuish guilty of the murder, and as required by law, Judge Law sentenced her to death by hanging. Said Law to Ocuish, "The sparing of you on account of your age would, as the law says, be of dangerous consequence to the public, by holding up an idea, that children might commit such atrocious crimes with impunity." Ocuish was hung on December 20, 1786.

Contemporary historians and organizations have attempted to claim that Ocuish may have been innocent, or Law's decision was based on race. Of course, it is now impossible to prove these allegations. Others have been critical of Law's harshness without realizing that, in those times, age was not a factor in sentencing.

Federal service called again on September 24, 1789, when President George Washington named Law to the US District Court of Connecticut, appointing him as a US District Court Judge. Chief Justice John Jay and Associate Justice William Cushing joined Law in opening the court on April 22, 1790. Law remained in this role until his death.

Judge Law died on January 26, 1806, at age 72. He was buried at Cedar Grove Cemetery in New London, Connecticut. The large obelisk at his grave reads, "To the Memory of the Hon. Richard Law. Judge of Connecticut District. Mayor of the City, and for many years, Chief Justice of the Superior Court in this State."

Son Lyman Law (1770–1841) served as a Federalist in the US House of Representatives (1811–17). Grandson John Law (1796–1873) served as a Democrat in the US House of Representatives (1861–65).

Samuel Chase
(1741–1811)

First to be Impeached

Buried at Old St. Paul's Cemetery,
Baltimore, Maryland.

**Continental Association • Declaration of Independence
Supreme Court Justice**

In 1766 town officials in Annapolis, Maryland published an article in the *Maryland Gazette Extraordinary* that described one young citizen as "a busy, restless incendiary, a ringleader of mobs, a foul-mouthed and inflaming son of discord and faction, a common disturber of the public tranquility, and a promoter of the lawless excesses of the multitude." The man who may well have embraced the description would later serve in the Continental Congress, sign the Declaration of Independence, and serve as an Associate Justice on the United States Supreme Court. Born on April 17, 1741, his name was Samuel Chase.

Chase's background and upbringing were not what one would expect of a fiery revolutionary. His father was an Episcopalian clergyman who moved to what was then the village of Baltimore to minister to the congregation of St. Paul's Church. His mother, Matilda, passed away soon after giving birth to the couple's only son. Chase was homeschooled by his father before leaving for Annapolis to study law. He was admitted to the bar in 1761. He started a law practice and soon earned the reputation of a man unafraid to speak his mind regardless of whom, including the rich and powerful, might be offended. He had a reddish-brown complexion that seemed to grow more colorful when he engaged in a debate or argument. This trait earned him the nickname "Bacon Face."

SAMUEL CHASE (1741–1811)

Portrait of Samuel Chase, circa 1811, by John Wesley Jarvis.

In 1762 Chase married Ann Baldwin and the couple had seven children though only four survived to adulthood. Ann passed away in 1776 and Chase remarried eight years later. The second Mrs. Chase was the daughter of an English physician and she bore the American patriot two daughters.

Chase got his start in politics when he was elected to the Maryland General Assembly in 1764. He was also active in a group known as the Sons of Liberty whose purpose was to protect American colonists from oppressive British laws. This was close to the heart of the young Chase. After the Stamp Act was passed in 1765, Chase led a group of fellow patriots on a raid of public offices in Annapolis where they destroyed the stamps and burned the tax collector in effigy. Criticized publicly by the Loyalist mayor for these acts, Chase responded in the newspaper where he admitted to taking part in the raid adding that he did so while others who shared his beliefs "meanly grumbled in your corners and not daring to speak your sentiments." He was 24 years old at the time.

Though he may not have been popular with local officials his reputation among patriots earned him an appointment to the First Continental Congress in 1774. When it came to the work of Congress, Chase was a popular member owing to his willingness to serve on multiple committees and his effectiveness in carrying out his duties. He remained a member of Congress until 1778.

In 1776 Chase returned from Canada with Charles Carroll and Benjamin Franklin after the trio had been unsuccessful in convincing those colonies to provide military support in the Revolutionary War. Back in Maryland, the legislature had yet to decide on how the state should vote on the question of American independence. Chase returned to his home state to lobby support for separation from England. Thanks in part to his efforts, Maryland instructed its delegation to vote in favor of independence.

Chase, much to his chagrin, was not present when the historic vote was taken. He remained in Maryland tending to his ailing wife until the middle of July. It wasn't until August 2, in what may well have been his proudest moment, that he was able to affix his signature to the Declaration of Independence.

In 1778 Chase left Congress after being discredited in newspapers for using inside information to profit from the wartime flour market. Returning to Maryland he made a number of bad investments that left him bankrupt. He went back to practicing law in order to remedy his financial situation.

In 1787 Chase declined an appointment to the Constitutional Convention. By this time he was leading a campaign in Maryland for paper money emission, a matter of vital importance when it came to his personal finances as a result of debts he had incurred while speculating on confiscated estates of those who had remained loyal to the English. When the ratification of the Constitution was debated in Maryland, Chase, joined by fellow Declaration of Independence signer William Paca, opposed it. George Washington and James Madison used their influence in the state to overcome the objections raised by Chase and Paca.

After the Constitution was ratified Chase became a firm Federalist and supporter of the new government. On January 26, 1796, President Washington appointed Chase to the United States Supreme Court. Though he was now a member of the nation's highest court this exalted position did nothing to curb his tendency, some might say need, to express his views. Some held that he bullied defendants and their lawyers. Nor was he shy about continuing to express his political views.

When Thomas Jefferson was elected President in 1800, Chase was an unapologetic critic of the nation's new leader. He said that under Jefferson's leadership "our Republican Constitution will sink to mobocracy, the worst of all possible governments." Jefferson was determined to purge the judiciary of Federalist judges. Urged by the President, the House of Representatives impeached Chase for allegedly showing extreme partisan conduct while on the

SAMUEL CHASE (1741–1811)

bench while deciding several cases. Chase was the first and only Supreme Court Justice ever impeached. His trial took place early in 1805 with the United States Senate presided over by then Vice President Aaron Burr sitting in judgment. Chase was acquitted of all charges in a case that many historians credit with ensuring the independence of the judiciary.

Chase was still serving on the court in 1811 when he suffered a heart attack and passed away. He was laid to rest In Baltimore's Old St. Paul's Cemetery. Though the cemetery has been designated as a historic site by the United States government it sits behind a locked fence and is overgrown and neglected. Were Chase alive today he would likely be quite outspoken and leading protests relative to the lack of care being shown to what should be a revered property.

The worn tombstone of Samuel Chase at Old St. Paul's Cemetery in Baltimore, Maryland (photo by Lawrence Knorr).

James Lovell
(1737 – 1814)

Teacher, Orator, Signer, Spy

Buried at unknown location,
Windham, Maine.

Continental Congress • Signer of the Articles of Confederation

James Lovell was a teacher from a Loyalist Boston family who was imprisoned by the British for spying. Upon his release, he was immediately elected to the Continental Congress, representing Massachusetts. Lovell signed the Articles of Confederation. Despite participating in the Conway Cabal and believing George Washington to be "overrated," President Washington appointed him to a lucrative Customs House position in Boston after the Revolution.

Lovell was born in Boston, Massachusetts, on October 31, 1737. He was the son of John Lovell, headmaster of the Boston Latin School, and his wife, Abigail (née Green). The elder Lovell graduated from Harvard in 1728. Ten years later, he succeeded Dr. Nathaniel Williams as the headmaster of the school where young James, Samuel Adams, and John Hancock received their preparatory education.

James also attended Harvard, graduating in 1756. He then worked with his father at the Latin School. In 1759, James earned a Master of Arts from Harvard, continuing with his father until the school closed in April 1775, as the Siege of Boston was underway.

James and his father were close during these early years. In 1760, James married Mary Middleton, with whom he had more than ten children, nine of whom survived to adulthood. Lovell also became a noted orator. One such speech was delivered at Boston's Old Faneuil Hall to a massive crowd following

JAMES LOVELL (1737–1814)

James Lovell

the Boston Massacre in April 1771. Lovell's father was not pleased with the speech. Said James, "The horrid bloody scene we here commemorate, whatever were the causes which concurred to bring it on that dreadful night, must lead the pious and humane of every order to some suitable reflections. The pious will adore the conduct of that Being who is unsearchable in all his ways, and without whose knowledge not a single sparrow falls, in permitting an immortal soul to be hurried by the flying ball, the messenger of death, in the twinkling of an eye, to meet the awful Judge of all its secret actions."

Lovell continued to deviate from his father's Loyalist leanings and joined with patriots James Warren, Josiah Quincy, and the Adams cousins, Samuel and John, in demanding increased freedoms from England. However, Lovell did not openly participate in the Boston Tea Party or the First Continental Congress. He wrote from Boston on May 3, 1775:

> Mrs. Lovell has suffered extremely in the Head, fears a fixed Disorder there, but is I hope only suffering thus thro Weakness. My Family is yet w[ith] me. Children are prepared to go away, and Mrs. Lovell w[ith] the rest will follow when able, if I so judge

proper. I am not yet ripe to determine, I shall tarry if 10 Seiges [sic] take place. I have determined it to be a Duty which I owe the Cause & the Friends of it, and am perfectly fearless of the Consequences. An ill Turn, of a most violent Diarhea [sic], from being too long in a damp place, has contirm'd Doctr Gardners [sic] advice to me not to go into the Trenches, where my whole Soul lodges nightly. How then can I be more actively serviceable to the Friends who think with me, than by keeping disagreeable post among a Set of Villains who would willingly destroy what those Friends leave behind them.

When the body of James Warren was searched by the British after the Battle of Bunker Hill on June 17, 1775, documents were found written in James Lovell's hand showing British troop movements. Ten days later, Lovell's home was searched, and additional documents were found confirming he was a spy for the rebels. He was taken into custody and jailed in Boston. Lovell spent nine months in Boston's stone jail until the British left, at which point he was taken to Halifax, Nova Scotia, where he was imprisoned with Ethan Allen for another nine months. While Lovell could have been executed for spying, he was only imprisoned. Curiously, his father, the Loyalist, followed him to Nova Scotia and later died there in 1778. There is no record of the elder Lovell appealing to the British to spare his son, but the scenario is very likely.

Lovell must have made an impression on his friends in Boston who were in Congress and also with the new commander of Continental forces, George Washington, to whom he had written about his imprisonment. Wrote Washington on December 19, 1775:

> Inclosed [sic] is a letter I lately received from Mr. James Lovell. His case is truly pitiable. I wish some mode could be fallen upon to relieve him from the cruel situation he is now in. I am sensible of the impropriety of exchanging a soldier for a citizen: but there is something so cruelly distressing in regard to this gentleman, that I dare say you will take it under your consideration.

While the letter from Lovell no longer survives, it also made an impression upon Congress, noting Lovell maintained "under the severest trials the warmest attachment to public liberty, and an inflexible fidelity to his country." Congress agreed to an exchange of Major Andrew Skene, a British prisoner, for Lovell. Washington noted it in a letter to Jonathan Trumbull on September 23, 1776.

JAMES LOVELL (1737–1814)

Months after being freed, Lovell was elected to a seat in the Continental Congress on December 10, 1776, joining John Hancock, Samuel Adams, John Adams, Robert Treat Paine, Elbridge Gerry, and Francis Dana as representatives from Massachusetts. Lovell was the only Continental Congressman to be "continuously present" for five contiguous years through 1781. Lovell served on the Committees of Foreign Correspondence and Secret Correspondence. He was known for his ciphers, which were impossible to crack without the key, though Ben Franklin tried.

During the summer of 1777, following the loss of Fort Ticonderoga to the British, Lovell was a supporter, along with Dr. Benjamin Rush, of General Horatio Gates to take command of the army. Gates had just taken over the Northern Department from Philip Schuyler. Washington managed to survive the intrigue known as the "Conway Cabal" to remain as the commander-in-chief.

Lovell seems to have been closest to John and Abigail Adams, frequently corresponding with them. He especially seemed close to Abigail when John was in France. He wrote Abigail, whom he called by a pet name, "Portia," wondering what John was doing with his private time in France. The letters were flirtatious in nature.

Lovell signed the Articles of Confederation on July 9, 1778. During this time, Lovell was part of a group known as the anti-Gallicans, who feared a subordinate relationship with France and desired a more open relationship with all of Europe. Among them were Francis Dana, the Adams cousins, and the Lees of Virginia. They were suspicious of Ben Frankin's actions at Versailles. They were also behind sending Dana as Minister to Russia in 1780.

During the Revolution, Lovell's oldest son, James, served as a low-level officer in the Continental Army. He saw action at the Battle of Monmouth and served under "Lighthorse Harry" Lee in the Southern Campaign. He was wounded several times.

Following his service in Congress, Lovell returned to teaching. He also was a tax collector in Massachusetts in the 1780s. Despite their prior differences, President Washington appointed Lowell to a customs position in Boson in 1789, holding the position for the rest of his life.

On July 14, 1814, while visiting his friend, Reverend Peter T. Smith, at Windham, Maine, James Lovell died. He was 86. His burial location remains lost.

Lovell's grandson, Joseph Lovell, was the first Surgeon General of the USA, serving from 1818 to 1836. A connection to *Apollo 13* commander James Lovell has not been proven.

Thomas Burke
(1747 – 1783)
States' Rights Congressman

Buried at Governor Burke Gravesite,
Hillsborough, North Carolina.

Continental Congress • Governor

Thomas Burke was a physician and lawyer of Irish descent who lived in Hillsborough, North Carolina. He was a delegate to the Continental Congress and served as the third governor of North Carolina.

Burke was born circa 1747, in Tiaquin, County Galway, Ireland, the son of Ulick Burke and Leticia (née Ould) Burke, the sister of Sir Fielding Ould, a well-known physician. Both parents were Protestants.

As a youth, Burke lost his sight in his left eye and was also scarred by smallpox. He received some training in medicine, likely from his uncle, but the family was impoverished, and he was unable to complete his studies.

Burke emigrated to America when he was about fifteen years old. By 1764, he had relocated to Virginia, where he completed his medical studies and established a medical practice. However, he was unable to earn a living and began to study law. He also began to write about political matters, such as the Stamp Act, in the *Virginia Gazette*.

Burke was admitted to the Virginia colonial bar and established a law practice in Norfolk. It was here that he met a teacher named Mary Freeman. The two were married in March 1770. Not long after, their only child, a daughter named Polly, was born.

THOMAS BURKE (1747–1783)

Thomas Burke

In 1772, now experiencing financial success, Burke moved his family to Hillsborough, North Carolina. He purchased a large estate and dubbed it Tyaquin, after his hometown. He opened a law practice there.

In 1775, Burke was elected to the first of four provincial congresses held at New Bern, Hillsborough, and Halifax. These continued into 1776, when, on April 12, he was part of a committee with Cornelius Harnett, Allen Jones, Abner Nash, John Kinchen, Thomas Person, and Thomas Jones, who penned what became known as the "Halifax Resolves," which illustrated North Carolina's protest against the king.

On December 20, 1776, Burke was appointed to the Continental Congress, arriving in Philadelphia on February 4, 1777. He attended sessions from February 4, 1777, until about September 10, 1777. Rather than fleeing with the Congress as the British invaded, Burke joined with General Nash's North Carolina troops to defend the city and was then at the Battle of Brandywine on September 11. Burke rejoined the Congress at Lancaster on September 27, and then at York from September 30 until October 14, 1777. Burke was deeply involved in the formulation of the Articles of Confederation and consistently prioritized the rights of the states. Wrote one historian, "Burke took a most active part in framing those articles, and wrote repeated letters to Governor

Richard Caswell, of his State, detailing the course of events. They are all of one tone and show a great jealousy of giving to Congress any powers that could possibly be retained by the States. Burke impressed upon Congress all through his career the necessity for guarding against any encroachment upon the power and dignity of the State . . . at one time, when standing out for what he thought were the prerogatives of the State, and desiring that a question under discussion be postponed for a day he threatened to secede unless his views were agreed to."

Burke served in the Continental Congress until 1781. He was known to be irascible at times, refusing to attend sessions during which matters he disagreed with were discussed, sometimes leaving Congress without a quorum. When threatened with arrest if he did not take his seat, Burke instead left and was seen as a folk hero back home. Wrote Congressman Thomas Rodney of Delaware on March 8, 1781:

> Doctr. Burk [sic], of N. Carolina, tho[ugh] not equal To Many Who have been in Congress, May Justly be Stiled [sic] the ablest And Most useful Member there at present. He has been in Congress five Years, is very Attentive and well Acquainted with business-is Nervous tho[ugh] Not Eloquent in his language, he is Correct and pointed in his debates, possesses the Honest integrity of a republican and is for preserving inviolable the rights of the people Without being lured away by power. Yet he is Some times not fully guarded from Dictatorial language and does not Attend Sufficiently To System, order and Arrangement, in a general view but Confines himself Too Much To particular Objects.

In June 1781, the North Carolina Assembly elected Burke as the third governor of North Carolina. He left the Continental Congress to assume his new role.

During the summer of 1781 in North Carolina, the Continental Army and militia were engaged in active combat against British troops and Loyalists. On September 12, Loyalists led by David Fanning raided the state legislature at Hillsborough and rounded up 200 Patriots, including Governor Burke. Burke was taken to Charleston, then Sullivan's Island, and finally, James Island. During this time, Patriots under the command of John Butler attempted a rescue but failed at the Battle of Lindley's Mill.

On James Island, Burke was paroled to live freely, but the conditions were deplorable, and he was mistreated. On January 16, 1782, he broke his parole

THOMAS BURKE (1747–1783)

agreement by escaping back to North Carolina. He wrote to the British authorities that he still considered himself under the terms of his parole, but he resumed his governor duties before he was properly exchanged. Many considered his behavior dishonorable. In April 1782, the North Carolina Assembly appointed Alexander Martin to succeed him.

In bad health and broken spirit, Burke returned to Tyaquin. There, ashamed, his wife took their daughter and left him. Burke died on December 2, 1783, at only thirty-six years of age. He was buried on his plantation near Hillsborough. His gravesite is about 350 feet north of Governor Burke Road.

Burke County, North Carolina, was named in his honor.

Henry Marchant
(1741–1796)

Liberty Lawyer

Buried at Common Burial Ground,
Newport, Rhode Island.

Articles of Confederation

Henry Marchant was an attorney from Newport, Rhode Island, who served as the attorney general of that state and a member of the state legislature. As a delegate to the Continental Congress, he signed the Articles of Confederation. He supported the U.S. Constitution and was appointed the first federal judge for the U.S. District Court of Rhode Island.

Henry Marchant was born on April 9, 1741, in Edgartown, on the island of Martha's Vineyard, in Massachusetts, the son of Huxford Marchant, a sea captain, and his wife, Sarah (née Butler) Marchant. The Marchant family descended from John Marchant, born in 1571, in Yeovil, Somerset, England. Sarah Marchant died in 1745 when Henry was a toddler. His father then married Isabel Ward, the daughter and sister of the governors of Rhode Island, Richard Ward and Samuel Ward. When Huxford Marchant died while in Liberia or the West Indies in July 1747, stepmother Isabel remained to raise her young stepson in a world of wealth and privilege.

When Henry was of school age, Isabel sent him to a prestigious academy in Newport. He then went to Philadelphia College (now the University of Pennsylvania), where he was introduced to Benjamin Franklin. Marchant graduated in 1762. Next, he studied law in the offices of Judge Edmund Trowbridge of Cambridge, Massachusetts.

HENRY MARCHANT (1741–1796)

Henry Marchant

Following his legal training, Marchant was admitted to the Rhode Island bar and opened a practice in Newport. He was the only "liberty lawyer" in the colony but was well-connected with local officials and the church. Marchant was the personal attorney for his uncle Samuel Ward.

On January 8, 1765, Marchant married Rebecca Cooke at Trinity Church in Newport. The couple had four children between 1766 and 1771: Sarah, Henry, William, and Elizabeth. Only Sarah and Elizabeth lived to adulthood.

Marchant then got involved in local politics. On December 4, 1767, he was elected to the Council of Newport. About three years later, Marchant was elected the attorney general for the colony, serving from October 1770 to May 1777.

Marchant was a bright young man, curious about science, and mathematically inclined. In 1769, he assisted Dr. Ezra Stiles, a well-known intellectual, Congregationalist pastor, and founder of Brown University, in observing and plotting the transit of Venus. Stiles was a member of the American Philosophical Society in Philadelphia and later became the president of Yale University.

In 1771, Marchant was named an agent for Rhode Island in England, and he visited the mother country for eleven months seeking recompense for the colony for a couple of court cases. He had quite a send-off, as recounted by David Lovejoy in the *William and Mary Quarterly*:

The Congress at York

Henry Marchant's departure for England on July 8, 1771, was a significant occasion in the social life of Newport. Nearly a score of friends, reluctant to see him leave, accompanied him in chaises and on horseback as far as Bristol Ferry, eight miles northward on the way to Providence and Boston. His well-wishers included his wife, of course, and his "honord Mother in Law," but also Joseph Clarke, General Treasurer of the colony; William Ellery, later member of the Continental Congress; Josias Lyndon, former Governor; and the Reverend Ezra Stiles, Marchant's minister. (Stiles had good reason to be pleasant since Marchant had tucked three guineas "gratuity" into his pocket before they left Newport.) At Bristol Ferry, there was "heavy parting from such good Friends"; several crossed over to the mainland with him and after a "Repetition of parting Feelings," dropped by the wayside at the homes of relatives. Richard Olney accompanied young Marchant to Providence; Mrs. Marchant prolonged her leave-taking and stayed with her husband all the way to Boston, where he was to embark.

Marchant kept a descriptive journal of his thoughts and encounters while in London. He conducted business before the Privy Council in London and traveled through Scotland with Ben Franklin, traveling in the highest intellectual and political circles. In Scotland, the two dined together often and met with David Hume. They toured the universities in Edinburgh and Glasgow. Marchant also participated in the sixty-sixth birthday party for Franklin. Back in London, Marchant was introduced to the historian Catharine Macaulay, and the two had numerous dinners together, discussing English history and the politics of the time. He maintained correspondence with Macauley, who was a radical thinker. Macauley later visited the United States, calling on Richard Henry Lee, George Washington, and others.

With the burning of the *Gaspee* off Rhode Island in June 1772, Marchant's business became more difficult. He bade farewell to Franklin, who was "ill of the Gout in one Foot," and headed home in late July 1772. The voyage turned out to be difficult when, in mid-ocean, a fire consumed the ship's galley thanks to a pot of boiling pitch left unattended. Fortunately, the fire did not reach the thirty barrels of gunpowder in the hold, and Marchant was safely back in Boston on September 20.

By May 1773, Marchant was active in the heated political discussions of the time, fresh off his experiences in England. As tensions mounted with

Great Britain, Marchant was a member of Rhode Island's Sons of Liberty and Committee of Correspondence. A son, William, was born in 1774.

When Marchant's term as attorney general concluded, the Rhode Island General Assembly appointed him to the Continental Congress on May 7, 1777. He was then re-elected twice, serving until November 30, 1779. During his tenure, he was interested in military and naval matters. An interesting episode involved the proposed creation of a black battalion in the Rhode Island militia created from purchased slaves who had been freed. Marchant and William Ellery, his counterpart in Congress, were asked to petition Congress to raise funds to reimburse the slave masters. Ultimately, despite their best efforts, Marchant and Ellery could not convince Congress, citing the lack of funds.

Marchant was present in York, Pennsylvania, for the discussions and negotiations that resulted in the Articles of Confederation. He then signed the document on July 9, 1778. Marchant was again elected to Congress in 1780 and 1783 but did not attend. When he came up for election in 1784, he resigned his

The stone of Henry Marchant.

seat. That year, he was back in local politics as a member of the Newport Town Council. He was elected Recorder for the city and, in 1785, was elected to the state General Assembly. In 1788, Marchant was active with the committee that approved the U.S. Constitution in Rhode Island.

On April 22, 1790, during the early days of the first Washington administration, Marchant was nominated as the first federal district judge in Rhode Island. The Senate confirmed him on July 2, 1790. Early in his term, Marchant presided over *West v. Barnes* in 1791, which was the first case appealed to U.S. Supreme Court.

Marchant served as a federal judge until he died in Newport on August 30, 1796, at age 55. A local newspaper said he was "much lamented." After a well-attended funeral, he was buried in the Common Burying Ground in Newport. His tombstone reads, "The Honorable Henry Marchant. Member of the Revolutionary Congress and U.S. Judge for the District of Rhode Island. Died Aug. 30, 1796."

Rebecca Cooke Marchant died in 1819. Son William Marchant inherited the Henry Marchant Farm, a historic site located in South Kingstown, Rhode Island.

William Smith
(1728–1814)

Merchant Congressman

Buried at Old Westminster Graveyard,
Baltimore, Maryland.

Continental Congress • 1st US Congress

William Smith was a native of Lancaster County, Pennsylvania, who moved to Maryland, where he became a state legislator, Continental Congressman, and member of the House of Representatives.

Smith was born on April 12, 1728, in Donegal Township, Lancaster County, Pennsylvania, the son of James Smith and his wife, Mary.

In 1761, Smith and his brother, John, relocated to Baltimore to establish themselves as merchants.

As tensions increased with Great Britain, Smith was appointed to the Committee of Correspondence in 1774 and the Committee of Observation in 1775, overseeing the implementation of the Continental Association's boycott. He also served in the Continental Army as deputy adjutant general to Generals Horatio Gates and Nathanael Greene while the hostilities were in the Mid-Atlantic region.

On February 15, 1777, the Maryland legislature appointed Smith to the Continental Congress. He attended sessions in Baltimore from February 18 to February 27, 1777, and then in Philadelphia from April 2 until May 5, 1777, and from July 5 until September 18, 1777. He then attended the Congress in York, Pennsylvania, from October 4 through December 19, 1777.

The Congress at York

William Smith

Within the papers of Robert Morris, the financier, there is a mention of Smith: "William Smith, [a] prominent merchant of Baltimore, attended Congress in 1777, where on 5 July he was elected, along with Robert Morris, to the Committee of Commerce that replaced the earlier Secret Committee of Trade. On 9 May 1778, Congress elected him to the Navy Board of the Middle Department, from which he resigned on 22 July to devote his full attention to private business. He engaged with John Holker and Morris in supplying flour for the French and Spanish forces."

Following his brief term, Smith returned to his mercantile business, most likely in Baltimore.

After the war was over and the new US Constitution was adopted, Smith was elected to one of Maryland's seats in the new US House of Representatives in November 1788, opposing the administration. He served in the First Congress from March 4, 1789, until March 3, 1791.

Despite being opposed to the administration, Smith was named as the first auditor of the US Treasury but only served from July 16 through November 27, 1791.

WILLIAM SMITH (1728–1814)

Smith's final public duties were as a Maryland state senator from 1801 to 1802.

Smith died on March 27, 1814, two weeks shy of his 76th birthday. He was buried in the Westminster Burial Ground in Baltimore.

Smith's daughter, Mary Smith, later married General Otho Holland Williams, the founder of Williamsport, Maryland. His nephew, Robert Smith (1757–1842), served as the secretary of the Navy (1801–1809) and acting attorney general (1805) in the administration of President Thomas Jefferson, and as the secretary of state (1809–1811) in the administration of President James Madison.

Jonathan Elmer
(1745 – 1817)

America's First Doctor

Buried at Old Broad Street Presbyterian Church Cemetery, Bridgeton, New Jersey.

Continental Congress • Military

Jonathan Elmer was a physician from Bridgeton, New Jersey, who became a jurist and politician. He was elected to the Continental Congress three times as a representative of New Jersey and later served in the first U.S. Senate.

Elmer was born on November 29, 1745, in Cedarville, New Jersey, the son of Reverend Daniel Elmer, a minister, and Abigail (née Lawrence) Elmer. The Elmers had four children, including three sons and one daughter. The Elmers were of English origin. Grandfather Daniel Elmer was a minister born in East Windsor, Connecticut. Daniel Elmar, the father, was born in Springfield, Massachusetts, and emigrated to New Jersey.

According to some sources, Elmer was a sickly child and was tutored at home, including French and Latin. In 1765, at age 20, he attended the first class of medical students at the College of Philadelphia, now the University of Pennsylvania. He received his Bachelor of Medicine in 1768.

In 1769, Elmer married Mary Seeley, the daughter of Colonel Ephraim Seeley of Bridgeton, New Jersey. The couple would have eight children, five of whom survived to adulthood.

In 1771, Elmer was among the first Doctors of Medicine (along with Jonathan Potts, James Tilton, and Nicholas Way) to graduate in America, also from the College of Philadelphia.

JONATHAN ELMER (1745–1817)

The following year, Elmer became a lifelong member of the American Philosophical Society and a member of the New Jersey Medical Society. He had opened several medical practices in the area and entered the political arena for the first time, being elected sheriff of Cumberland County, New Jersey, a position he served in until 1775.

Elmer was pulled to the Revolutionary cause by his brother, Ebenezer, who participated in the Greenwich Tea Burning incident in December 1774 in Greenwich, New Jersey. The brig *Greyhound* was tied up in Greenwich harbor and was known to be carrying tea from the East India Company. Rebels boarded the ship, seized the tea, and burned it. The authorities captured Ebenezer and other perpetrators and put them on trial. The jury was comprised of locals, one of whom was the Elmers' other brother, Daniel Jr., who happened to be the jury foreman. Daniel was able to get the grand jury to dismiss the case, and the charges were dropped.

Stirred to the cause, Elmer joined the local militia and ultimately rose from captain to major of an infantry company. In May 1775, he was elected to the New Jersey Provisional Congress, serving until October, when he was replaced by his uncle, Theophilus Elmer.

The following year, Elmer became the clerk of Cumberland County, ending his military involvement. He served in this capacity until 1779.

On 30 November 1776, Elmer was elected to a seat in the Continental Congress for the first time. Elmer first attended the Congress on January 3, 1777, and attended sporadically through the end of his term on November 20. During this time, he visited hospitals as a member of the medical committee. It appears he returned to the Congress on Septmber 15, prior to their evacuation of Philadelphia on September 18, 1777. He would have attended the Congress in Lancaster, for one day, and then in York, Pennsylvania, through November 20, when he returned home.

That day, November 20, Elmer was reelected to Congress, but left Congress without a New Jersey representative. New Jersey did not immediately sign the Articles of Confederation when passed the prior week because of underrepresentation.

Elmer returned to York in January 1778 and then followed the Congress back to Philadelphia in July but resigned from his seat in September, complaining about the inadequacy of the compensation in covering his travel expenses. His replacement and three other New Jersey Congressmen signed the Articles of Confederation on November 26, 1778.

Elmer stayed in New Jersey for the next two years, serving as a representative of Cumberland County in the New Jersey Legislative Council in 1780. The following year, he returned to the position of clerk of Cumberland County. He was also appointed to the Continental Congress once again on November 28, 1781. Elmer served through 1783.

In 1782, Elmer was honored with an appointment as trustee of the College of New Jersey, now known as Princeton. He served in this role until 1795.

In 1784, Elmer returned to the New Jersey Legislative Council, representing Cumberland County. He also served as a judge of the New Jersey surrogate court from 1784 to 1792.

In 1786, Elmer returned to the role of clerk of Cumberland County from 1786 to 1789.

In 1787, Elmer became president of the New Jersey Medical Society. Later that year, he was appointed to the last Continental Congress, from 1787 through 1788. It was his third and final sting in the body.

After the passage of the U.S. Constitution, Elmer was appointed by the New Jersey Legislature to the U.S. Senate on March 4, 1789. He was of the group serving only two years, until March 3, 1791. Others served four and six years to stagger the terms.

In 1792, Elmer failed in his bid to win election to the U.S. House of Representatives. Instead, he focused on his role as the presiding judge of the Court of Common Pleas of Cumberland County, a position he held until his retirement in 1804.

Elmer's last attempt at elective office was a failed bid for the U.S. Senate in 1798. Retired after 1804, Elmer was called to public service again in 1813, when he was appointed to a judgeship. However, now in his late sixties, Elmer's health declined, and he resigned months later, in February 1814.

The grave of Jonathan Elmer.

JONATHAN ELMER (1745–1817)

A devout Presbyterian, Elmer died on September 3, 1817, and was laid to rest in the Old Presbyterian Cemetery, now known as the Old Broad Street Presbyterian Church Cemetery in Bridgeton. His large gravestone reads: "Here rests in hope of glorious resurrection the body of Jonathan Elmer, M.D., and fellow of the American Philosophical Society. An eminent Physician and Civilian, a distinguished Christian who departed this life, Sept. 3, 1817, in the 72nd year of his age."

Two years after his death, it was reported that the "legacy of Dr. Jonathan Elmer, deceased, late of Bridgetown West, New Jersey, to the American Bible Society 'to be added to their fund for circulating the Holy Scriptures,' paid by Isaac Snowden, Esq. on account of Dr. William Elmer, Executor."

Elmer's younger brother, Ebenezer, who was embroiled in the tea incident, and his son, Lucius Elmer, were both members of the U.S. House of Representatives.

John Harvie
(1742 – 1807)

Friend of Jefferson

Buried at Hollywood Cemetery,
Richmond, Virginia.

Articles of Confederation

John Harvie was an attorney and builder from Virginia, the son of Thomas Jefferson's guardian, John Harvie Sr. He served in the Virginia House of Delegates and operated a prison camp during the Revolution. He was elected to the Second Continental Congress, where he signed the Articles of Confederation. Later, he was the mayor of Richmond and was a lifelong friend of Jefferson.

Harvie, born in 1742 at the family's 2500-acre estate, Belmont Plantation, in Albemarle County, Virginia, was the son of Scottish immigrant John Harvie Sr., a planter, and his wife, Martha (née Gaines) Harvie. When Thomas Jefferson's father, Peter Jefferson, died in 1757 during Thomas's fourteenth year, neighbor John Harvie Sr. became his legal guardian. Young Harvie and Jefferson, only a year apart, became like brothers and were close for the rest of their lives.

Harvie studied law and was admitted to the Virginia bar. In 1767, he inherited Belmont Plantation when his father died and continued to live there. His mother moved to Georgia with his eight siblings, leaving the 25-year-old to run the estate. Harvie then married Margaret Morton Jones, the daughter of Gabriel Jones, a longtime member of the House of Burgesses, and Margaret Strother Morton Jones. The couple had seven children: Lewis, John, Edwin, Jacquelin, Gabriella, Emily, and Julia.

Prior to the American Revolution, Harvie grew his business interests. He was also one of the first lawyers to practice at the Albemarle bar. In 1774,

JOHN HARVIE (1742–1807)

John Harvie

following what was later called Dunmore's War, he helped negotiate a peace treaty with the Shawnee following the Battle of Point Pleasant, which occurred in what is now West Virginia.

When Governor Dunmore abolished the House of Burgesses, Harvie was elected to Virginia's new assembly, the Virginia House of Delegates. He attended in 1775 and 1776 and was elected to the Second Continental Congress on behalf of Virginia. He was also a colonel in the Virginia militia in 1776 and helped to organize and purchase supplies.

While in the Continental Congress at York, Pennsylvania, Harvie worked on the Articles of Confederation. He also served on the Board of War for the Congress and inspected the camp at Valley Forge in the Winter of 1777/78. Congress was very concerned about the conditions there. Harvie said to Washington, "My dear General, if you had given some explanation, all these rumors [denigrating Washington] would have been silenced a long time ago."

Harvie signed the Articles on July 9, 1778, and promptly resigned from the Congress afterward. He also procured from Richard Anderson a 240-acre property west of Charlottesville called The Barracks. There, he established a prison camp that held 6000 Hessians and British soldiers by January 1779. The camp had brick buildings to house the troops as well as animals, poultry, gardens, and other outbuildings. Some of the prisoners deserted and headed into the hills. There, they married Native American women. When the camp closed in November 1780, the remaining soldiers were moved north.

In 1780, Harvie was appointed the registrar of Virginia's Land Office and moved to Richmond. He oversaw transactions in the Northwest Territory, western Virginia, Ohio, and Kentucky.

Harvie was elected the mayor of Richmond, Virginia, from 1785 to 1786. His holdings included the magnificent Belmont plantation, as well as the estates at Pen Park and The Barracks. In 1789, he was a presidential elector.

In 1798, Harvie added Judge Bushrod Washington's Belvidere estate in Richmond. Some compared it to Mount Vernon and said it was "an extremely handsome house, and of decidedly superior architecture, being beautifully proportioned."

Harvie died from injuries sustained following the fall from the roof of a building he was inspecting that was under construction. He passed on February 6, 1807, and was buried at Belvidere, which later became part of Hollywood Cemetery in Richmond.

Harvie is remembered by a street in Richmond. Jacquelin Street was named after his son, General Jacquelin Harvie. In 1982, Harvie descendant

The Harvie family crypt is within these walls.

JOHN HARVIE (1742–1807)

James Beverly Harvie Jr. placed a plaque near his ancestor's grave, which reads: "Within, and without, these walls rest members of the family of Col. John Harvie, 1742–1807. A guardian of Thomas Jefferson, and signers of the Articles of Confederation and the Bill of Rights. Here, too, lie his son, Jacquelin, and Mary, his wife, daughter of Chief Justice John Marshall. This area, part of the Harvie lands, became Hollywood Cemetery in 1847."

Benjamin Rumsey
(1734 – 1808)

Soldier, Congressman, Judge

Buried at Old St. John's Church Cemetery,
Joppa, Maryland.

Continental Congress • Military • Judge

Benjamin Rumsey was a militiaman, jurist, and Continental Congressman from Maryland. For nearly twenty-eight years, he served as the first chief judge of the Maryland Court of Appeals, a record that still stands.

Rumsey was born on October 6, 1734, at Bohemia Manor in Cecil County, Maryland, the son of William Ramsay and his wife, Sabina (née Blaidenburgh) Rumsey.

Rumsey graduated from the College of New Jersey (Princeton), then read law and was admitted to the Maryland bar. On March 24, 1768, he married a widow, Mary Hall Maxwell, with whom he had three children: Benjamin Jr., John, and Hannah. Around this time, he settled in Joppa, moving into the home of his wife's late husband.

In 1771, Rumsey was elected to Maryland's lower house, representing Cecil County. When Harford County was formed in 1773, he represented it.

As the Revolution began, Rumsey represented his county in the Maryland conventions of 1775 and 1776. In September 1775, he was appointed captain of Company 6 in the Harford County militia and rose to colonel of the Lower Battalion of that same militia on January 6, 1776. He built a fort in the area near his home.

Rumsey served on the Committees of Observation and Safety for Maryland, established in each colony to enforce the boycott of British goods banned by the

BENJAMIN RUMSEY (1734–1808)

Continental Association. He was also a member of the Council of Safety for the Western Shore of Maryland.

On November 10, 1776, the Maryland assembly elected Rumsey to the Continental Congress. He attended from November 19, 1776, until December 12, 1776, in Baltimore, Maryland. He was reelected on February 15, 1777, and served from February 17, 1777, until an unknown date, from April 8 to May 5, 1777, all in Philadelphia, and about November 5 to December 24, 1777, in York.

After his service in the Congress, Rumsey was the first chief justice of the new Maryland Court of Appeals, created in 1778. He held this seat until he retired in 1806.

Rumsey died at his home on March 7, 1808, at age 73, and was buried at the Old St. John's Church Cemetery in Joppa, Maryland.

The homestead now known as Rumsey Mansion, in Joppa, Maryland, is on the Historic American Buildings Survey and is the only remaining building of Old Joppa, northern Maryland's first town. The home was built in the 1720s and converted to a plantation. This example of Colonial Georgian architecture remains in private hands.

Rumsey's cousin James (1743–1792) was an engineer known for his steamboat experiments on the Potomac.

Benjamin Rumsey's house, Joppatowne, Maryland.

William Clingan
(1721–1790)
Chester County Continental Congressman

Buried at Upper Octorara Church Cemetery,
Parkesburg, Pennsylvania.

Articles of Confederation

William Clingan was a Continental Congressman born circa 1721 who attended the Congress from 1777 to 1779, including the months when it met in Lancaster and then York, Pennsylvania during the British occupation of Philadelphia. During this time, Clingan signed the Articles of Confederation which was later ratified by the states in 1781.

Born near Wagontown in Caln Township, Chester County, Pennsylvania, Clingan was likely the son of immigrants from Northern Ireland or Scotland. His educational details are lost to history, but he did marry twice: first to Catherine (maiden name unknown) with whom he had a son before her death in 1785; and second to Rachel Gilleylen (1756–1843), a widow with six children from her first marriage, who survived him.

Clingan owned hundreds of acres of land in the Wagontown area and resided along the King's Highway from Philadelphia to Lancaster, the current Route 340, just west of Wagontown. The current address for the property is 101 Hatfield Road, Coatesville, Pennsylvania. From 1757 to 1786, he served as a justice of the peace in Chester County and, for the last six years, President of the Chester County Courts.

William Clingan was elected to the Continental Congress as a delegate from Pennsylvania on September 14, 1777. He attended sessions from November

WILLIAM CLINGAN (1721–1790)

William Clingan

1 to about November 28, 1777; from January 1, 1778 to about March 24, 1778; from about April 25, 1778, to about May 19, 1778; from about June 16, 1778 to about June 27, 1778; and from about September 14, 1778 to about December 2, 1778. He was re-elected on November 20, 1778.

These dates of service put William Clingan in the room for the final debates on the Articles of Confederation and then the adoption on November 15, 1777, in York. Beginning on July 9, 1778, the delegates began signing the document. Along with Clingan, Robert Morris, Daniel Roberdeau, Jonathan Bayard Smith, and Joseph Reed signed for Pennsylvania.

William Clingan's nephew and namesake married Jane Roan, the beautiful daughter of revered pastor John Roan and his wife Anne, on June 11, 1778. Jane's uncle John Cochran was a distinguished surgeon in the Revolutionary army. The wedding was noteworthy enough to receive a lot of coverage in *The Pennsylvania Packet* newspaper:

> Was married, last Thursday, Mr. William Clingan, Jr., of Donegal, to Miss Jenny Roan, of Londonderry, both of the County of Lancaster—a sober, sensible, agreeable young couple and very sincere Whigs. This marriage promises as much happiness as the state of things in this our sinful world will admit.

> This was indeed a Whig wedding, as there were present many young men and ladies, and not one of the gentlemen but had been out when called on in the service of his country, and it was well-known that the groom, in particular, had proved his heroism, as well as Whiggism, in several battles and skirmishes. After the marriage was ended, a motion was made, and heartily agreed to by all present, that the young unmarried ladies should form themselves into an association by the name of the "Whig Association of the Unmarried Ladies of America," in which they should pledge their honor that they would never give their hand in marriage to any gentleman until he had first proved himself a patriot, in readily turning out when called to defend his country from slavery, by a spirited and brave conduct, as they would not wish to be the mothers of a race of slaves and cowards.

The younger Clingan was a soldier who participated in the battles at Trenton, Princeton, Brandywine, and Germantown and had served in the army elsewhere. The couple later moved northwest to the Buffalo Valley near Lewisburg, Pennsylvania.

Following his service in Congress, the elder Clingan returned to his duties on the court in Chester County. He was a Justice of the Peace for the district of West Caln, Sadsbury, and West Fallowfield Townships, and Justice of the Court of Common Pleas of Chester County. He also presided in the Court of Quarter Sessions and the Orphans' Court there. Clingan was instrumental in the planning and construction of a new prison and court facilities in Chester County.

Throughout his life, William was a leading member of the Upper Octorara Presbyterian Church, which is along present-day Route 10 near Parkesburg, Pennsylvania. According to an early *History of Chester County, Pennsylvania*, Clingan was robbed of the church collections:

> At one time during the career of the noted robbers, the Doanes, Mr. Clingan was visited by them. In some business transactions, he had received a large amount of money in gold, and the visit of the Doanes had reference to this treasure, which they supposed was in the house. While searching for it, one of them announced that he had found it. Mr. Clingan's desk had been opened, and there stood a large leathern bag full of money, and seizing a violin which was in the house, as they said, to have a jubilation over their good luck,

they mounted their horses and were off. The bag, however, which they supposed to contain the gold was simply filled with coppers, the church collections as he had brought them home from Sunday to Sunday, and which, when he had a quantity on hand, he exchanged for larger money. One of the gang, afterward executed, was visited by Mr. Clingan in prison, and he told him of their chagrin when they discovered their mistake.

William Clingan died on May 9, 1790, and was laid to rest in the Upper Octorara Burial Grounds. His tombstone reads:

Here lyeth the Body of WILLIAM CLINGAN, Esq. Who departed this Life, The 9th Day of May 1790. Also CATHERINE, his Wife, Who departed this Life, The 8th Day of Feby 1785.

William Clingan left no descendants.

The grave of William Clingan

William Ellery
(1727–1820)

Early Abolitionist

Buried at Common Burying Ground,
Newport, Rhode Island.

Declaration of Independence • Articles of Confederation

This Founder once wrote a letter to one of his grandsons enumerating the jobs he had been employed in over the years. Putting pen to paper he stated, "I have been a clerk of the court, a quack lawyer, a member of Congress, one of the Lords of the Admiralty, a judge, a loan officer, and finally a collector of the customs, and thus, not without many difficulties, but as honestly, thank God, as most men, I have got through the journey of a varied and sometimes anxious life." As part of that journey, he added his signature to the document declaring American independence. His name was William Ellery.

Ellery was born on December 22, 1727, in Newport, Rhode Island. His father was a graduate of Harvard and a wealthy merchant. He was initially educated by his father and eventually also found his way to Harvard from which he graduated at the age of twenty. He then returned to Newport where he first attempted to follow in his father's shoes as a merchant.

Ellery married twice, first in 1750 to Ann Remington who died in 1764 and again in 1767 when he wed Abigail Cary. In the course of these marriages, he fathered at least sixteen children, though some put the number at nineteen. Only one other signer, Carter Braxton, is recorded as fathering more. Needless to say, providing for a family of this size took a lot of his energy, though clearly not all of it.

WILLIAM ELLERY (1727–1820)

Portrait of William Ellery, artist unknown.

Ellery, as stated in his aforementioned letter, worked a number of jobs until at age forty he achieved a life's ambition and began to practice law. He was a successful lawyer working in both his home state and nearby Massachusetts. At this same time, he became involved in the political scene becoming active in the Sons of Liberty. Like many of the patriots of his day he strongly opposed the Stamp Act and the Intolerable Acts.

In 1776, Samuel Ward, a former Rhode Island governor who was one of the two Rhode Island representatives to the Continental Congress, died after contracting smallpox. Ellery was the choice to replace him. Thus he arrived in Congress shortly before the Declaration of Independence was adopted and signed. In both the play and the movie *1776* it is the other Rhode Island delegate, Stephen Hopkins, who is portrayed as finding a spot where he could see each man's face as he signed the Declaration. In reality, it was Ellery who did so. Describing the scene he said, "I was determined to see how they all looked as they signed what might be their death warrant. I placed myself beside the secretary Charles Thomson and eyed each closely as he affixed his name to the document. Undaunted resolution was displayed on every countenance."

During the Revolution, the British seized Newport and burned Ellery's home to the ground. During the occupation, he and his family fled to Dighton,

Marker honoring William Ellery.

The grave of William Ellery at Common Burying Ground & Island Cemetery in Newport, Rhode Island (photo by Lawrence Knorr).

WILLIAM ELLERY (1727–1820)

Massachusetts where they resided until it was safe to return to their home and begin the rebuilding process.

After joining Congress, Ellery would remain a member of that body for eight of the next ten years. In 1922, the *Altoona Tribune* described him as one of its most influential members. During this period, he also signed the Articles of Confederation and served on numerous committees including war wounded, army purchases, and public accounts.

In 1786, Ellery left Congress and returned to Rhode Island to attend to his personal affairs, most notably shoring up his financial situation. He worked a number of jobs until 1790 when President Washington appointed him customs collector for Newport. The appointment solidified him financially and he held the post until his death.

Ellery was one of three signers of the Declaration of Independence who lived into their nineties, dying at the age of 92 on February 15, 1820. He was laid to rest in the Common Burying Ground in Newport, Rhode Island.

There is an annual commemoration held at his grave every July 4th sponsored by the Sons of the Revolution and the William Ellery Chapter of the Daughters of the American Revolution. A town in New York and an avenue in Middletown, Rhode Island are named in his honor.

Edward Langworthy
(1738 – 1802)
An Orphaned Founder

He was initially buried at the Old Episcopal Church in Baltimore, Maryland. The church was demolished in 1891, and the location of his remains is unknown.

Articles of Confederation

This founder's parents were likely among the first colonists shipped to Georgia. This conclusion is because he was born within five years of James Oglethorpe recruiting those in poorhouses and debtors' prisons to be the first to settle in the region. It appears his parents died when he was very young as he was raised in the Bethesda Orphan House in Savannah. Despite these challenging beginnings, he would rise to represent Georgia in the Continental Congress during the American Revolution and sign the Articles of Confederation. This document officially united the thirteen colonies as a country. Described by Burton Alva Knokle in *The Georgia Historical Quarterly* as a patriot, teacher, statesman, editor, writer, historian, and eminent citizen of two states, this founder's name was Edward Langworthy.

Edward Langworthy

Langworthy was born in Savannah circa 1738. It appears his parents died when he was relatively young as he was raised and educated in Savannah's Bethesda Orphan House. He took his studies seriously as he became one of the instructors at the orphanage. At one point, he took out an advertisement in a Georgia newspaper which read, "The subscriber having taken a convenient House, proposes to board eight young gentlemen at 22 per annum, and to instruct them in the Latin and Greek Languages. The greatest care will be taken to improve them in the English language and to accustom them to a just and agreeable manner in pronunciation and reading. Young ladies may be taught English Grammar, Writing, &c. privately." It appears that teaching as a profession appealed to him since he would take up the profession again later in life.

In 1774, when the fires that became the American Revolution were already burning, Langworthy remained loyal to the British crown, as evidenced by his signing the Loyalist protest of the Savannah Resolutions. His Loyalist leanings did not last long as, within a year, he reversed his position entirely and was chosen secretary to the Revolutionary body known as the Council of Safety. Two months later, he became a member of the Georgia Provincial Congress, where he was appointed secretary of that body. In this position, Langworthy signed the initial delegates' credentials to represent Georgia at the Continental Congress meeting in Philadelphia. Among the credentials he signed was one for a good friend of his, Button Gwinnett. Gwinnett would affix his signature to the Declaration of Independence.

On June 7, 1777, the Georgia legislature elected Langworthy to serve as a delegate to the Continental Congress. As a representative from Georgia, he signed the Articles of Confederation on July 24, 1778. The Articles formally brought the thirteen states together, forming the United States of America. He was not a vocal member of Congress as he is not recorded as ever having made a motion though he did second on two occasions. He was among the representatives who spent time in York, Pennsylvania, when the Congress was moved there after the British army occupied Philadelphia. Based on a letter he wrote at the time, he had little liking for the city. After completing his service in Congress, Langworthy returned to Georgia, where he may well have begun the research on the state's first history, which he would work on for years but never complete. His papers involving this project have never been recovered.

In 1785, Langworthy moved to Baltimore, where he became part owner and the editor of the *Maryland Journal & Baltimore Advertiser*. The newspaper flourished and proved to be a successful business venture. In one open letter to the paper's readers, Langworthy and his co-owner, William Goddard, stated, "It would perhaps be to little Purpose to descant on the many Advantages derived from the Art of Printing; that the present Age is esteemed an Enlightened One, and that we are in the enjoyment of Political Independence, and Perfect

The Congress at York

Freedom in the important Concerns of Religion, may, in a great Degree, be ascribed to the Liberty of the Press."

When Langworthy was busy with his newspaper, the Baltimore religious heads of the Catholic, Episcopalian, and Presbyterian churches established the Baltimore Academy. The institution's purpose was to provide the young men in the area an opportunity to pursue a higher education without leaving home. Langworthy was chosen to head the school where he also taught the classics. It is not clear how long he labored at the Academy. It is known that he sold his interest in the newspaper on January 1, 1787, and that in March of that year, he completed his memoir of General Charles Lee. In 1792 this work was published in both New York and London.

In 1795, Langworthy was appointed to the post of Baltimore's Clerk of Customs. He would serve in this position until he died on November 2, 1802. He had impressed many in the Baltimore area relative to his conduct and life in his adopted second city.

His obituary stated, "After a severe illness of six days . . . the spirit of Edward Langworthy, Esq. deputy naval officer of the port of Baltimore, took its flight for 'another and a better world.' To eulogize the defunct is not the intention of the writer of this paragraph, suffice it to say, that his public and private walks in life were such as many may endeavor to imitate, but a few will attain to equal perfection."

Langworthy was laid to rest in the yard of Baltimore's Old Episcopal Church. That church was demolished in 1891, and the records of the graveyard were lost.

Joseph Wood
(1712–1791)

Pennsylvania Transplant

Burial location unknown,
Sunbury, Georgia.

Continental Congress • Military

Joseph Wood was a Pennsylvanian who moved to Georgia as a young man. When Georgia hesitated to join with the other twelve colonies in revolt, Wood joined the Continental Army in Pennsylvania and rose to the rank of colonel. When Georgia entered the fray, he returned to his new state and was selected to the Continental Congress.

Wood was born circa 1712 in Pennsylvania. His precise lineage is unknown. He likely had a military background.

On December 10, 1747, he received 200 acres of land in Georgia. Around this time, he married Catholena (or Catherine) Reading, likely a native of Delaware born circa 1730. The couple had six children, including Henry (1754), Joseph (1760), John (1762), Hester (1765), Elizabeth (1765), and Jacob (1768), all of whom lived in Georgia.

Through 1770, Wood was listed as living in Savannah, Georgia, west of Bull Street near the wharf. He likely also owned a plantation in what is now the ghost town of Sunbury, Georgia, in St. John's Parish (now Liberty County), about thirty-five miles southwest. Wood was listed as living in Sunbury in 1774.

As the Revolution was underway, Wood was a leading voice for liberty. When the colony of Georgia did not immediately join the other twelve colonies in the First Continental Congress on August 10, 1774, the following February,

Wood, Daniel Roberts, and Samuel Stevens requested to join with the South Carolinians in implementing the Continental Association, which involved boycotting British goods.

Frustrated by the lack of movement in his adopted state, Wood returned to Pennsylvania to fight. He was appointed to the rank of major and then rose to lieutenant colonel and then colonel in the 2nd Pennsylvania Regiment led by Arthur St. Clair. Wood saw action in June 1776 with General Sullivan in Canada at Trois-Rivières and in October 1776, when he was wounded at Lake Champlain.

On November 9, 1776, a Philadelphia newspaper referred to Colonel Joseph Wood, in charge of the 3rd Regiment of twelve Pennsylvania regiments in the Continental Army.

On June 7, 1777, Georgia appointed Wood to the Continental Congress. He joined the Congress in York from November 17, 1777, until February 27, 1778. He was again elected on February 26, 1778, but in his 66th year, he returned to Georgia, where he served on the Georgia Council of Safety.

Wood lived the rest of his life on his plantation in Sunbury, Georgia. He died there on October 2, 1791. His burial location has been lost.

Francis Lewis
(1713–1802)

"All That Glitters Is Not Gold"

Trinity Church Cemetery
New York, New York

Declaration of Independence • Articles of Confederation

Francis Lewis was a Welsh-born merchant from New York City who was elected to the Continental Congress, where he signed the Declaration of Independence and the Articles of Confederation.

Lewis was born March 21, 1713, in the village of Llandaff, Glamorganshire, Wales, slightly northwest of the capital, Cardiff. He was the only child of Reverend Francis Lewis, an Anglican clergyman, and his wife, Amy (née Pettingal) Lewis, the daughter of an Anglican clergyman. Lewis was orphaned at age five and went to live with relatives, including a maternal aunt. He grew up in both Wales and Scotland and learned the Gaelic and Welsh languages. The Pettingal family, especially an uncle who was the dean at St. Paul's Cathedral, saw to his education at the prestigious Westminster School in London.

Upon graduation, Lewis became an apprentice at a mercantile business in London. When he turned 21, he inherited properties left by his father. He sold them and used the proceeds to start his own business in partnership with Edward Annesley. He acquired merchandise and sailed for New York City, arriving in 1734 or 1735. He left some of the goods with his partner in New York and took the rest to Philadelphia. There, he lived for two years before returning to New York.

Back in New York, Lewis was involved in the trans-Atlantic trade, making trips to several northern European ports, Saint Petersburg, Scotland, and Africa.

Francis Lewis

Twice, he survived shipwrecks off the Irish coast. Circa 1743, Lewis broke up his business partnership with Annesley but married his sister, Elizabeth Annesley, on June 15, 1745. The couple had seven children, three of whom survived to adulthood:

- Ann Lewis (1748–1802) married Captain George Robertson (1742–1791) of the Royal Navy.
- Francis Lewis Jr. (1749–1814) served as churchwarden of St George's Parish in Flushing, New York, from 1791 to 1794. He married Elizabeth Ludlow (d. 1831), daughter of Gabriel Ludlow, Esq.
- Morgan Lewis (1754–1844) married Gertrude Livingston, the daughter of Judge Robert Livingston of Clermont. He was a governor and attorney general of New York.

In 1756, at the outbreak of the French and Indian War, Lewis supplied uniforms to the British. He was at Fort Oswego that August, delivering uniforms, when General Montcalm's forces and Indian allies attacked. Lewis was standing next to Colonel James Mercer, the fort's commander, when a cannonball killed him. The fort was surrendered to Montcalm, who permitted the natives to select thirty prisoners to keep or kill. Lewis was among them. While being tortured

FRANCIS LEWIS (1713–1802)

by his Indian captors, Lewis spoke in Welsh. The natives recognized similarities in the language and stopped and spoke with him. The chief then took Lewis to Montreal where he requested to return to his family. However, he was instead sent to France as a prisoner, where he remained until the end of the war.

In 1763, Lewis was exchanged and returned to New York. There, the British granted him 5,000 acres for his service. He re-established his mercantile business and quickly accumulated a large fortune, permitting him to retire at age 52 in 1765. The *Encyclopedia of American Wealth* estimated that his holdings ranked him fifth among all the signers of the Declaration.

In 1765, with the passage of The Stamp Act, Lewis turned against the British government. He was appointed to the Stamp Act Congress, held in New York. In 1877, granddaughter Julia Delafield wrote, "On October 25 [1765] they met for the last time, and had the honor of being the first body to pass the resolution that the colonies ought to be united and act in common. Among the members of the New York committee we find the names of Francis Lewis and Robert R. Livingston. This Congress had not in its ranks a more consistent and energetic opponent of the tyranny of the mother country than Lewis."

During the crisis, Lewis moved his business and family to Whitestone, now part of Flushing, Queens County, New York. In 1771, he moved the business back to New York City and, with his son, Francis Lewis Jr., became one of the leading merchants under the banner of Francis Lewis and Son. He also became a founding member of the Sons of Liberty there.

To protest the closing of the port of Boston in 1774, New Yorkers formed the Committee of Fifty to oversee the city. Lewis, by unanimous consent, became the 51st member on May 16. The committee eventually included sixty members who established the colony's new government.

In 1775, sensing the risk of invasion, Lewis again moved the family and their belongings to Whitestone. He was elected to the Second Continental Congress on April 22, 1775, serving until November 19, 1779. He signed the Olive Branch Petition and used his own resources to help supply the army with clothing. On October 9, 1775, Lewis, John Alsop, and Philip Livingston were contracted by the Secret Committee of the Continental Congress to supply arms and ammunition. Benjamin Rush called Lewis "a very honest man and very useful in executive business."

When the vote for independence was called on July 2, 1776, New York's delegation abstained due to the lack of instructions from the provincial assembly. Thus, when independence was declared unanimously, 12 to 0, on July 4, New York was not among the colonies. Finally, the New York delegation received instructions to approve the measure, and Francis Lewis and the others signed the Declaration of Independence on August 2.

Only a few weeks later, on August 27, 1776, during the Battle of Brooklyn Heights, the British captured the Lewis estate at Whitestone. British Captain Birtch and a troop of light horsemen were sent to destroy the Lewis home. As the soldiers approached and a British warship opened fire on the house, Elizabeth remained calm. Thinking her shoe buckles were made of gold, a soldier bent down and tore them off.

"All that glitters is not gold," said Elizabeth to the young man. The buckles were just pinchbeck.

The soldiers ransacked the house, destroying books, papers, pictures, and furniture. They also took Elizabeth Lewis as a captive and imprisoned her without a bed or a change of clothes and little food.

Upon learning of this, General Washington ordered the arrest of two Loyalist women in Philadelphia and said these captives would receive the same treatment as Mrs. Lewis. Finally, an exchange was arranged, but Elizabeth's health was weakened.

That winter, while the troops were at Valley Forge, Lewis was a strong supporter of General Washington when the Conway Cabal became public. Meanwhile, in York, Pennsylvania, Lewis worked on the Articles of Confederation, which he signed in November 1778. He was just one of sixteen men to sign both the Declaration and the Articles.

Grave of Francis Lewis

FRANCIS LEWIS (1713–1802)

He returned home in 1779 to be with his ailing wife. She passed in June 1779, and Lewis did not seek re-election after his term was up in November of that year. He then served as the chairman of the Continental Board of Admiralty until he retired from public service in 1781.

In his later years, from 1784 to 1786, Lewis was a vestryman at Trinity Church. He enjoyed the company of his family, especially his grandchildren. Lewis died on December 31, 1802, at age 89. He was buried in an unmarked grave at Trinity Church Cemetery in New York City. The descendants of the Signers of the Declaration of Independence added a granite marker and plaque in 1947.

Francis Lewis had many interesting descendants:

- His son Morgan served in the Continental Army during the Revolutionary War and later held many offices in New York, including governor (1804–1807). He was a major general in the War of 1812.
- Through Morgan, he was a grandfather of Margret Lewis (1780–1860), who married New York lawyer and politician Maturin Livingston and became parents to twelve children.
- Through his son Francis Jr., he was a grandfather of Gabriel Ludlow Lewis.
- Through his daughter Ann, he was a grandfather to Marianne Robertson (1779–1829), who married John Bird Sumner, the Archbishop of Canterbury and brother of Charles Richard Sumner, bishop of Winchester.
- Great-grandson Manny Livingston died at the Battle of Gettysburg during the Civil War.
- Great-great-great-grandson William A. Wellman was a Hollywood director.

Francis Lewis is also remembered in many ways:

- John Trumbull's 1819 painting *Declaration of Independence* includes Lewis, near Richard Stockton and John Witherspoon. This painting hangs in the Rotunda of the Capitol in Washington, D.C.
- A granite boulder bears his name in the memorial park of the 55 signers near the Washington Monument in Washington, D.C.
- Francis Lewis High School and P.S. 79, "The Francis Lewis School" in Queens, New York, are named after Lewis.

The Congress at York

- Francis Lewis Boulevard, known locally as "Franny Lew" or "Franny Lewie," stretches almost the entire north/south length of Queens.
- Francis Lewis Park is located under the Queens approach of the Bronx-Whitestone Bridge, on the site of the Lewis home.
- A society of the Children of the American Revolution located in Queens, New York, is named for him.
- A Masonic lodge, Francis Lewis #273, is in Whitestone.

George Frost
(1720 – 1796)

Sea Captain Congressman

Buried at Pine Hill Cemetery,
Durham, New Hampshire.

Continental Congress

George Frost was a sea captain from Durham, New Hampshire, who became a jurist later in life. He was elected to the Continental Congress as a representative of New Hampshire.

Frost was born on April 26, 1720, at New Castle, Rockingham County, New Hampshire, the son of John Frost, a British naval officer, and Mary (née Pepperell) Frost. The elder Frost was born in Kittery, Massachusetts Bay Colony (now Maine) in 1682, the son of Major Charles Frost from Tiverton, Devon, England, who had emigrated to America with his wife. Mary Pepperell Frost's father, William Pepperell, was also from Devonshire and emigrated in 1647. Mary's brother, William Pepperell, was the 1st Baronet Pepperell (1696–1759), a distinguished soldier who fought at Fort Louisburg during King George's War. Besides George, John and Mary Frost had fifteen other children before John died in 1732, when George was 12.

Mary Frost, a widow, was unable to care for so many children. Frost was sent to his uncle, William Pepperell, where he went to sea on his uncle's ships. He spent over twenty years as a seaman, many as the captain of a merchant vessel. Frost then opened a merchant business at Kittery Point, near Portsmouth, New Hampshire.

Circa 1760, Frost returned to Newcastle and continued as a merchant. In 1769, he moved to Durham and married. There, he studied law. In 1773, he was made a justice on the court of common pleas in Strafford County, a post he retained until 1791.

On April 1, 1777, Frost was elected to the Continental Congress along with Nathaniel Folsom to represent New Hampshire. He served from May 16, 1777, through September 17, 1777, the day before the Congress fled Philadelphia. He then joined the Congress in York from December 20, 1777, through December 31, 1777. During his absence, Frost missed the completion of the Articles of Confederation on November 15, 1777.

After his service in the Congress, Frost returned to New Hampshire, where he was named to the state's governor's council in 1781, serving until 1784. At that point, it appears Frost, in his mid-sixties, retired from public life.

Frost died at his home in Durham, New Hampshire, on June 21, 1796. He was buried at Pine Hill Cemetery. The Portsmouth, New Hampshire, newspaper *The Oracle of the Day* said:

> As a respectable statesman and patriot, he was early known in the general Congress, and for many years in the offices of Judge in this state. His humanity, his cheerfulness and his great philanthropy gave evidence of his truly christian [*sic*] temper—and his unexampled hospitality and kindness, rendered him dear to society. His consort [wife] and children feel the loss of unceasing affection and tenderness and the sons and daughters of poverty and distress within the compass of his knowledge, now fighting, say, "We have lost our friend."

Grave of George Frost.

Abraham Clark
(1726–1794)

House burned, sons tortured

Buried at Rahway Cemetery,
Rahway, New Jersey.

**Continental Congress • Declaration of Independence
United States House of Representatives**

Abraham Clark suffered much for the independence of the United States. He served in the Continental Congress as a representative from New Jersey, voted for independence, and signed the Declaration of Independence. This, of course, was an act of treason and all the signers risked their lives and welfare. Many lost their homes and land, and property and many families were split up during the war.

Abraham Clark was born in Elizabethtown (now Elizabeth), New Jersey, on February 15, 1726, the only child of Thomas Clark and Hannah Winans. At a young age, he established himself as a math prodigy. He was tutored in surveying, which gave him a steady income that allowed him to pursue an education in law. He was admitted to the state bar and quickly gained the reputation as a man for the little man as he would represent many who could not afford a lawyer. He became known as the "Poor Man's Counselor," was known for his integrity and generosity, and was very popular, particularly among the middle class.

Clark met Sarah Hatfield at the age of 22, and the couple was soon married. They had ten children, eight of whom survived to adulthood. He entered politics in 1752 when he served as clerk of the New Jersey colonial legislature. He

The Congress at York

Abraham Clark

later became Sheriff of Essex County and, in 1775, was elected to the Provincial Congress. The Provincial Congress was a transitional governing body of the province of New Jersey with representatives from all New Jersey's then thirteen counties to supersede the Royal Governor.

As the issue of independence heated up, Clark was highly vocal in favor of independence. Early in 1776, the New Jersey delegation to the Continental Congress was opposed to independence. On June 21, 1776, the state replaced all five delegates with delegates favoring separation, including Clark, John Hart, Francis Hopkinson, Richard Stockton, and John Witherspoon. They arrived in Philadelphia on June 28, 1776 and voted for the Declaration of Independence. On August 2, he signed the famous document. Few of the signers suffered as much as he did. The British invaded and burned his home and captured and tortured his sons.

Clark had two sons who were officers in the Continental Army. Aaron and Thomas were both officers in the New Jersey state artillery in Henry Knox's Regiment. Both were captured by the British and incarcerated on the prison ship *Jersey*, notorious for its brutality. Records said when the British discovered who they were, they were tortured and beaten. Thomas, for some reason, was put in the dungeon where he lay in his own urine, feces, and blood, and the only food he received was that pressed through a keyhole by fellow prisoners. Thomas most likely crossed the Delaware with George Washington, but in any event, he fought at the Battles of Trenton and Princeton and later at Brandywine, Germantown, and Monmouth. Abraham Clark never spoke of his sons' service and plight. He did not want them targeted by the enemy, nor did he seek special treatment for his sons. Now that Clark became aware of his sons' situation, he broke down and raised the issue in Congress. The British offered Abraham Clark the lives of his sons if he would recant the signing and support of the Declaration of Independence. He refused. When other members of Congress heard of the plight of Abraham's son, they were outraged. They ordered George Washington to take a British officer as a prisoner and starve him to death in a dark hole. The communication of that congressional order to General Howe was enough to end the persecution of Thomas, and he survived his imprisonment. He survived, but this cruel treatment permanently ruined his health, and he died at the age of thirty-five on May 13, 1789.

Clark knew what the signers were getting themselves into, and soon after the signing wrote to his friend, Colonel Elias Drayton: "as to my title, I know not yet whether it will be honorable or dishonorable; the issue of the war must settle it. Perhaps our Congress will be exalted on a high gallows . . . I assure you, Sir, I see, I feel, the danger we are in."

Clark remained in the Continental Congress until April 1778, when he was elected to the New Jersey Legislative Council. He was subsequently re-elected to Congress in 1780 until 1783, and then again from 1786 to 1788. He was one of New Jersey's representatives at the Annapolis Convention of 1786, at which representatives of five of the thirteen states gathered to address grievances that had arisen over the cumbersome Articles of Confederation. Among those attending were Alexander Hamilton, John Dickinson, Edmund Randolph, and James Madison.

Clark was elected to the Constitutional Convention of 1787 but was too ill to attend. The Constitution established a U.S. House of Representatives and a U.S. Senate and a plan for national elections. In 1790, Clark was elected to a seat in the House, serving in the Second (1791–93) and Third (1793–95) Congresses. He remained in Congress until his death. On September 15, 1794, Clark watched some men build a bridge on his land in what is now Roselle, New Jersey when he suddenly felt ill. Believing that he had suffered a bout of severe sunstroke, he staggered to his carriage and got himself home. There he was put to bed and died hours later. He was sixty-eight. He was buried in Rahway

Cemetery next to his father. His wife survived him by a decade, and when she died, she was laid to rest with her husband. These words are inscribed on his tombstone: "he loved his country and adhered to her cause, in the darkest hours of her struggles against oppression."

On July 4, 1848, the citizens of Rahway erected a ten-foot obelisk monument in Clark's honor near his burial site. In 1924 the stone slabs marking both Abraham and Sarah's burial site were encased in a concrete monument. In 1941 a replica of Clark's original house was built about a block away from his original house. The original was destroyed in a fire in 1900. The replica is located at 101 West Ninth Avenue, Roselle, New Jersey. Visitation is by appointment. Abraham Clark High school stands just a few blocks from the home.

Clark is also memorialized in Washington, DC, in a large mural in the rotunda of the National Archives and John Trumbull's famous painting in the U.S. Capitol building.

Abraham Clark memorial.

James Smith
(1719 – 1806)

York's Radical Revolutionary

Buried at First Presbyterian Memorial Gardens,
York, Pennsylvania.

Declaration of Independence • Continental Congress

James Smith organized a volunteer company of militia in York County. It was the first volunteer company raised to oppose the British, and he was among the first of colonial leaders to call for a continental congress to discuss the problems with the home country. He served as a delegate from Pennsylvania to the first and second Continental Congresses and signed the historic Declaration of Independence.

Exactly when James Smith was born is open to question. He was born in Ulster, Northern Ireland but would never admit to the year. In 1805 a fire destroyed his office and all his official papers. We know the family emigrated to America in 1727 and that James was a young boy. They settled in Chester County, Pennsylvania and James' father John died in 1761.

Young James was tutored in the classical education of the day by local clergy and attended the Philadelphia Academy (later known as the University of Pennsylvania). There he came to study under the distinguished provost Dr. Allison. He studied Latin and Greek and excelled at the art of surveying, which at that time was of great importance.

When he completed his studies at the Philadelphia Academy, he decided to study law under his brother George and in the office of Thomas Cookson in Lancaster, Pennsylvania. He was admitted to the Pennsylvania Bar in 1745 and

James Smith

began a practice in Shippensburg, Pennsylvania but soon moved the practice to the flourishing town of York, Pennsylvania.

In 1760 at the age of 41, Smith married a woman from New Castle, Delaware, Eleanor Armor. They would have five children, four of whom would die without having children. James Smith has no living descendants.

Smith early perceived the gathering storm and was among the first Pennsylvanians to speak out fearlessly on the side of the patriots from Massachusetts and Virginia. In 1774 he attended a provincial assembly where he presented a paper he had written entitled "Essay on The Constitutional Power of Great Britain Over The Colonies In America." In that paper, Smith recommends that the colonies boycott all British goods. He felt that such action would pressure the British Parliament to back away from some of their oppressive laws.

Later that same year, Smith organized a volunteer militia company in York which elected him captain. It was the first volunteer corps raised in Pennsylvania. In soon increased in size to a regiment and he was appointed its colonel, a title which in respect to him was honorary, sine he never assumed actual command.

Emerging as one of the regions radical leaders, he was elected a delegate to the state convention in Philadelphia in January 1775. He concurred in the spirited declaration of that convention that "if the British administration should determine by force to effect a submission to the late arbitrary acts of the British Parliament, in such a situation, we hold it our indispensable duty to resist such force, and at every hazard to defend the rights of liberties of America." These were strong words considering that many Pennsylvanians hoped for some form of "accommodation" with the mother country. Also, in Pennsylvania, many of the delegates and citizens were Quakers and against any violence.

Smith did not take part in the debates in the Continental Congress that led to independence. He was added to Pennsylvania's delegation on July 20, 1776, by a provincial convention in time to sign the Declaration of Independence

The grave of James Smith

on August 2, 1776. On the evening of August sixth, he rode off to York with a printed broadside copy to read to the public in the town square.

Smith continued to serve in Congress and the state assembly through 1778. He lent his law office in York to the Board of War in 1777 when Congress had to flee Philadelphia and move operations there. He was elected a Brigadier General of the state militia in 1781 and resumed his law practice when the war ended.

In 1785, Smith was elected to Congress again but declined to serve because of his age. He never said how old he was and any legal papers that might have shed light on his age were destroyed in the aforementioned fire about a year before his death. Smith died on July 11, 1806, and was buried in the First Presbyterian Memorial Gardens in York, Pennsylvania. His grave marker says he was ninety-three.

Jonathan Bayard Smith
(1742–1812)

Quaker Educator

Buried at Mount Vernon Cemetery,
Philadelphia, Pennsylvania.

Military • Articles of Confederation

This founder was a native Pennsylvanian born and bred in Philadelphia. A graduate of Princeton, he entered the mercantile business owned and operated by his father. An ardent patriot he embraced the at times unpopular stance, especially among Quaker Pennsylvania, of taking up arms against the British. Elected to the Continental Congress, he endorsed and signed the Articles of Confederation. He was a great promoter of education in the new nation. His name was Jonathan Bayard Smith.

Smith was born on February 21, 1742. His father Samuel Smith moved to Philadelphia from New Hampshire. Once settled in Pennsylvania he opened a business and quickly became a prosperous and respected merchant. The elder Smith saw to it that his son received a quality education. In 1760 he graduated from Princeton, a university he would later serve as a trustee. It may have been his father who instilled in Smith his devotion to education that he exhibited throughout his life.

By 1775 Smith was already supporting independence for the American colonies. That same year he was elected secretary of the committee of public safety. An election to the Continental Congress followed in 1777. He served in Congress until November of 1778 and signed the Articles of Confederation on behalf of Pennsylvania. The Articles were finally ratified in 1781 which for the first time formally formed the states into a union.

The Congress at York

Jonathan Bayard Smith

During this same time, he put his money where his mouth was. On December 1, 1777, Smith presided at a public meeting in Philadelphia where it was resolved, "That it be recommended to the council of safety that in this great emergency... every person between the age of 16 and 50 be ordered out under arms." Smith joined the militia becoming a lieutenant colonel in John Bayard's regiment. His commanding officer was his brother- in- law. It was after marrying Susannah Bayard that Smith took his wife's maiden name as his middle name.

After leaving Congress, Smith returned to running his business though he remained active in civic affairs. He promoted education and in 1779 was one of the founders of the University of the State of Pennsylvania. In 1795 when it merged with two other schools to form the University of Pennsylvania Smith became a trustee—a position he would hold until his death. He also put in thirty years of service as a trustee at his alma mater, Princeton.

He remained active almost to his last days. When the War of 1812 broke out public meetings were held in Philadelphia sponsored by the Democratic Young Men, but it was the 70-year-old Smith who headed these meetings as

JONATHAN BAYARD SMITH (1742–1812)

the organization's president. He passed away on June 16, 1812, and was laid to rest with Masonic honors in the Cemetery of the Second Presbyterian Church. When that cemetery closed in 1867 Smith's was one of the approximately 2,500 graves moved to the Mount Vernon Cemetery where he now rests behind locked gates. We were unable to visit his grave because the cemetery, though still in operation, is not open to the public, has suffered from neglect and is widely overgrown. It is our understanding that local volunteers are looking at taking action to clean up what was once, and could be again a beautiful cemetery.

The locked gateway to Mount Vernon Cemetery, Philadelphia.

Francis Dana
(1743 – 1811)
Congressman at Valley Forge

Buried at Old Burying Ground,
Cambridge, Massachusetts.

Articles of Confederation • Diplomat

Francis Dana was an American statesman, lawyer, and jurist from Massachusetts. He served as a delegate to the Continental Congress in 1777–1778 and again in 1784. He was a signer of the Articles of Confederation.

He was born on June 13, 1743, in Charlestown, Massachusetts. His parents were wealthy and respectable and gave him the benefit of an excellent education. He graduated from Harvard in 1762 and took up the practice of law. He was admitted to the bar and set up a practice in Boston in 1767. He opposed British colonial policy and became a leader of the Sons of Liberty. He was elected to Massachusetts' provincial congress in 1774. In the spring of 1774, the Continental Congress felt it important to send someone to England to represent the patriots and to ascertain the real feeling among England's rulers. Dana was selected. He was just 31 years old. The question was whether we should seek to adjust our differences with England as its colony or whether we should declare absolute independence. He returned in March 1776 convinced that all hope for a friendly settlement must be abandoned. He threw his whole influence for independence. He impressed his convictions upon the Continental Congress and just over three months after his return they voted for Independence.

He was a member of the Massachusetts executive council from 1776 to 1780 and served as a delegate to the Continental Congress from 1776 to 1778.

FRANCIS DANA (1743–1811)

Portrait of Francis Dana etched circa 1885.

He signed the Articles of Confederation in 1778. In January 1778, Congress appointed him chairman of the committee assigned to visit George Washington at Valley Forge and confer with him about the reorganization of the army. The committee spent about three months at Valley Forge and assisted Washington in preparing the plan of reorganization which Congress in the main adopted. In that same year, he was a member of the committee that considered a peace proposal offered by Lord North of Great Britain, which he vigorously opposed and which Congress rejected.

In 1779, France went to war with England and took the side of the colonists. Congress needed to send able and discreet persons to Europe and selected Dana to accompany John Adams and his son John Quincy Adams. In December 1780, Dana was appointed minister resident to the Russian court. He was never officially received at the court of Catherine the Great and left Russia in August 1783. After his return, he was again elected to Congress in 1784. He resigned from Congress 1785 to accept a seat on the Supreme Court of Massachusetts.

Dana was named a delegate to both the Annapolis Convention and the Constitutional Convention but attended neither due to poor health. He was, however, a member of the Massachusetts Ratifying Convention. He left there briefly during its proceedings, after a spat with Elbridge Gerry who opposed the ratification.

Dana was appointed Chief Justice of the Massachusetts Supreme Court in 1791, a position he held until his retirement from the bench in May 1806. He became a charter member of the American Academy of Arts and Sciences in 1780.

Francis Dana died at Cambridge, Massachusetts, on April 25, 1811, and is buried in Cambridge's Old Burying Ground.

The Dana family marker at the Old Burying Ground in Cambridge, Massachusetts (photo by Lawrence Knorr).

Thomas McKean
(1735 – 1817)

The Simultaneous Governor of Delaware and Chief Justice of Pennsylvania

Buried at Laurel Hill Cemetery,
Philadelphia, Pennsylvania.

**Military • Declaration of Independence • President of Congress
Articles of Confederation**

This founder was known for his very brusque take-charge attitude that at times upset his fellow patriots. This may have contributed to the fact that while serving in the Stamp Act Congress, two other delegates challenged him to duels which he speedily accepted. Only the departure of one representative and the existence of cooler heads avoided the shedding of blood. His resume is lengthy and in addition to service in Congress included service in the military. He also served as Governor of Delaware and as Chief Justice of Pennsylvania at the same time. He would later attend the Pennsylvania convention that ratified the United States Constitution and serve as the Governor of that state. He also affixed his signature to both the Declaration of Independence and the Articles of Confederation. Some contend that he served as one of the first Presidents of the United States under those Articles. His name was Thomas McKean.

McKean was born on March 19, 1734, in New London Township located in Chester County, Pennsylvania. His parents were both Irish born Ulster-Scots who came to America from Ballymoney, County Antrim, Ireland. When McKean was 16 years of age, he traveled to New Castle, Delaware to study the law under one of his cousins. By 1756 he had been admitted to the bar in both

The Congress at York

Thomas McKean

Delaware and Pennsylvania. By the mid-1760s he was serving in the Delaware General Assembly and as a judge of the Court of Common Pleas. Delaware at the time had two political factions which were commonly referred to as the "Court Party" and the "Country Party." The former party urged reconciliation with England while the latter, of which McKean was a leading member, supported American independence.

In 1765, Mckean and Caesar Rodney represented Delaware at the Stamp Act Congress. McKean was an active member of this group and along with John Rutledge and Philip Livingston served on the committee that drafted the Declaration of Rights and Grievances. Timothy Ruggles, a delegate from Massachusetts who served as president of the body, refused to sign the Memorial. Ruggles also declined to state the reasons for his objection. McKean wouldn't let the matter drop and demanded that Ruggles explain himself. The Massachusetts delegate then explained that his conscience would not permit him to address complaints to the king. McKean responded with scorn twice bellowing out the word conscience in a sarcastic manner that Ruggles viewed as an insult. He challenged McKean to a duel which was immediately accepted. Early the next morning Ruggles returned to his home state, so no duel was fought. The Massachusetts legislature officially censured Ruggles for "a neglect of duty." Ruggles wasn't the only delegate at the gathering to draw McKean's ire. Robert Ogden, a representative from New Jersey, also challenged McKean to a meeting on the field of honor. McKean accepted this invitation but cooler heads in attendance interceded, and the quarrel was settled without a shot being fired.

McKean would marry twice and father eleven children. His first wife, Mary Borden, passed away in 1773. A year later he married Sarah Armitage and moved his family to Philadelphia. Despite his Pennsylvania residence he was elected to represent Delaware in the Continental Congress. As a member of Congress, McKean is remembered for the part he played in fellow delegate Caesar Rodney's midnight ride. On July 1, 1776, McKean concluded that another delegate from Delaware, George Read, intended to vote against declaring American independence. Rodney, who like McKean favored independence, was absent from Congress due to a severe illness. Realizing that Rodney's vote would be needed McKean sent a messenger to Rodney who had returned to his home in Dover, Delaware. The message urged his fellow delegate to return to Philadelphia at once. Rodney immediately mounted a horse and began the eighty-mile trip back to Congress. As McKean later remembered in a letter to one of Rodney's nephews, he met Rodney "at the State-house door in his boots and spurs as the members were assembling; after a friendly salutation (without a word on the business) we went into the Hall of Congress together, and found we were among the latest: proceedings immediately commenced, and after a few minutes the great question was put; when the vote for Delaware was called, your uncle arose and said: 'As I believe the voice of my constituents and of all the sensible & honest men is in favor of Independence & my own judgment concurs with them I vote for Independence." Read voted nay but by a margin of two to one Delaware favored independence.

McKean did not get to sign the Declaration of Independence with his fellow members of Congress. Soon after casting his vote he led a militia group to assist George Washington during the unsuccessful defense of New York City. As a result of this military duty, McKean is considered to be the last signer of the Declaration of Independence. McKean insisted that he signed the document sometime in 1776 though most historians believe he affixed his signature to the document between 1777 and 1781.

The war years weren't quiet ones for McKean. He had been placed on the English hit list and wrote in a letter to John Adams that "he was being hunted like a fox." When the British captured the rebel governor of Delaware, McKean assumed the post. At the same time he was serving quite capably as Chief Justice of Pennsylvania in a post he filled from 1777 until 1799. According to his biographer John Coleman, "only the historiographical difficultly of reviewing court records and other scattered documents prevents recognition that McKean, rather than John Marshall, did more than anyone else to establish an independent judiciary in the United States. As Chief Justice under a Pennsylvania constitution he considered flawed, he assumed it the right of the court to strike down legislative acts it deemed unconstitutional, preceding by ten years the U.S. Supreme Court's establishment of the doctrine of judicial review."

In October of 1776 the during what was viewed as a conservative reaction against independence, the Delaware General Assembly did not re-elect McKean to the newly declared nation's Congress. Within a year British occupation of the state changed public opinion, and McKean was returned to Congress in

The grave of Thomas McKean.

1777. He would serve in this body until 1783. He helped draft the Articles of Confederation and voted for their adoption in 1781. That same year he was elected to the position of President of Congress. Though primarily a ceremonial position with little authority some have argued that McKean served as President of the United States.

Though he did not attend the Constitutional Convention, McKean took a leading role in securing Pennsylvania's ratification of the United States Constitution. He argued in favor of a strong executive and was a member of the state convention that voted to ratify the document. When American political parties came into being, he allied himself initially with the Federalists. By the mid-1790s he broke with that party because of disagreements with compromises that the administration in Philadelphia made with Great Britain. He became an outspoken Jeffersonian Republican.

In 1799 McKean was elected to the first of three terms he would serve as Governor of Pennsylvania. As Governor, he demanded that things be done his way. He removed his critics from government posts and rewarded his supporters with jobs. His administration was so stormy that he had to survive an impeachment attempt by his political foes in 1807. In this, he proved successful.

McKean passed away in 1817 at the age of 83. He was initially laid to rest in the First Presbyterian Church Cemetery, but his remains were moved to Philadelphia's Laurel Hill Cemetery in 1843. In a letter to one of McKean's sons, John Adams described his fellow founder as "among the best tried and firmest pillars of the Revolution."

McKean County, Pennsylvania is named in his honor. There is also a McKean Street in Philadelphia. Both the University of Delaware and Penn State University have buildings named for him.

Gouverneur Morris
(1752 – 1816)

The Penman of the Constitution

Buried at Saint Ann's Episcopal Churchyard,
Bronx, New York.

Articles of Confederation • U.S. Constitution • Military • Diplomat

He was a founding father who hailed from New York City. He argued with his family over the issue of American independence. He served in the army during the Revolutionary War. He signed both the Articles of Confederation and the United States Constitution. He is credited with writing large sections of the latter document including the preamble. He was also a United States Senator from 1800 to 1803. His name was Gouverneur Morris.

Morris was born on January 31, 1752, in what is now called the Bronx section of New York City at the family estate known as Morrisania Manor. As a boy, he exhibited a keen intellect. So keen in fact that, at the age of twelve, he enrolled in King's College which is now known as Columbia University. He began his studies in 1764 and graduated in four years. Since he was too young at age sixteen to start a career, he stayed at King's and received his Master's degree in 1771. Next Morris studied under the noted New York law scholar William Smith. It was through Smith, who opposed British tax policies in the colonies, that Morris met patriots such as John Jay and Alexander Hamilton.

In 1775, Morris was elected to the New York Provincial Congress. This Congress was organized by patriots who were seeking an alternative to the Province of New York Assembly, which was the official pro-British body. It was during his service in the Provincial Congress that Morris began supporting

GOUVERNEUR MORRIS (1752–1816)

Gouverneur Morris

turning the colony of New York into an independent state. This put him at odds with both his family and his mentor William Smith who had turned away from the patriot cause when it moved towards pursuing independence.

When the Revolutionary War began, Morris favored reasoning with those Americans who stayed loyal to the king. This is hardly surprising since this group, known as Tories, included his mother and his half-brother. His mother gave the family estate to the British army to be used for military purposes. As the war went on, Morris changed his views on the treatment of Tories and favored tarring and feathering, whippings and the confiscation of property.

In 1778, Morris was appointed to be a delegate to the Continental Congress. He was placed on a committee charged with reforming the Continental Army. Upon visiting the army at Valley Forge, he was so affected by the conditions that he became a spokesman for the military in Congress and was instrumental in reforms in training, methods, and financing. That same year, the Conway Cabal took place. Its purpose was to remove George Washington as Commander-in-Chief of the army. Morris cast the deciding vote that kept Washington in his job. In 1779, Morris was defeated in an election that cost him his seat in Congress. Most likely the defeat was caused by his support for a strong central government, a view not popular in New York at the time. After his defeat, he left New York and moved to Philadelphia.

In 1780, Morris shattered his left leg, and it had to be amputated. He said he had done it by getting his leg stuck in the spokes of a carriage he was driving. However, Morris had a reputation for having affairs with both married and unmarried women. There was gossip that the accident occurred while a jealous husband was chasing him.

In Philadelphia, he served as superintendent of finance from 1781 to 1785. He also worked as a merchant who put him in contact with the financier and founding father, Robert Morris (no relation). With the support of both George Washington and Robert Morris, he was appointed to be a Pennsylvania delegate to the 1787 Constitutional Convention.

Morris certainly made his presence known at the Convention. According to Catherine Drinker Bowen in her book *Miracle at Philadelphia*, Morris has been described as the most brilliant man at the Convention. She noted that he often spoke, giving 173 speeches, while never saying anything foolish or tedious. She describes his tactics as abrupt, first an eloquent explosive expression of his position and then cynically waiting for the Convention to catch up with him. He continued to favor a strong central government. He said, "When the powers of the national government clash with the states, only then must the states yield." Many others at the Convention, including Washington, shared his desire for a strong central government. Morris served on the Committee of Style and Arrangement who drafted the final language of the proposed constitution. Bowen called Morris the Committee's "amanuensis" meaning that he was responsible for most of the draft, as well as its final form. Also, Morris was one of the few delegates at the convention who spoke openly against slavery. According to James Madison's notes, Morris attacked slavery calling it a nefarious institution. After the Constitution was adopted, Morris was proud to put his signature on it. He then moved back to New York.

Morris went to France on business in 1789. He would not return for a decade. He served as Minister Plenipotentiary to France from 1792 to 1794. His diaries from this period have become a valuable resource concerning the French Revolution. They also help to document his ongoing affairs with women. He was openly critical of the French Revolution which led to a request from the French government to recall him which the United States eventually did.

Upon his return to the States, he resumed his law practice and entered politics. In 1800 he was elected to the United States Senate as a Federalist representing New York. He would serve until 1803. During this time, he championed improving transportation from the eastern part of the country to the interior. After being defeated in his reelection bid, he became Chairman of the Erie Canal Commission from 1810 to 1813. The canal was instrumental in transforming New York into a financial capital. That much was clear to Morris when he said: "The proudest empire in Europe is but a bubble compared to what America will be, must be, in the course of two centuries, perhaps of one."

Morris married at the age of 57. His wife was Ann Cary Randolph, the sister of Thomas Mann Randolph who was the husband of Thomas Jefferson's daughter Martha. Morris and his wife had one son, Gouverneur Morris Jr., who became a railroad executive.

On November 16, 1816, Morris passed away after causing himself internal injuries while using a piece of whalebone to clear a blockage in his urinary tract. He was laid to rest in Saint Ann's Episcopal Churchyard Cemetery along with his brother Lewis Morris who signed the Declaration of Independence.

Morris's grandson, William Walton Morris, a graduate of West Point, was a brevet Major General during the Civil War. He is also buried at Saint Ann's.

During the early twentieth century, a great-grandson, also named Gouverneur Morris (1876–1953), authored novels and short stories. The Lon Chaney film *The Penalty* (1920) was adapted from one of them.

Morris was a substantial landowner in St. Lawrence County in upstate New York. There, the town and village of Gouverneur are named for him. During World War II, the liberty ship S.S. *Gouverneur Morris* was named after him.

In *Pennsylvania History* in July 1938, Philip Wild summed up Morris's life:

> Endowed with all that aids a man to achieve much for the common good, namely sterling character, wisdom, worthwhile place and wealth, Morris, on the contrary, chose to use these gifts to advance and strengthen the position of the small group of property men to which he belonged, instead of setting for his goal, the securing of the greatest good for all the people. His narrow conservatism led to his failure to secure political gifts from the people about whom he so often manifested his lack of faith. Lacking political backing, Morris became embittered and adopted positions which have brought rather caustic criticisms to him from historians. But it must be remembered that in public office, his efforts controlled as they were by the more liberal tendencies of his higher officers, produced much of significance for the United States.

Monument to Morris in the Bronx. His grave is beneath the church nearby.

James Forbes
(1731 – 1780)

Forgotten Congressman

Buried at Christ Church Cemetery,
Philadelphia, Pennsylvania.

Continental Congress

James Forbes was a justice of the peace in Maryland and a member of the Maryland General Assembly who was elected to serve in the Continental Congress from 1778 until he died in 1780.

Forbes was estimated to have been born in 1731 near Benedict in Charles County, Maryland. Details of his family life are not known. Perhaps there was a connection to Brigadier General John Forbes of French and Indian War fame, who led the building of Forbes' Road across the Pennsylvania wilderness, from Carlisle to Fort Duquesne. John Forbes, the soldier, was also buried at Christ Church in Philadelphia after his untimely death in 1759.

Forbes served as a state court judge in Maryland in 1770 and was appointed justice of the peace for Charles County, Maryland, on April 1, 1777, and also served as tax commissioner for the county that same year. He was a member of the Maryland House of Delegates from 1777 to 1778, which elected him on December 22, 1777, to the Continental Congress. He served in this role from 1778 until his death in 1780.

During 1778, Forbes attended Congress in York from January 17 through April 17. Forbes' letter to Maryland Governor Tom Johnson was written on February 13, 1778, and hints at a lack of formal education:

I should have don my self the honour to have wrote you before now, had I any thing worth communicating. This is to inform you that the appointment of

The Congress at York

Commershall agents in France has been moved for in Congress, in consequence of Mr. Wm. Lee's being appointed, a Commissioner, to the Courts of Vienna and Berlin, and of a Letter from Mr. Robt. Morris, recommending Mr. Jno. Ross, to suckseed [sic] his Brother. I put Mr. Joshua Johnson in the nomination, and I believe, had Congress made the appointment, he would have been chosen, but they resolved that the Commissioners in France shoud appoint them, and they are wrote to on the 9th Instt, for that purpose. had I known how to have directed to your Brother, I would have wrote him on the Subject . . . Ten States only, are represented in Congress, and one half of them, by one member only Masechusits [sic], New York and Virginia have noe representation. I shall doe my self the honour of writing you when any thing offers worth communicating and am very respectfully Sir.

He followed this with another letter to Johnson from York on March 24, 1778:

> Mr. [Samuel] Chase [a delegate from Maryland] is just arrived, but seems to be determined to make but a short stay, on Account of the very bad accommodations this place affords . . . Your Lettr to Genl. [Horatio] Gates on the Subject of an Embargoe [sic] and the Virga. Frigate was committed and a report ready but it has not yet been taken up in Congress I apprehend an Embargoe [sic] on provisions will take place, but am affraid [sic] a general one will not be agreed to' when any thing material occurs shall do my self the honour of writing you . . . Virga. and N. York only, have agreed on form to the ratification of the Confederation most of the other States have proposed amendments, but the Members say they are instructed to ratefy, if the amendments cant be obtained. noe [sic] time fixt [sic] for taking up this matter in Congress.

The Congress then moved back to Philadelphia that summer. Forbes arrived in Philadelphia on July 13, 1778, and attended Congress until October 2. He was elected to a second term on November 13, 1778, and attended from July 12 to December 31, 1779. He was elected to a third term on December 22, 1779, and attended from January 1 through March 10, 1780.

Forbes died suddenly on March 25, 1780, and was buried at Christ Church Burial Ground in Philadelphia.

John Henry Jr.
(1750–1798)

First Senator

Christ Episcopal Church Cemetery
Cambridge, Maryland

Continental Congress • Senator • Governor

John Henry was a Continental Congressman from Maryland. He also later became a US Senator and the eighth governor of the state.

Henry was born in November 1750 at *Weston*, the family's estate on the Nanticoke River near Vienna, Dorchester County, Maryland, the son of Colonel John Henry, a planter, and his wife, Dorothy (née Rider) Henry. Reverend John Henry, the paternal grandfather, was a Presbyterian minister who emigrated to America. The maternal grandfather was Colonel Rider, who also emigrated from England. Colonel Henry, a lawyer, represented Dorchester County in the colonial legislature.

Young Henry was first educated at the West Nottingham Academy in Cecil County, Maryland. He then attended the College of New Jersey (now Princeton), graduating in 1769. An Anglican, Henry next studied law at the Middle Temple in London. In 1775, he returned to the colonies and opened a law practice in Dorchester County.

In his 27th year in 1777, Henry ran for a seat in the Maryland House of Delegates and won. Soon after taking his seat, he was appointed, on December 22, 1777, as a Continental Congressman. Henry served in the Maryland legislature until 1780. Henry appeared at the Congress from January 20, 1778, until May 30, 1778, in York, Pennsylvania, and then from August 29, 1778, until December 31, 1778, in Philadelphia. He was reelected on November 13, 1778. During his tenure, Henry pushed for the adoption of the Articles of Confederation by his state, ultimately signed by John Hanson and Daniel Carroll in 1781. Henry also supported the war effort on behalf of his state.

In 1780, Henry left the Continental Congress and served as a senator in the Maryland state senate until 1790. During this time, he was reappointed to the Continental Congress in 1785 and 1786 and worked on the formation of what would become the Northwest Territory.

On March 6, 1787, Henry married Margaret Campbell, the daughter of John and Elizabeth(née Goldsborough) Campbell of Caroline County, Maryland. At this time, the US Constitution was being drafted and passed. Son John Henry Campbell was born this year (1787–1857).

In late 1788, Maryland elected members of the new House of Representatives, and the Maryland legislature selected two members of the new US Senate. At first a Federalist, Henry was elected to both seats but chose the Senate, where he joined Charles Carroll of Carrollton as the first two Senators from Maryland seated on March 4, 1789.

During this time, a son, Francis Jenkins Henry (1789–1810), was born. However, his mother, Margaret, did not survive the childbirth, dying on March 6, 1789, at age 20.

Grave of John Henry Jr.

JOHN HENRY JR. (1750–1798)

Henry was reelected to the Senate in 1795 and served ten years altogether, resigning on December 10, 1797, because he had been elected Governor of Maryland, having become a Democratic-Republican.

Henry had received two electoral votes in the 1796 presidential election but now focused on his duties as governor, working with the Jefferson administration. Due to ill health, he served less than one year.

On December 16, 1798, Henry died at *Weston* and was buried at Christ Episcopal Church Cemetery in Cambridge, Maryland. The obelisk at his grave is inscribed: "John Henry. Lawyer, Statesman, Governor. Born in Dorchester Co. 1750. Died 1798. Honored for His Wisdom and Political Integrity."

Thomas Sim Lee was elected as his successor.

Nathaniel Scudder
(1733 – 1781)

"The Only Congressman to Die in Battle"

Buried at Old Tennent Churchyard,
Tennent, New Jersey.

Articles of Confederation • Military

Nathaniel Scudder was a physician and Continental Congressman who signed the Articles of Confederation. He was also an officer in the New Jersey Militia during the American Revolution and was killed in action. Scudder was the only former member of the Continental Congress killed in battle.

Scudder, born May 10, 1733, in Monmouth Court House, New Jersey, was the son of Jacob Scudder and his wife, Abia (née Rowe) Scudder.

Scudder was a 1751 graduate of the College of New Jersey (now Princeton University). He studied medicine and then opened a practice in Monmouth County. He married Isabella Anderson with whom he had five children. He was also, as of December 1766, one of the board members of Mattisonia Grammar School in Lower Freehold, New Jersey, along with Reverand William Tennent and Reverand Charles M. Knight.

In 1774, as hostilities increased with England, Scudder joined the county's Committee of Safety and was elected to attend the Provincial Congress of New Jersey. By 1776, Scudder was elevated to the New Jersey Committee of Safety and became the Speaker of the New Jersey Assembly. He also joined the New Jersey Militia as a lieutenant colonel.

On November 20, 1777, Scudder was elected to the Continental Congress which met in York, Pennsylvania. He was re-elected the following year, serving

NATHANIEL SCUDDER (1733–1781)

Portrait of Nathaniel Scudder.

with Abraham Clark, Elias Boudinot, Jonathan Elmer, and John Witherspoon back in Philadelphia.

The summer of 1778 was especially busy for Scudder, who had abandoned his medical practice and was splitting his time between Congress and the New Jersey Militia. On June 28, 1778, he led his regiment at the Battle of Monmouth, very close to his birthplace. He also wrote a series of impassioned letters about the progress of the Articles of Confederation. In a letter to John Hart on July 13, 1778, he worried about the delay in the ratification of the Articles of Confederation:

> I do myself the Honor to address you upon an Affair to me one of the most serious and alarming Importance. The Honorable Council and Assembly of this State have not thought proper to invest their Delegates with Power to ratify and sign the [Articles of] Confederation; and it is obvious that unless every [one] of the thirteen States shall accede to it, we remain an unconfederated [sic] People. These States have actually entered into a Treaty with the Court of Versailles as a Confederated People and Monsieur Girard their ambassador Plenipotentiary to Congress is now on our Coast with a powerfull [sic] Fleet of Ships, which have taken

Pilots on Board for Delaware. He probably may be landed by this Time, and will at all Events be in Philadelphia in a few Days. How must he be astonished & confounded? [A]nd what may be the fatal Consequences to America, when he discovers (which he will immediately do) that we are ipso facto unconfederated [sic], and consequently, what our Enemies have called us, 'a Rope of Sand'? Will he not have just Cause to resent the Deception? [A]nd may not insidious Britain, knowing the same, take Advantage of our Disunion? For my own Part I am of Opinion She will never desist from her nefarious Designs, nor ever consider her Attempts upon our Liberties fruitless and vain, untill [sic] she knows the golden knot is actually tied. I left Congress last Wednesday Evening. The Affair of Confederation was to be taken up next Day. The Magna

The grave of Nathaniel Scudder.

NATHANIEL SCUDDER (1733 – 1781)

Charta of America was amply engrossed and prepared for signing. Ten States had actually authorised [sic] their Delegates to ratify; a Delegate from an eleventh (vizt. Georgia) declared he was so fully possessed of the Sense of his Constituents, that he should not hesitate to subscribe it.

New Jersey ratified the Articles of Confederation on November 19, 1778. John Witherspoon signed with Nathaniel Scudder. Scudder was elected to the Continental Congress again in 1779.

Finished in the Continental Congress, Scudder next served in the New Jersey General Assembly in 1780. He also continued his military service and was promoted to colonel in 1781. On October 17, 1781, he led part of his regiment to counter a foraging party from the British Army near Shrewsbury, New Jersey and was killed in the skirmish at Blacks Point. He was buried at the Tennent Church Graveyard in Tennent, Monmouth County, New Jersey, three days later, the same day the British surrendered at Yorktown.

Scudder was the only member of the Continental Congress to die in battle. He was also the last colonel to die in battle during the American Revolution.

Scudder's tombstone reads, "In Memory of the Honorable Nathaniel Scudder, Who Fell in Defence of His Country October the 16th 1781 Aged 48 Years."

Samuel Huntington
(1731 – 1796)

First President of the United States?

Buried at Colonial Cemetery (aka Old Norwichtown Cemetery),
Norwich, Connecticut.

**Continental Congress • Articles of Confederation
Declaration of Independence**

This founder happened to be the President of Congress on March 1, 1781, when the Articles of Confederation officially went into effect. The Articles essentially brought the individual colonies together and created the United States of America. It is because of his position in the Congress at the time that some point to this founder as the first president. Whether one agrees with that view is not important. The man can and should be remembered for his efforts on behalf and his contributions to the young country. Known for his great dignity and exceptional gentleness, he was described by those who knew him as "a sensible, candid and worthy man." He was among those who risked all by affixing his signature to the Declaration of Independence. His name was Samuel Huntington.

Huntington was born on July 16, 1731, in what is now Scotland, Connecticut. He was the firstborn of Nathaniel and Mehetabel Huntington's ten children. Since he was the oldest of ten children, he was expected to work the family farm. As a result, according to multiple sources, he never received any formal education. However, one researcher has written that Huntington graduated from Yale College in 1755. Considering his later success, this is entirely possible. When he reached the age of 16, he apprenticed with a barrel maker while at the same

SAMUEL HUNTINGTON (1731–1796)

Samuel Huntington

time continuing to assist his father with the farm. He somehow found the time to educate himself by borrowing books from local attorneys and his future father in law, the Reverend Ebenezer Devotion. It appears possible that the studies he undertook on his own could have prepared him for Yale. What is not in dispute is fueled by his industry; he became a practicing attorney after being admitted to the Connecticut bar in 1754.

In 1761 Huntington married Martha Devotion, the daughter of the aforementioned Ebenezer. The couple did not have any children of their own, but when one of Huntington's brothers died, they adopted his two children. Huntington and his wife stayed together until she died in 1794. The couple's adopted son, Samuel Huntington, became the third governor of Ohio.

By the age of thirty, Huntington was one of the most important lawyers in Connecticut. In 1765 he was named the King's Attorney for the colony apposition, making him Connecticut's attorney general. When Huntington first entered politics a year before being appointed as the King's Attorney, as a member of the Connecticut General Assembly, he held conservative views and was loyal to the king. However, as the British Parliament began imposing oppressive measures on the colonies, his position changed, and he became an outspoken critic of the crown and resigned his office. In 1775 he was chosen along with Roger Sherman and Oliver Walcott to represent Connecticut in the Continental Congress. All three members of the Connecticut delegation were ardent advocates of independence. As a member of Congress, he voted for American independence and signed the declaration that proclaimed the separation of the colonies from the British empire.

In terms of his congressional service, in 1846 the historian Robert T. Conrad wrote that Huntington "devoted his talents and time to the public service. His stern integrity, and inflexible patriotism, rendered him a prominent member, and attracted a large share of the current business of the house; as a member of numerous important committees, he acted with judgment and deliberation, and cheerfully and perseveringly dedicated his moments of leisure to the general benefit of the country."

Huntington was not known as a great orator, nor did he write much or very well. He earned the respect of his fellow delegates through his diligence and hard work. When John Jay left Congress to become minister to Spain, Huntington was elected to succeed him as president in 1779. On March 1, 1781, the Articles of Confederation were signed, which made the thirteen colonies the United States of America. Because Huntington was the President of Congress, some point to him as the first President of the United States.

Five months after the signing of the Articles, Huntington was forced to resign from Congress and return to Connecticut due to illness. Despite battling health issues for the rest of his days, he remained active in public affairs. He served as chief justice of the Connecticut Supreme Court and as lieutenant governor of the state before serving as the third governor of the Constitution State. He advocated for religious tolerance, the abolition of slavery, and the ratification of the United States Constitution under which George Washington served as the generally recognized first president of the country. Huntington presided over the state convention that gathered to debate ratification.

In 1900 Susan Huntington wrote about her ancestor in the *Connecticut Magazine*:

> Among the phalanx of Patriots who fearlessly and unbrokenly resisted the menaces and efforts of the British government to prevent the Declaration of Independence, it is remarkable to observe the great proportion that arouse from the humble walks of life who by the vigour [sic] of their intellect, and unwearied fearlessness compensated the deficiencies of early education and enrolled themselves with honor and capacity among the champions of Colonial freedom. Such a man was Samuel Huntington ... His extreme

SAMUEL HUNTINGTON (1731–1796)

modesty and the fact that he left no descendants perhaps account for so little appreciation of the value of his services in these days of revival of interest in all things relating to the American Revolution.

Huntington was serving as governor when he died on January 5, 1796. He was laid to rest just 15 miles away from the place of his birth in the Old Norwichtown Cemetery that is now known as the Colonial Cemetery. In 2003 the citizens of Norwich raised $31,000 and used the funds to exhume both Huntington and his wife. The tomb was restored, and the bodies of the founder and his wife were placed in new caskets and reinterred. There rests a man who went from being a barrel maker to a signer of the Declaration of Independence, to become, at least according to the people of Norwich, the first President of the United States.

Tomb of Samuel Huntington.

Oliver Wolcott
(1726 – 1797)

Connecticut Yankee

Buried at East Cemetery
Litchfield, Connecticut

Declaration of Independence • Articles of Confederation

Oliver Wolcott was a Revolutionary War hero who went on to serve as a member of the Continental Congress and sign the Declaration of Independence and later the Articles of Confederation. He commanded fourteen regiments of troops during the Revolutionary War and rose to the rank of Major General. He served for ten years as Connecticut's Lieutenant Governor beginning in 1786 and in 1796 became Governor until he died in 1797.

Wolcott was born in Windsor, Connecticut on November 20, 1726, the youngest of ten children to Colonial Governor Roger Wolcott and Sarah Drake Wolcott. He attended Yale College and graduated at the top of his class in 1747. Immediately upon graduating, he received a captain's commission from New York Governor George Clinton to fight in King George's War. He served on the northern frontier defending the Canadian border against the French until the Treaty of Aix-La-Chappelle of 1748. After the war, his regiment was disbanded and Wolcott returned to Connecticut to study medicine with his uncle, Dr. Alexander Wolcott. He completed his training but rather than pursue a career in medicine he settled in the newly developed area of Litchfield County where his father owned land and pursued an entirely different career. He was elected sheriff of the county at the age of twenty-five and founded a successful business. He served as Sheriff from 1751 to 1771. He also represented Litchfield in both

OLIVER WOLCOTT (1726–1797)

Oliver Wolcott

houses of the colonial and state legislatures and later was appointed as judge of the Litchfield Probate and County Courts.

Wolcott married Lorraine (Laura) Collins, the daughter of a sea captain. The couple had five children, four of whom survived to adulthood. Wolcott remained active in the militia during the period leading up to the Revolutionary War, devoting portions of each year to militia duty. He rose through the ranks, serving as captain and then major in 1771, and was promoted to colonel in 1774, and later rose to Major General.

As tensions escalated between the colonies and Britain Wolcott became an active participant in the Patriot cause. He was elected to the Continental Congress in 1775 and was an ardent proponent of independence noting "a final separation between the countries I consider as unavoidable." The Congress named him a Commissioner of Indian Affairs and asked him to persuade the northern Indian nations to remain neutral. His experience in the French and Indian War led to that assignment.

In the summer of 1776, a brief illness and Wolcott's role in military affairs drew him away from his political responsibilities, resulting in his absence from Congress during the adoption of the Declaration of Independence. When he recovered from his illness, rather than returning to Philadelphia, the Connecticut

Governor Jonathan Trumbull appointed him to command a detachment of fourteen regiments of Connecticut militia to defend New York, which he did.

On July 9, he was in New York City when George Washington read the Declaration of Independence to the troops. A demonstration followed and a group of soldiers toppled a large statue of King George III. The statue was made of lead and shattered into many pieces. The head was put on a spike outside a tavern. Wolcott arranged for the collection of the pieces and had them shipped off to the general's house. There, Wolcott, his family, and some local patriots melted the lead and made over 42,000 bullets for the war effort. In October 1777 he used some of these bullets in the defeat of General Burgoyne's troops at Saratoga, New York. The victory was a turning point in the war, bolstering American morale and convincing France to support the revolution.

In the fall of 1776, Wolcott returned to Philadelphia and signed the Declaration of Independence. After the victory at Saratoga Wolcott returned to Congress which was then meeting in York, Pennsylvania due to the British occupation of Philadelphia. There he signed the Articles of Confederation, the nation's first constitution.

In 1786 Wolcott was elected Lieutenant Governor of Connecticut, a post he would hold for ten years. He was a member of the Connecticut State Convention which ratified the Constitution of the United States in 1787. He

Wolcott's grave

OLIVER WOLCOTT (1726–1797)

became governor when Samuel Huntington died on January 5, 1796. He held the office until his own death at age 71. He died on December 1, 1797, and was buried at East Cemetery beside his wife.

Oliver Wolcott Jr, his son, served as Secretary of the Treasury under George Washington and John Adams and as Governor of Connecticut. A plaque commemorating Wolcott signing the Declaration of Independence can be found on the Signers Walk on the six hundred block of Chestnut Street in Philadelphia. His home in Litchfield, Connecticut was declared a National Historic Landmark in 1971. The town of Walcott, Connecticut was named in honor of Oliver and his son.

William Henry Drayton
(1742 – 1779)
Died in Philadelphia

Buried at Christ Church Burial Grounds,
Philadelphia, Pennsylvania.
In 1979, soil from the grave reburied at "Drayton Hall,"
Charleston, South Carolina.

Articles of Confederation

This Founder initially opposed the growing colonial resistance to British rule after the Stamp Act. As a matter of fact he wrote a series of articles defending the actions taken by England. When these articles were published in Europe he was appointed as a member of the Colonial Council in 1772. Over the next two years his views on colonial rule changed drastically and in 1774 he authored a pamphlet titled the *American Claim of Rights* which supported the call for a Continental Congress. As a result he was removed from his government position which only served to strengthen his views on the rebel cause. During the revolution he represented South Carolina in the Continental Congress. As a member of that Congress he signed the Articles of Confederation. He died before reaching the age of forty and before the end of the Revolution. He remains one of our lesser-known Founders. His name was William Henry Drayton.

Drayton was born in the month of September in 1742 at his father's plantation, "Drayton Hall," located on the banks of the Ashley River near Charleston, South Carolina. His birth took place shortly after his father completed construction of the main house located on the large rice plantation. His mother was Charlotta Bull Drayton the daughter of the colony's governor William Bull.

WILLIAM HENRY DRAYTON (1742–1779)

Portrait of William Henry Drayton courtesy of the Library of Congress.

His well-connected family sent him to England in 1750 for his education. He attended the Westminster School and Balliol College, Oxford before returning to America in 1764. Upon his return, he studied law and was admitted to the South Carolina bar.

As mentioned above, Drayton's conversion to the American cause was not complete until the mid-1770s. By 1775, he was a member of South Carolina's Committee of Safety and the provisional Congress that functioned as the rebel government of South Carolina. In 1776, he was appointed to the position of Chief Justice on his state's Supreme Court. That same year Drayton raised two battalions to fight in the war against England. South Carolina sent him to Georgia for the purpose of proposing that Georgia, with its smaller population, would benefit by being annexed to its eastern neighbor. Though the proposal was debated, Georgia rejected the idea. A year later, Drayton appealed directly to the citizens of Georgia attempting to convince them of the advantages of joining South Carolina. This resulted in Georgia's governor offering a reward of 100 pounds for the capture of Drayton. Though he accused the governor of "nonsense and falsehoods," Drayton returned to South Carolina and abandoned the effort to annex the neighboring state.

In 1778, South Carolina sent Drayton to Philadelphia as a representative in the Continental Congress. As a member of Congress, he was a strong supporter of the military and a signer of the Articles of Confederation. Drayton didn't live long enough to see the Articles ratified or the revolution he championed succeed. While serving in Congress he passed away from typhus on September 3, 1779. He was laid to rest in Philadelphia's Christ Church Burial Ground in a now unknown location. In 1979 dust from what was believed to be his grave were taken to "Drayton Hall" in South Carolina.

On September 25, 1779, the *Virginia Gazette* reported Drayton's death. The paper noted that Drayton had been honored by his country through his appointment to the "most important and confidential offices." The report went on to say that at the time of his death he was Chief Justice of his state and one of its representatives in Congress. The paper also proclaimed that Drayton's writings were well-known and studied in both America and Europe. Since he passed away before he reached the age of forty, there is little doubt that had he lived he would have made an even greater mark on the young country he well represented. His past service and reputation would have assured him a voice as the new nation found its footing after the war with England was won.

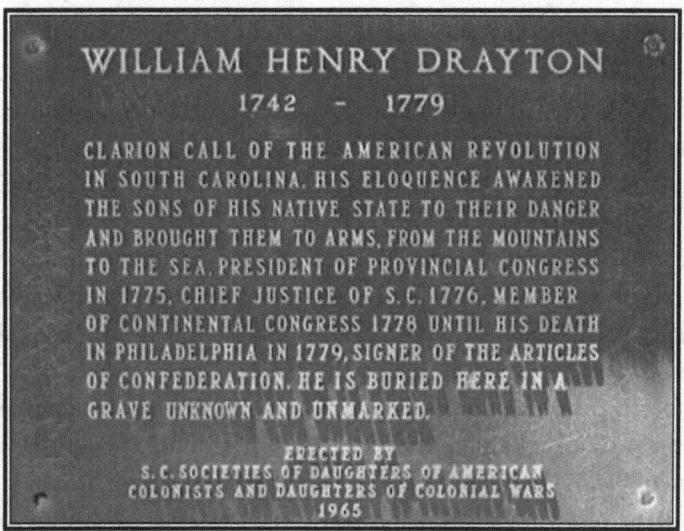

Plaque honoring William Henry Drayton at Christ Church Burial Ground in Philadelphia, Pennsylvania (photography by Lawrence Knorr).

Joseph Reed
(1741–1785)

President of Pennsylvania

Buried at Laurel Hill Cemetery,
Philadelphia, Pennsylvania.

Military • Continental Congress • Articles of Confederation

Joseph Reed served in the Continental Congress and signed the Articles of Confederation. He was one of George Washington's aides-de-camp early in the Revolutionary War and held the ranks of colonel and adjutant-general. Given his background, money, education, and marriage, he was an unlikely revolutionist. He was an enigma to many as he at first believed that reconciliation with Britain was both desirable and possible. His reluctance to commit to the cause made him seem to be trying to be on the winning side for his gain. George Washington was a big supporter of Joseph Reed, but Reed even turned on Washington when things weren't looking very good for the general.

Joseph Reed was born in Trenton, New Jersey on August 27, 1741. He was the son of Andrew Reed, a merchant, and Theodora Bowes. Reed's ancestors had come to America from Northern Ireland and were well established by the time Joseph was born. The family moved to Philadelphia from Trenton shortly after Joseph's birth, and he was enrolled at Philadelphia Academy. He received his bachelor's degree in 1757 at the age of sixteen from the College of New Jersey, which became Princeton University. Soon after, he studied law under Richard Stockton the able, eloquent Princetonian who was acknowledged to be one of the best lawyers and who would become a signer of the Declaration of Independence. In 1763 Reed went to England to study law at the prestigious

The Congress at York

Joseph Reed

Middle Temple in London. He studied there for two years often attending debates in the House of Commons. During this time he met an Englishwoman named Esther deBerdt. They married in May of 1770. Reed returned to America with his wife and widowed mother-in-law in October of 1770. He set up a law practice in Trenton at first but soon moved to Philadelphia. There the couple had five children. Esther started an organization called the Daughters of Liberty, to raise money in support of the war. She died in September 1780, and Ben Franklin's daughter Sarah Bache took over the organization.

Reed focused on becoming a leading lawyer in Philadelphia and confronted suspicions that he was a Loyalist as he had marital and familial ties with the mother country. He slowly came to feel that independence was the only course for the colonies to take. In the two years before the war, he worked as a member of Philadelphia's Committee of Correspondence and as president of Pennsylvania's second Provincial Congress.

When the army was formed in April 1775, Reed became a lieutenant colonel. On June 19, 1775, four days after George Washington was elected commander in chief, he was asked to join Washington's staff. He joined Washington in Cambridge and was appointed as his secretary. Three months later, Reed departed, pleading the press of cases pending in his law practice. Washington requested that he return, but Reed was reluctant to do so. In March 1776,

Washington offered him the job of Adjutant General, and he reluctantly accepted. He performed well and became one of Washington's most trusted officers. His judgment in military matters was consistently good and his advice to Washington excellent. However, to many, he seemed irresolute and wavering, wondering which current would become the mainstream.

After the loss of Fort Washington, the last outpost in colonial hands on Manhattan Island, Reed along with other generals, questioned Washington's judgments, especially allowing New York City to be dangerously open to invasion. Reed had not told Washington of his feelings but wrote to General Charles Lee, a letter that was a stunning criticism of Washington and praised Lee. Unhappily for all involved, when Reed was absent from headquarters, Washington opened a communication from Lee to Reed that indicated that they were both questioning Washington's abilities. This was extremely upsetting to Washington as Reed was one of his most trusted and relied upon officers. The aftermath was an awkwardness between the two that could not be repaired. The intimate relationship they had once was gone for good. Washington remained professional however and allowed Reed to continue. As a former resident of Trenton and Princeton, Reed knew that area well and supplied Washington with vital information before and during the battles of Trenton and Princeton. Three weeks after the victory at Princeton, Reed resigned as Adjutant General and then curiously volunteered as an aide without pay in time to serve at the battles of Brandywine, Germantown, and Monmouth.

In 1777, Reed was offered the positions of brigadier general and Chief Justice of the Supreme Court of Pennsylvania. He declined both in favor of being elected as a delegate to the Continental Congress. In 1778 he was one of five Pennsylvania delegates to sign the Articles of Confederation. Also that year he was elected to the equivalent position to Pennsylvania Governor, President of the Supreme Executive Council of Pennsylvania, with an almost unanimous vote. He was re-elected to this position twice. During his administration, he helped oversee the passage of a statute that abolished slavery in Pennsylvania. He also was successful in getting Revolutionary War soldiers placed on half-pay for life. Also during this time, he pressed charges against Benedict Arnold for corruption and military malpractice while he was in command at Philadelphia. The subsequent court-martial largely exonerated Arnold, but his resentment over this matter is thought to have fueled his later traitorous behavior.

Also in 1778, he was caught up in a scandal in which he was accused of traitorous correspondence with England. Until his name was cleared long after his death, some people questioned his loyalty which may be why he took such a strong stance against Loyalists. He was very strongly anti-Loyalist, advocating in

Congress for property seizure and treason charges against anyone who sympathized with the Crown. As President of Pennsylvania, Reed oversaw numerous trials of suspected Loyalists. After James Wilson defended 23 people accused of treason, a mob, stirred up by Reed's speeches, attacked Wilson in what was to become known as the "Battle of Fort Wilson." The arrival of militia saved Wilson and his friends after one casualty from inside Wilson's house. A number of the mob were arrested, but Reed pardoned and released them.

After Reed's term as President of Pennsylvania ended in 1781, he returned to practicing law. He was again elected to Congress in 1784 but declined to serve because of deteriorating health. Joseph Reed died at his house in Philadelphia on March 5, 1785. He was initially buried in the Arch Street Presbyterian Burial Grounds in Philadelphia but was removed to Laurel Hill when that cemetery was abolished in 1868.

The grave of Joseph Reed

Thomas Adams
(1730–1788)

Delegate from Virginia

Body lost or destroyed / burial site unknown

Articles of Confederation

Some of the founders of our country are well known to almost all Americans. Others we become aware of through American History courses. Still, others are known to only serious students of United States history. There are a few founders whose memory has been lost to all but those who have examined the revolutionary period under a microscope. This founder falls into the latter category. When one sees or hears the name Adams associated with the founding of the United States, thoughts immediately are drawn to the state of Massachusetts and Samuel, John, and Abigail. This founder was not even a relative of that trio, and he hailed from Virginia. His name was Thomas Adams, and he served in the Continental Congress during the American Revolution, where he added his signature to the Articles of Confederation.

Adams was born sometime in 1730 in New Kent County, Virginia. His grandfather was a tailor and has been described as one of London's leading merchants. He was educated at what was known as the common school, which was a reference to nonurban institutions of learning. It is unknown if he attended any institutions of higher learning, but whatever education he did receive qualified him to work as the clerk of Henrico County, Virginia.

According to his Congressional biography, from 1762 until 1774, Adams lived in England, where he had extensive business interests. When he returned to America, tensions between the mother country and the colonies were high. He

The Congress at York

Thomas Adams

sided with his fellow colonists in opposing the harsh economic policies adopted by the English Parliament. Shortly after returning to the country of his birth, he was elected to the Virginia House of Burgesses. He was among the delegates who signed the Articles of Association. This document strongly criticized the British government and its "ruinous system of colony administration." The Articles, in Virginia, were the result of the action taken by the colonial governor, John Murray, when he dissolved the House of Burgesses. It was at this time that Adams became chairman of the New Kent County Committee of Safety.

In 1778 Adams was elected to represent Virginia in the Continental Congress. He would serve in the Congress for two years, and it was in this capacity that he affixed his signature to the Articles of Confederation.

In 1780 Adams left the Congress and moved to Augusta County, Virginia. He was elected to the Virginia State Senate, where he served from 1783 until 1786. After retiring from public service, he lived the remainder of his days on his estate known as the "Cowpasture." It was here he passed away on July 8, 1788. Very little detail exists relative to this Founder's life. Almost none of his letters have survived. The College of William and Mary has nine letters that involve Adams though most deal with his family's burial ground. The location of his burial site is unknown.

THOMAS ADAMS (1730–1788)

Even with so little information left behind, it is possible to surmise the qualities that Adams possessed. His business success suggests that he was intelligent and industrious. The faith his fellow citizens had in him is attested to by the many positions he held as an elected representative. His courage is evident because he supported the revolution against England even though he had significant business interests in the mother country. In short, his character was in keeping with the many well and better-known founders who were his contemporaries.

John Banister
(1734 – 1788)

The Master of Hatcher's Run

Buried at Hatcher's Run Estate,
Dinwiddie County, Virginia.

Articles of Confederation

Colonel John Banister was an attorney and plantation owner from Petersburg, Virginia. He served in the Virginia House of Burgesses and as an officer in the Virginia Militia. He was elected to the Second Continental Congress, where he signed the Articles of Confederation.

Banister, born December 26, 1734, at the family's estate, Hatcher's Run, near Petersburg, Dinwiddie County, Virginia, was the son of Captain John Banister, a ship's captain, and his wife, Martha Wilmette (née Munford) Banister. Banister's grandfather, John Baptist Banister (1654–1692), was one of the first university-trained naturalists in North America, referred to as "the first Virginia botanist of any note."

Young Banister traveled on his father's ship, crossing the Atlantic to England, where he attended Wakefield, a private school south of Leeds. He then studied law at the Temple Inn in London, admitted on September 27, 1753. Upon graduation, Banister was admitted to the Virginia bar and opened a law practice in Petersburg. He also managed his plantation.

Banister married Elizabeth Munford in 1755. He was first elected to the Virginia House of Burgesses in 1765 and served until 1769. During this time, he and Elizabeth built a suburban villa in Petersburg called Battersea. It was in the five-part Palladian style and completed in 1768. John Banister Jr., known as

JOHN BANISTER (1734–1788)

John Banister

Jack, was born to this couple, though the exact year is not recorded. Likewise, a daughter, Maria Ann, was born, though the date is lost. She later married the physician George Wilson from Petersburg. Unfortunately, Elizabeth died in 1770.

Banister next married Elizabeth "Patsy" Bland, the daughter of Theodorick Bland of Cawsons, a descendant of one of Virginia's first families, and a son of Continental Congressman Richard Bland. She was also the sister of Colonel Theodorick Bland, who later became a Continental Congressman and member of the First Congress. The couple gave birth to son Robert Bannister in 1771, but he lived only until 1794.

Banister returned to the House of Burgesses in 1772 until 1775, when his wife died that year.

As tensions rose with England, Banister was a member of the Virginia Convention, which declared Virginia independent in 1776. He was elected to the new Virginia House of Delegates in 1776 and served until 1778.

The Congress at York

Home of John Banister

On November 19, 1777, Banister was elected to the Second Continental Congress, which met in York, Pennsylvania. There, he was one of the framers of the Articles of Confederation, which he signed on July 8, 1778.

Banister next joined the Virginia Militia as a cavalry officer in 1778 at the major, rising to the rank of lieutenant colonel by 1781. During this time, Banister became good friends with Thomas Jefferson.

In 1779, Banister married Agan Blair of Williamsburg, Virginia, the daughter of John Blair Sr., a nephew of James Blair, the founder of William and Mary College, and the father of John Blair Jr., who signed the Constitution. John Blair Sr. was a longtime member of the House of Burgesses and acting governor. The couple had sons Burrell Banister (1779–1837) and Theodorick Blair Banister (1780–1829) early in their marriage.

During the weeks before the Battle of Yorktown in 1781, Lieutenant Colonel Banister, highly regarded by George Washington, aided in supplying and repelling the British army from Virginia. In so doing, he lost most of his personal property to the British led by General William Phillips, who often stayed at Battersea and confiscated his valuables.

After the war, Banister returned to the House of Delegates from 1781 until 1784. By 1782, he appears to have recovered his assets, as Dinwiddie County records note: three free males, 46 adult slaves, 42 underage slaves, 28 horses, 126 cattle, and one chariot. He and Agan had another son, John Monro Banister (1784–1832). Also, in 1784, son "Jack" accompanied Thomas Jefferson to France.

JOHN BANISTER (1734–1788)

Sign pointing the way to John Banister's estate, Battersea.

In 1785, Banister was appointed the first mayor of Petersburg and was noted for his knowledge of current affairs and his writing accomplishments.

Banister died on September 30, 1788, at Hatcher's Run, three months short of his 54th birthday. He was buried in the family plot there. His eldest son, "Jack" Banister, died eleven weeks later, owing Thomas Jefferson 3173 livres following his time in Europe. This great debt may have greatly impacted the Banisters, leading to small or no inheritances for the minor children, Burrell and Monro.

Daughter Maria Ann Wilson died in October 1792. Ann Blair Banister died on December 23, 1813.

George Plater
(1735 – 1792)

Master of Sotterley

Buried at Sotterley Plantation,
Hollywood, St. Mary's County, Maryland.

Continental Congress

George Plater III was a planter and attorney from one of the leading families of colonial Maryland. He was a member of the Maryland Provincial Congress, elected to the Continental Congress from late 1778 to 1780. He was also a state senator and, at the end of his life, briefly the Governor of Maryland.

Plater was born on November 8, 1735, at Sotterley Plantation, St. Mary's County, Maryland, the son of George Plater II, attorney and planter, and Rebecca (née Addison) Bowles Plater, the widow of the plantation's founder. Plater's grandfather, George Plater I, a naval officer, emigrated from England and was very involved in the colonial Maryland government. Through marriage, the elder Plater was able to increase his holdings to become one of the leading landholders in the colony. "Sotterle" was the name of the seat of the Plater family in England, purchased from the Sotterle family. Plater's siblings included his sister Rebecca, wife of John Tayloe II; Anne; Thomas Addison (died in infancy); and Elizabeth Norton.

Plater's early education was on the plantation with private tutors. He then attended the College of William and Mary in Williamsburg, graduating in 1752. The following year, he studied law in England and was later admitted to the bar in Maryland.

GEORGE PLATER (1735–1792)

Portrait of George Plater

At only twenty-two, Plater's first foray into politics was his election to the lower house of the Maryland colonial legislature as a member of the Proprietary Party. He served until 1759.

In December 1762, Plater married Hannah Lee, the daughter of Richard Lee of Charles County, who owned Blenheim Plantation. The two had a daughter, Charlotte, born in September 1763, who died young. Hannah did not survive the childbirth.

In July 1764, Plater married Elizabeth Ann Rousby, with whom he had four sons and two daughters. Rebecca married Uriah Forrest, who was an aide to George Washington and lost a leg at the Battle of Germantown. The sons' names were George IV, John, Thomas, and Edward. Daughter Ann married Philip Barton Key, an uncle of Francis Scott Key, who composed "The Star Spangled Banner."

Around this time, Plater, a devout Protestant, became a vestryman at St. Andrews Episcopal Church, which he helped found and build. His indentured servant, Richard Boulton, was the architect of the church, built circa 1766. Plater served as a vestryman for the rest of his life. The church survives to this day and is on the National Register of Historic Places.

The Congress at York

From 1766 to 1771, Plater again was a representative in the colonial legislature. He was also a justice of the peace in St. Mary's County. From 1767 through 1777, Plater was a naval officer in the Patuxent District. From 1771 through 1774, Plater served on the colonial governor's Executive Council.

In February 1776, now in his 41st year, he had clearly shifted his loyalties to the Revolution. He was appointed to the Maryland Council of Safety, where he assisted with the collection of funds for military operations against Canada. In March, he and George Dent were selected by the Council of Safety to work with the Virginians to construct beacons along the Potomac River. On May 9, Plater took his seat, representing St. Mary's County, in Annapolis at the new Maryland Provincial Congress. While there, on August 14, 1776, he was appointed to assist in drafting Maryland's first constitution.

The Maryland legislature elected Plater to the Continental Congress on December 22, 1777. At the time, the Congress was meeting in York, Pennsylvania, having adopted the Articles of Confederation. He attended the Congress for the last two months of the session in York, from April 18 through June 27, 1778. He then moved with the Congress back to Philadelphia, attending from July 22 until September 22, 1778. He was reelected on November 13, 1778, and served from February 10, 1779, through June 8, 1779, and October 11, 1779, through the end of the year. He was elected for a third term on December 22, 1779, and continued from January 1, 1780, through May 5, 1780, on about May 19, 1780, and from September 22, through November 28, 1780.

Plater returned to state politics in 1781, becoming a state senator, a role he maintained through 1790.

In April 1788, Plater attended the Maryland convention, representing St. Mary's County, to ratify the new US Constitution. He was appointed the president of the convention and voted in favor on April 28, 1788.

During the first presidential election under the new United States Constitution, Plater was chosen as a presidential elector early in 1789 but did not vote.

On December 6, 1791, Plater reached the pinnacle of state politics when he was unanimously elected governor. He took office soon after but only lasted three months. On January 17, 1792, *The Federal Gazette* of Philadelphia reported the governor was "dangerously ill."

Plater died on February 10, 1792, while serving in Annapolis, Maryland. He was buried on the plantation at Sotterley.

On February 22, 1792, *The Carlisle Gazette* wrote:

GEORGE PLATER (1735–1792)

With a heartfelt Regret, in which every patriotic Citizen of Maryland, every Lover of Honour and Virtue throughout the Union, must feelingly participate, we announce to the public the Demise of our late worthy Governor, his Excellency George Plater, Esq. who closed his truly honourable and invaluable Life, on Thursday last, after a long and distressing Illness, aged 56 Years. Scarcely was he elected, by the unanimous voice of the Legislature, to fill the first station in Government, when painful disease assailed him, and, by terminating his life, deprived the state of the blessings of an administration of which, from his uniformly just and dignified conduct in various important trusts and the most flattering passages were entertained.

The Sotterley Plantation remains a historic site, now known as Historic Sotterley. At the time of Plater's death, at least 93 slaves lived on the plantation, which is now maintained as a museum and operated by a foundation. It is located on Route 245, near Hollywood, Maryland.

Unfortunately, the location of Plater's grave has been lost.

John Mathews
(1744 – 1802)

"The Disagreeable One"

Buried at Circular Congregational Church Burying Ground
Charleston, South Carolina

**Signer of Articles of Confederation • Continental Congress
Governor • Militia**

John Mathews was a lawyer from Charleston, South Carolina, who was involved in politics. He served in local positions and was elected to the Continental Congress in time for the Articles of Confederation, which he signed. Near the end of the American Revolution, he was elected governor of South Carolina for one term. For the remainder of his life, he served in state judicial positions.

Mathews was born in 1744 in Charleston, South Carolina, the son of John Mathews and his wife, Sarah (née Gibbes). His paternal lineage was from Captain Anthony Mathewes (1661–1734), who emigrated to South Carolina from London in 1680.

Early in the 1760s, Mathews fought the Cherokee in South Carolina as an ensign in the South Carolina Provincial Regiment. He was promoted to lieutenant in the process.

Mathews next studied law and went to England, where he entered the Middle Temple in 1764. He graduated in 1766 and returned to South Carolina, where he initially clerked for Colonel Charles Pinckney before he was admitted to the colonial bar. However, Mathews did not practice law in South Carolina. Rather, he became a politician, speaking against the various actions of the British Parliament following the French and Indian War.

JOHN MATHEWS (1744–1802)

John Mathews

In December 1766, Mathews married Mary Wragg, the half-sister of Charlotte Wragg, who married William Loughton Smith, a fellow delegate to the Continental Congress from South Carolina. The couple had no children. Mathew's sister, Elizabeth, was married to another Continental Congressman, Thomas Heyward Jr.

In 1772, Mathews was elected to the South Carolina Commons House of Assembly. There, he called for a boycott of British goods. From June 1774 until June 1775, Mathews was a member of the Committee of Ninety-Nine, which formed a rebel government in the colony. Mathews also returned to the military as a lieutenant in the provincial militia, guarding Fort Charlotte on the Savannah and Fort Moore near present-day Augusta.

During 1775 and 1776, following the hostilities commencing at Lexington and Concord, Mathews was appointed an associate judge on the state circuit court and a member of the First and Second Provincial Congresses in South Carolina. From 1776 to 1780, Mathews served in the South Carolina House of Representatives, serving as speaker in 1777 and 1778. He also continued his military service as a captain in the Colleton County regiment.

On January 22, 1778, after Christopher Gadsden and Henry Middleton declined to continue serving, Mathews was elected to the Continental Congress.

He immediately found himself embroiled in the debates about the Articles of Confederation following the meetings in York, Pennsylvania. Mathews was unhappy from the start, describing the trip from South Carolina to York, Pennsylvania, "A most disagreeable journey, indeed." He followed this with a complaint about the indecision in Congress to John Rutledge on July 7, 1778:

> We are thrown into a good deal of confusion with regard to the Confederation. Before we left York-Town, Congress proceeded to the consideration of the amendments offered by the different States to the Confederation, every one of which have been rejected. It was then ordered to be engroced [sic] to [be] ready for ratification when we came to Philadelphia. Now, that it is so, Mr. Laurens, Mr. Drayton, and Mr. Hutson say they will not sign it because they do not think themselves authorized by our instructions to do so unless the other twelve states will agree to sign it likewise. Maryland has refused to ratify. Mr. Heyward and my self [sic] are of a different opinion, and think we are authorized, not withstanding [sic] one or even two States were to refuse, nor do I apprehend that inconsistancy [sic] will arise in the Confederation, from the Defection of one or two States which these three Gentlemen seem to imagine, however they mean, I believe, to write to the Prest. or to you, to be laid before the Assembly. I do not think it necessary for Heyward and myself to write on the subject, in our public Characters, as we think we are authorised [sic] to sign it, but as Three are necessary to a final Ratification, we must wait for your decision. This I am clear in, from what I have seen, and know, since I have been in Congress, that if we are to have no Confederation until the Legislatures of the Thirteen States agree to one, that we shall never have one, and if we have not one, we shall be literally a rope of sand, and I shall tremble for the consequences that will follow at the end of this War.

Mathews quickly developed a reputation as a complainer in Congress. He did not enjoy his time in the sessions, complaining about his fellow Congressmen, "Those who have dispositions for jangling and are fond of displaying their Rhetorical abilities, let them come. I never was so sick of anything in my life." He wrote to others about his frustrations with the slow pace of things. Regardless of his mood, Mathews signed the Articles of Confederation on July 21, 1778. His complaints about his fellow members continued, and they also described his temperament as hot, "like the country of his nativity."

Mathews was reelected to the Congress in 1779 and 1780, joining Henry Laurens, Francis Kinloch, Arthur Middleton, and Thomas Bee as delegates from South Carolina. During his tenure, he served on the Committee of Congress, which dealt with military matters. When Mathews got word of Charleston's fall in 1780, he wished to return from Congress. Only John Rutledge, the governor, remained, now in exile in North Carolina. Britain was trying to pry away the Southern states from the rest, but the patriots would not hear it. Rutledge urged Mathews to stay in Congress to help manage affairs there.

After Nathanael Greene's victory at Eutaw Springs on September 9, 1781, the tide turned against the British, who now fell back to Charleston. Rutledge prepared for the re-establishment of South Carolina's government in late 1781. On January 24, 1782, the South Carolina House met and announced the return of John Mathews from Philadelphia. After both Christopher Gadsden and Richard Hutson were elected and declined the post of governor, Mathews was elected. The house voted that Mathews could not refuse the post! Mathews then retired from Congress and became the governor. He was sworn in on January 31, 1782, and served until February 4, 1783. During this time, the British evacuated Charleston in December 1782, and Mathews threatened the nonpayment of British merchants if the soldiers carried off any goods from the citizens of the city. The negotiation worked.

After his governorship, Mathews was a judge on the state Court of Chancery in 1784 and again served in the South Carolina House. He remained involved in Charleston's affairs and sold off his merchant sloop. He also advertised for a fugitive slave in August 1790, seeking the recovery of Jemmy "of the African country." Mathews was a judge on the state Court of Equity in 1791. He was also a founding trustee of the College of Charleston.

After Mary's passing, Mathews married Sarah Rutledge in May 1799. She was the sister of John and Edward Rutledge, both Continental Congressmen. The couple had no children.

Mathews followed his wife to the grave on October 30, 1802, in Charleston. He was buried at the Circular Congregational Church Burying Ground in Charleston.

Roger Sherman
(1721 – 1793)

Three-Fifths Compromise

Buried at Grove Street Cemetery,
New Haven, Connecticut.

**Continental Association • Declaration of Independence
Articles of Confederation • U.S. Constitution**

Roger Sherman, of Connecticut, was the only person to sign all four founding documents of the United States of America: Continental Association, Declaration of Independence, Articles of Confederation, and Constitution. A lawyer and statesman, he with James Wilson proposed the Three-Fifths Compromise during the Constitutional Convention. Sherman later served as a member of the U.S. House of Representatives and as a U.S. Senator.

Sherman was born in Newton, Massachusetts, on April 19, 1721, to William Sherman and his second wife Mehetabel (née Wellington) Sherman. Others in his family tree include Senator, Secretary of the Treasury, and Secretary of State John Sherman (1823–1900), Civil War General William Tecumseh Sherman (1820–1891), and Senator William Maxwell Evarts (1818–1901), who was also Attorney General and Secretary of State.

William Sherman was variously a cordwainer, farmer, and shoemaker in Stoughton, Massachusetts. He married first Rebecca Cutler of Watertown with whom he had a son, William, who died in infancy. He then married Mehetabel Wellington of Watertown on September 3, 1715. Roger was born in 1721 and lived on the farm in Stoughton until 1743, studying his father's trades and never receiving a formal education. From pastor Reverend Samuel Dunbar, Roger

ROGER SHERMAN (1721–1793)

Portrait of Roger Sherman by Ralph Earl, circa 1776.

privately learned the classics and theology. When William Sherman died in 1741, 18-year-old Roger cared for his widowed mother and the rest of the family.

In 1743, Roger literally followed in his older brother William's footsteps, setting out on foot with his cobbler's tools to find work in New Milford, Connecticut. Soon, a local attorney took notice of his writing ability and urged him to become a lawyer. In 1745, Sherman was named the surveyor of New Haven County, remaining in that position until 1752, after which he was the surveyor for Litchfield County until 1758. During this time, he turned his earnings and observations into great wealth through well-played land speculation.

Sherman married Elizabeth Hartwell of Stoughton, Massachusetts, in November 1749. The two had seven children, four of whom lived to adulthood. After Elizabeth passed in 1760 at the age of 34, Sherman moved to New Haven and married Rebecca Prescott in May 1763. The couple had eight children, seven of whom lived to adulthood.

Beginning in 1750, like Benjamin Franklin, Sherman began publishing a series of almanacs on a variety of subjects expressing his ideas and showcasing his writing ability. He studied law and was admitted to the Connecticut colonial bar in 1754. In 1755, he was elected to the Connecticut colonial Assembly, serving until 1766. He was also a justice of the peace for Litchfield County from 1755 to 1761. Later, he served in the state Senate (1766–1785), and as a judge of the Superior Court (1766–67 and 1773–88).

Beginning in the mid-1760s, Sherman was a leader in opposition to the British Parliament, personally urging protest of The Stamp Act. Though he was not initially one of the radical Sons of Liberty, he did eventually join the Committee of Correspondence to communicate with the other colonies following the Boston Tea Party.

As royal rule collapsed in Connecticut, Jonathan Trumbull was named the governor. He was a friend of Sherman's and named him one of 12 assistants including Eliphalet Dyer and William Samuel Johnson. For the first Continental Congress in 1774, Connecticut sent Sherman, Dyer, and Silas Deane.

In Philadelphia, Silas Deane was not impressed with his fellow delegate, writing in a letter to his wife, "Mr. Sherman is clever in private, but I will only say he is as badly calculated to appear in such Company as a chestnut-burr is for an eye-stone. He occasioned some shrewd countenances among the company, and not a few oaths, by the odd questions he asked, and the very odd and countrified cadence with which he speaks; but he was, and did, as well as I expected."

Sherman served in the Continental Congress from 1774 to 1781 and then again in 1784 during which he did more than Jefferson, or Adams, or any other delegate, signing the Continental Association, the Olive Branch Petition, the Declaration of Independence, the Articles of Confederation, and, eventually, as a delegate to the Constitutional Convention, the U.S. Constitution. He also wrote hundreds of letters, documents, and other correspondence "to establish regulations and restrictions on the trade of the United States; to regulate the currency of the country; to furnish supplies for the army; to provide for the expenses of the government; to prepare articles of confederation between the several states; and to propose a plan of military operations for the campaign of 1776."

Roger Sherman's biggest contribution in the Continental Congress may have been on June 11, 1776, when he was named to the committee to draft a declaration of independence from England along with Thomas Jefferson, John Adams, Benjamin Franklin, and Robert Livingston.

After the Revolution, Sherman was selected to represent Connecticut at the Constitutional Convention. He again played a prominent role as a key player in many votes. After the ratification of the Constitution, Sherman was elected to the First Congress (1789–1791). However, he did not quite finish his term, instead taking the vacant Senate seat of William Samuel Johnson on March 4, 1791.

ROGER SHERMAN (1721–1793)

In 1987, a draft of the Bill of Rights was found among James Madison's papers at the Library of Congress written in Sherman's hand. Historians have argued since over whether Sherman was a collaborator with Madison, or just made a copy for the record. According to Christopher Collier, the former Connecticut State Historian, Sherman was simply making a copy. He had been against a Bill of Rights even after the draft was recorded.

Sherman served as a senator until his death at home in New Haven on July 23, 1793. He was 72. Sherman was buried at the New Haven Green. A few years after his death, a new cemetery was started a few blocks away to deal with the overcrowding under the Green. By 1821, many of the families had moved their loved ones' graves and headstones to the new cemetery. However, for thousands, this was not done. Only the headstones were moved, but the remains were not. Thus, perhaps 5,000 to 10,000 people remain buried under the New Haven Green. We believe some or all of Roger Sherman was moved to Grove Street Cemetery.

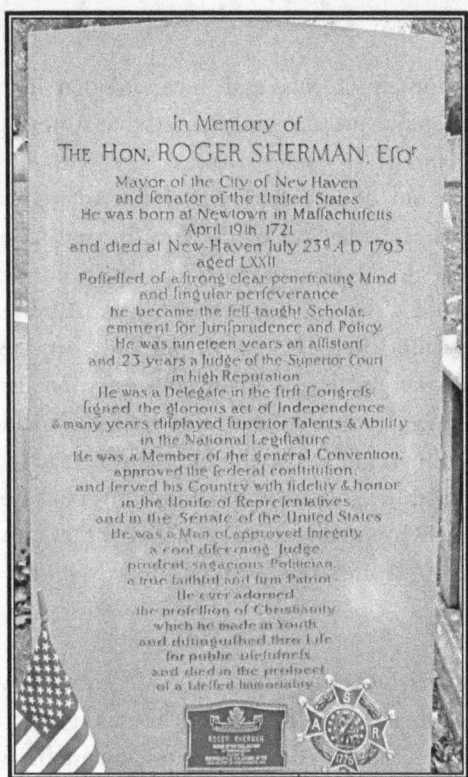

Grave of Roger Sherman at Grove Street Cemetery in New Haven, Connecticut (photo by Lawrence Knorr).

Philip Livingston
(1716 – 1778)

Died in York

Buried at Prospect Hill Cemetery,
York, Pennsylvania.

Continental Association • Declaration of Independence

Philip Livingston opposed violence and once said that independence was "a vain shallow and ridiculous project" and warned that America would collapse if separated from England.

On his first trip out of Massachusetts, John Adams was on his way to Philadelphia to serve as a member of the Continental Congress. On a stop in New York, he was able to arrange meetings with some of New York's representatives that would serve in Congress with him. Among these was Philip Livingston. Adams found that Livingston not only opposed revolution but that he distrusted New Englanders. Livingston questioned Adams as to why Massachusetts had once hanged Quakers and used the incident to argue that a revolution would only result in the colonies fighting each other. Adams later said that it was impossible to reason with Livingston. However, the behavior of the British government eventually turned the New Yorker into an ardent patriot and an active promoter of efforts to raise and fund troops for the war.

Livingston was born on January 15, 1716, in Albany, New York into a prosperous family. His father Robert Livingston had emigrated to America from Scotland in 1673. He settled in Albany and quickly established himself in the fur trade. In 1687 the English Royal Governor granted him ownership of a tract of land consisting of 160,000 acres on the east bank of the Hudson River. The

PHILIP LIVINGSTON (1716–1778)

Portrait of Philip Livingston by Pompeo Girolamo Batoni, circa 1783.

land became known as the "Manor of Livingston" and remains in the family to the present day.

Robert saw to it that young Philip was tutored at home and then attended and graduated from Yale University in 1737. After marrying Christina Broeck, the daughter of the mayor of Albany, the couple settled in New York City where he became a very successful merchant and took an active part in civic affairs. His accomplishments during this time included pushing for the founding of Kings College (known today as Columbia University), the establishment of a Professorship of Divinity at Yale, the building of the first meeting house for the Methodist Society in America, and providing aid to organize the New York Public Library. In 1754 he was elected an alderman in the City, his first venture into public life. He would continue to be elected alderman for nine consecutive years. His success in these elections suggests that he was perceived as an effective representative by those who were able to cast ballots. In 1758 he was also elected to the Colonial Legislature and would urge moderation in dealings with England.

The Congress at York

In 1765 he attended the Stamp Act Congress which produced the first formal protest to the Crown. In July 1775, he signed The Olive Branch Petition, a final attempt to achieve an understanding with the Crown. The petition appealed directly to King George III to cease hostilities and restore harmony. The King refused to respond to the plea and proclaimed the Colonies to be in a state of rebellion. Livingston was elected to the First and Second Continental Congress and during this time he changed his mind and supported the Revolution and signed the Declaration of Independence in 1776. He accepted independence reluctantly, dreading the social upheaval.

In September 1775, he was one of nine men appointed to the Secret Committee—later known as the Committee on Commerce—charged with arranging the importation of arms and gunpowder for the patriot forces He remained a member throughout his time in Congress and spent a large part of his own money to purchase supplies for the army. When the British army captured New York City, they seized his two houses forcing his family to flee

Grave of Philip Livingston at Prospect Hill Cemetery, York, Pennsylvania (photo by Joe Farley).

to Kingston. They used his Duke Street home as a barracks and his Brooklyn Heights residence as a Royal Navy Hospital.

Unfortunately, Livingston did not live to see the American victory. He was elected to Congress in October 1777. During this particularly critical and gloomy period in the Revolution, Congress was forced to meet in York, Pennsylvania because the British had seized Philadelphia. Livingston's health was precarious, as he was diagnosed with dropsy in the chest (today it would be called congestive heart failure) with no rational prospect of recovery or improvement. Yet his love of his country was unwavering, and so he did not hesitate to give up the comforts of home and family.

With his health declining, he made the trip to York after bidding his friends and family a final farewell. He believed he would never return. He proved to be correct; on June 12, 1778, Philip Livingston died. He was sixty-two years old. The entire Congress attended his funeral and declared a mourning period of a month. He was first buried in a churchyard at the German Reformed Church on West Market Street in York but later moved to Prospect Hill Cemetery in York. In 2005, Descendants of the Signers of the Declaration of Independence honored him by attaching a plaque to his tombstone identifying him as a Signer of the Declaration. A number of the direct descendants took part in the dedication ceremony.

Richard Hutson
(1748 – 1795)

First Mayor of Charleston

Buried at Circular Congregational Church Burying Ground,
Charleston, South Carolina.

Articles of Confederation

Richard Hutson was a prominent lawyer, judge, and politician in Charleston, South Carolina. He was elected to the Second Continental Congresses and signed the Articles of Confederation. He also served as the eighth Lieutenant Governor of South Carolina and the first mayor of Charleston. He participated in the state constitutional convention to ratify the U.S. Constitution.

Richard Hutson was born July 9, 1748, in Prince William Parish, South Carolina, to Reverend William Hutson and his wife, Mary (née Woodward or Gibbes). The elder Hutson first studied law in England but disliked it. He came to America and as an actor in 1740, after which he was called to preach. Young Richard studied the classics. He then studied law and graduated from Princeton College in New Jersey in 1765. He was admitted to the South Carolina bar and opened a law practice in Charleston.

The young attorney was an early agitator for independence. He was elected to the provincial assembly in 1776. On January 18, 1777, he wrote Isaac Hayne, his brother-in-law, concerning the mood in South Carolina regarding a state religion:

> The Dissenters' Petition came before the House on Saturday last. It was introduced and warmly supported by General Gadsden. In

RICHARD HUTSON (1748–1795)

Richard Hutson

order to give you a general idea of the debates, it will be necessary to quote the paragraph, which it was the prayer of the Petition might be inserted into the [state] Constitution. It runs thus: That there shall never be any establishment of any one Denomination or sect of Protestants by way of preference to another in this State. That no Protestant inhabitant of this State shall, by law, be obligated to pay towards the maintenance and support of a religious worship that he does not freely join in or has not voluntarily engaged to support, nor to be denied the enjoyment of any civil right merely on account of his religious principles, but that all Protestants demeaning themselves peaceably under the government established under the constitution shall enjoy free and equal privileges, both religious and civil.

In early 1778, Christopher Gadsden, Arthur Middleton, Henry Laurens, and William Henry Drayton were elected to the Second Continental Congress. Middleton and Gadsden declined the honor, and a subsequent election for the three vacancies selected John Mathews, Thomas Heyward, Jr., and Richard Hutson. Wrote Historian David Duncan Wallace about the elections:

> During the spring and summer of 1778, Congress was considerably strengthened. [On] May 21st Samuel Adams returned from an absence of over six months, which, under the Massachusetts rule requiring three delegates, had deprived the State of her vote; Gouverneur Morris took his seat from New York [on] 20 January 1778; Roger Sherman returned [on] 25 April after a long absence. All the States, even Delaware at last, sent representatives; Laurens, who since the beginning of November 1777, had been the sole attendant from his State, was reinforced [on] 30 March by the brilliant young William Henry Drayton, [on] 13 April by Richard Hutson, [on] 22 April by John Matthews [sic; should be Mathews], and [on] 6 June by Thomas Heyward.

Hutson arrived at the Continental Congress when it was in York, Pennsylvania, having fled occupied Philadelphia. He served from April 13, 1778, until June 27, 1778. At that point, the Congress returned to Philadelphia. Hutson accompanied Elbridge Gerry and Francis Dana to Philadelphia by Wilmington and Chester, avoiding the public inns filled with other delegates and people returning to the city. The group crossed the Susquehanna at McCall's Ferry, southeast of York, and celebrated July 4th at City Tavern in Philadelphia. Hutson then served through February 26, 1779, during which he signed the Articles of Confederation on behalf of South Carolina.

Upon his return to Charleston in 1780, Hutson found himself on the front lines of a British invasion. When Charleston fell, he was captured along with Christopher Gadsden, Josiah Smith, Edward Blake, Jacob Read, and Alexander Moultrie. The group was taken by ship to St. Augustine, where they were held for many weeks.

Following his release, Hutson was elected to the state's Legislative Council, holding the position into 1782. Hutson had served in the South Carolina House of Representatives sporadically throughout the revolutionary years. In 1782, he was elected the lieutenant governor of the state and then, in 1783, was the first elected mayor of Charleston. In 1784, Hutson was elected to a court position, which he held until 1791. In 1788, he was a member of the state constitutional convention that ratified the U.S. Constitution. After 1791, Hutson was promoted to senior judge of the Chancery court.

RICHARD HUTSON (1748–1795)

Richard Hutson died in Charleston on April 12, 1795. He was buried in the Perrineau family vault in the Independent Congregational Church Cemetery, now the Circular Congregational Church Burying Ground, located in Charleston. A plaque placed on a wall next to his grave reads:

> Herein Lie the Remains of Richard Hutson 1747–1795. Son of Rev. William and Mary Woodward Hutson. South Carolina Patriot, Statesman, and Jurist. Graduated Princeton 1765. Founding Body the College of Charleston 1772–1794. Member S.C. General Assembly and Legislative Council 1776–1790. Served in Militia and Imprisoned by the British During the Revolutionary War. Delegate to the Continental Congress 1778–1779. Signer Articles of Confederation. Lieutenant Governor 1782–1783. Author of Act Incorporating City of Charleston 1783. First Intendant (Mayor) of Charleston 1783. Judge, Court of Chancery 1784–1794. Senior Judge 1791–1794.

Tomb of Richard Hutson.

Dr. Josiah Bartlett
(1729–1795)

First Vote for Independence

Buried at Plains Cemetery
Kingston, New Hampshire

**Continental Congress • Signer of the Declaration of Independence
Signer of the Articles of Confederation**

The first to vote for independence from Great Britain was the delegate from New Hampshire, who was also a physician. Dr. Josiah Bartlett said "Aye," and was then the second to sign the document after President John Hancock. Bartlett later signed the Articles of Confederation and served as Chief Justice of the New Hampshire Supreme Court. He was the first popularly elected governor of the state.

Josiah Bartlett was born on November 21, 1729, in Amesbury, Massachusetts, the fifth child and fourth son of Deacon Stephen Bartlett, a shoemaker, and his wife Hannah (née Webster) Bartlett. Stephen was the son of Richard and Hannah (Emery) Bartlett, and according to one genealogical study, the Bartlett line can be traced back to John Bartlett, Sr., who came to Newbury, Massachusetts, in 1634, on the ship *Mary and John*. Josiah's maternal grandfather was said to be "wealthy in landed property."

Young Josiah study Latin and Greek in his teens but likely due to the family's circumstances, received a limited education. Soon, he was apprenticed to a relative, Dr. Nehemiah Ordway, with whom he studied medicine. At just twenty years of age, in 1750, and after three years of studies, Josiah moved to Kingston, New Hampshire, and started medical practice. At the time, Kingston

DR. JOSIAH BARTLETT (1729–1795)

Dr. Josiah Bartlett

was a frontier community where his services were greatly needed, being the only doctor in the county. With the proceeds, in 1751, he purchased land and a farm.

Josiah married his first cousin, Mary Barton Bartlett (1730–1789), the daughter of his uncle Joseph and his wife, Sarah (née Hoyt) Bartlett, on January 15, 1754. Mary was from nearby Newton, New Hampshire. Together, the Bartletts had eleven children: Mary (1754), Lois (1756), Miriam (1758), Rhoda (1760), Hannah (1762, did not survive), Levi (1753), Josiah (1765, did not survive), Josiah (1768), Ezra (1770), Sarah (1773), and Hannah (1776, did not survive). Three sons and five grandsons later became physicians.

In years past, the Kingston area was the center of an epidemic of "throat distemper," serious for adults and often fatal for young children. In 1754, the illness was back, and Bartlett experimented with therapies and drugs, discovering that Peruvian bark aided recovery, saving many.

Josiah Bartlett next became involved in politics. In March 1757, he was elected as a selectman for the town of Kingston, a position he held until 1775 when the town's government was dissolved by the royal governor at the outset of the Revolution.

In 1763, Bartlett was behind several real estate ventures, settling the town of Warren, New Hampshire, where Bartlett was the original grantee. He served in the same capacity for the villages of Wentworth and Sudbury, and was the proprieter for Salisbury and Perrystown (now Sutton).

In 1765, Bartlett was elected to the colonial assembly and joined in a three-year partnership for a medical practice with Dr. Amos Gale in Kingston.

In 1767, Bartlett became the colonel of the county militia, was appointed justice of the peace by Governor John Wentworth, and was asked to propose reforms to provincial laws.

The governor and Bartlett continued their close collaboration in 1770 when Wentworth asked Bartlett to help establish a system of equitable taxation for the colony. Following the Boston Massacre in March 1770, Bartlett was commissioned a lieutenant in the 7th New Hampshire Regiment in November.

By 1774, the friendship with Governor Wentworth was greatly strained. That year, in response to the Intolerable Acts following the Boston Tea Party, Bartlett was appointed to a committee of correspondence and attended the First Provincial Congress, held in Exeter, New Hampshire, after Wentworth dissolved the colonial assembly. This body sent delegates to the new Continental Congress in Philadelphia.

As tensions mounted later that year, the Bartlett home was destroyed by fire, allegedly set by Tories. After moving his family to their farmhouse, he commenced on reconstruction. Bartlett was selected as a delegate to the Continental Congress but declined so he could attend to his family and home. While still in New Hampshire, Bartlett alerted the state militia about a raid on British arms and gunpowder at Fort William and Mary in Portsmouth Harbor on December 14 and 15, 1774. Bartlett helped prepare for the British response. Angered at Bartlett's behavior and attendance at the Second Provincial Congress in January 1775, Governor Wentworth revoked Bartlett's various positions prior to being expelled.

Bartlett was elected to the Third Provincial Congress in the Spring of 1775 and wrote letters of support to Massachusetts following the clashes at Lexington and Concord. On August 23, 1775, Bartlett was elected as a delegate to the Second Continental Congress, and through early 1776, was the only representative from New Hampshire in Philadelphia, forcing him to participate on all of the committees. Bartlett wrote often to his wife. In one of the letters, he worried about potential outcomes, but left the results to higher powers:

DR. JOSIAH BARTLETT (1729–1795)

> Kind Providence will order all things for the best, and if Sometimes affairs turn out Contrary to our wishes, we must make our selves Easy & Contented, as we are not Certain what is for the best.

During the second session, Bartlett was joined by delegates William Whipple and Matthew Thornton. On July 1, 1776, when the draft of the Declaration of Independence was circulating, Bartlett wrote to John Langdon, then the President of New Hampshire:

> The affair of Independency has been this day determined in a Committee of the whole House; by next Post, I expect you will receive a formal declaration with the reasons; the Declaration before Congress is, I think, a pretty good one. I hope it will not be spoiled by canvassing in Congress.

When the question of declaring independence from Britain was proposed, the vote was processed from the northernmost colony to the southernmost. Thus, New Hampshire was called first, and Bartlett the first delegate. He voted in the affirmative and became the first to vote for independence.

During the remainder of July 1776, Bartlett was very interested in what form the new government would take. He shared with John Langdon the arrival of the constitutions of Virginia and New Jersey, which he suggested would be good models for New Hampshire.

On August 2, 1776, when many of the delegates signed the Declaration of Independence, Bartlett was the second to sign, following John Hancock, the President of Congress. Bartlett returned to New Hampshire in December 1776 and declined another term in Congress. Instead, he joined the militia as a doctor under General John Stark. At the Battle of Bennington in August 1777, he cared for wounded soldiers.

In 1778, Bartlett was named to a legislative committee in New Hampshire to consider the adoption of the Articles of Confederation. Bartlett reluctantly agreed to again join the Continental Congress in Philadelphia, where he signed the Articles of Confederation on behalf of New Hampshire and then returned home.

In 1779, Bartlett served as a judge on the Court of Common Pleas and as a member of the State Executive Council. Bartlett was elected to the New Hampshire State Legislature and named a delegate to the state's constitutional convention.

Despite not being a lawyer, Bartlett was appointed a justice on the State Superior Court in 1781. In 1782, he was appointed to the New Hampshire Supreme Court. In 1784, he presided over the inaugural session of the new state legislature. In 1788, Bartlett was named Chief Justice of the New Hampshire Supreme Court and was a delegate, and part-time chairman, of the state's convention to adopt the U.S. Constitution. Bartlett supported ratification, which occurred June 21, 1788. The legislature then named Bartlett as one of the state's first Senators, but Bartlett declined, his wife had failing health and passed away on July 14, 1789.

In 1790, Bartlett was selected as the Chief Executive of New Hampshire ("governor") under the new state constitution. He was reelected three times. In 1792, he was the state's first popularly elected governor. He started the New

Grave of Dr. Josiah Bartlett

DR. JOSIAH BARTLETT (1729–1795)

Hampshire Medical Society, and upon his retirement as governor, became the society's first president.

Less than a year after his final term as governor, Bartlett suffered a stroke on May 19, 1795, and died in Kingston at age 65. He was buried next to his wife in the family sarcophagus at the Congregationalist Church in Kingston (now Plains Cemetery).

Bartlett's son of the same name (1768–1838) served in the US House of Representatives in the Twelfth Congress (1811–1813). A distant relative, Roscoe Gardner Bartlett also served as a Congressman more recently (1993–2013).

The town of Bartlett, New Hampshire, is named after Josiah. Relatives still live in the home at 156 Main Street in Kingston, now a historic landmark. A bronze statue of Bartlett stands in the town square in Amesbury, Massachusetts, and his portrait hands in the New Hampshire State House in Concord. It was drawn from the original by John Trumbull. Bartlett's name dons an elementary school, and he is the subject of a historical marker on New Hampshire Route 111 in Kingston. The Bartlett School operated in Amesbury, Massachusetts, and is now known as the Bartlett Museum, a nonprofit corporation.

The main character in the NBC drama series *The West Wing* was President Josiah Bartlet. Though a fictional character with a slightly different spelling, this Josiah played by Martin Sheen claimed lineage to the signer of the Declaration of Independence.

John Wentworth Jr.
(1745–1787)

New Hampshire Scion

Buried at Pine Hill Cemetery,
Dover, New Hampshire.

Continental Congress • Articles of Confederation

John Wentworth Jr. was an attorney from a famous New Hampshire family. As a member of the Continental Congress from 1778 until 1779, he was a signer of the Articles of Confederation on behalf of New Hampshire.

Wentworth was born on July 17, 1745, near the Salmon Falls River at Somersworth, Strafford County, New Hampshire, the son of Judge John Wentworth and Joanna (née Gilman) Wentworth, a descendant of "Elder" William Wentworth who emigrated to America in the mid-1600s and had blood ties to King Edward VI of England and Sir Thomas Wentworth, the Earl of Strafford, for whom Strafford County, New Hampshire, was named. Two other John Wentworths were descendants of "Elder" including John Wentworth (1672–1730), a lieutenant governor of New Hampshire, and Sir John Wentworth (1737–1820), the last colonial governor of New Hampshire, and a first cousin once removed to the signer.

Wentworth was tutored privately and then entered Harvard College, where he graduated in 1768. He then began studying law in Dover, New Hampshire. He was admitted to the New Hampshire bar in 1771, but did not open a law practice. Instead, Governor John Wentworth appointed him as the register of probate for Strafford County from 1773 until his death.

On January 1, 1774, siding with the revolutionaries, Wentworth was named to the New Hampshire Committee of Correspondence against the wishes of

JOHN WENTWORTH JR. (1745–1787)

his family. This put him at odds with the governor and other Loyalist family members. It was the various Committees of Correspondence that agreed to call for a Continental Congress.

On May 11, 1775, the New Hampshire Provincial Congress held a Convention of Deputies at Exeter, New Hampshire, of which young Wentworth, not yet thirty, was the chair. This committee elected John Langdon and John Sullivan to the First Continental Congress.

From 1776 through 1780, Wentworth, representing Dover, was elected to the New Hampshire House of Representatives, which succeeded the colonial government during the Revolution. In 1777, Wentworth was also named to the New Hampshire Committee of Safety.

On March 14, 1778, Wentworth was elected to the Continental Congress, still meeting in York, Pennsylvania, after the authoring of the Articles of Confederation. Wentworth attended the Congress from May 30 to June 18, 1778, and then affixed his signature on behalf of New Hampshire on July 9, 1778. A letter from Josiah Bartlett, New Hampshire Congressman, to Meshech Weare, the President of New Hampshire, on July 11, 1778, stated, "Mr. Wentworth had a fever at York Town; it was pretty bad. I tarried with him for four days after the Congress adjourned; left him better Thursday the 2nd instant; have not heard from him since; hope he will be here the beginning of the week."

On August 18, 1778, Bartlett wrote to William Whipple, "Mr. Wentworth is in town but does not attend public business." However, Wentworth was re-elected to Congress the next day on August 19, 1778.

York Courthouse where the Continental Congress approved the Articles of Confederation.

The Congress at York

The following month, on September 8, 1778, Bartlett again wrote to Weare: "I have Reced [received] a Copy of the appointment of Delegates to attend Congress the first of November next, and I must beg leave inform you That I can by no means attend Congress after the last of october [sic] next. By reason of Mr. Wentworth's Sickness I have not Recd. the least assistance from him, and am obliged to attend so Closely to public business without any interval of Relaxation, that it will be necessary for my Constitution of body and mind to be relieved then, if I am able to hold out till that time."

Grave of John Wentworth Jr.

JOHN WENTWORTH JR. (1745–1787)

It appears that Wentworth did not attend the Congress again. On April 3, 1779, Nathaniel Peabody and Woodbury Langdon were elected to the Congress in place of Bartlett and Wentworth, who had resigned. Rather, Wentworth remained in the New Hampshire House of Representatives. In 1781, he replaced his father as a member of the state executive council, in support of Meshech Weare. He was also a member of the New Hampshire Committee of Safety.

In 1783, Wentworth was elected to the New Hampshire Senate and left the executive council. He served through 1786.

Wentworth died at age 41 on January 10, 1787, at Dover, New Hampshire. He was interred at Pine Hill Cemetery in Dover.

John Collins
(1717–1795)

Rhode Island Representative

Buried at Collins Burial Ground,
Newport, Rhode Island.

Articles of Confederation

John Collins was the third governor of Rhode Island, a Continental Congressman, and a signer of the Articles of Confederation. He is credited with casting the deciding vote in Rhode Island to adopt the U.S. Constitution.

John Collins was born in Newport, Rhode Island, on June 8, 1717, the son of Samuel and Elizabeth Collins. He was a businessman and merchant by trade, selling merchandise in Newport that he had acquired through trade as far away as the Mississippi River. He married Mary Avery, the daughter of John Avery of Boston, and the couple had a son also named John Collins and a daughter Abigail.

During the War of Independence, Collins was sent by Rhode Island to the Continental Congress where he served from 1778 to 1780 and again from 1782 to 1783. Collins was involved in activities regarding the army, navy, and finance.

After the war, Collins was elected Governor of Rhode Island, serving from 1786 to 1790. An article in *The Universal Asylum* magazine from June 1790 related the closeness of Collins and Benjamin Franklin. The article stated:

> John Collins was one of Franklin's most intimate acquaintance. This was a boy who was very fond of reading. With him, Franklin

often disputed on various subjects. Like most young disputants, they were very warm and very desirous of consulting each other. One subject was started, which produced a longer discussion than usual. It was respecting the propriety of educating the female sex, and their abilities for acquiring knowledge. Collins endeavored to show, that they were naturally unequal to the talk of study and that a learned education was improper for them. Franklin supported the opposite opinion, with much warmth, though he was occasionally staggered, more by the greater fluency of his adversary, than by the strength of his arguments.

After the U.S. Constitution was drafted in Philadelphia in 1787, it was sent to the 13 states to be ratified. Each state had to decide whether or not to hold a state convention and then proceed to vote. Rhode Island lagged the other colonies in approving the Constitution, holding out for a Bill of Rights. During this time, Rhode Island was in effect an independent nation with Collins as its head of state. The state remained deeply divided even after the Bill of Rights was introduced, but Collins called for a vote for a convention anyway. In the end, he was the one to cast the deciding vote that called for a state convention in Rhode Island. Without his vote, Rhode Island would not have adopted the Constitution.

There is no known portrait of John Collins. This image is of the historic Colony House in Newport, Rhode Island, which was the seat of government in colonial times.

Following the ratification of the Constitution, Collins was nominated for a seat in the First Congress, but he refused it even though he was elected. Collins wife, Mary, had died in 1788 at the age of 53. Collins also left the governorship in 1790.

John Collins died in Newport on March 4, 1795, at the age of 78. He was laid to rest in the Collins family burial ground on their Newport, Rhode Island estate, "Brenton Neck." By 1854, the burial ground had become so rundown that relatives restored the graves and stones. In 2002, the Sons of the American Revolution placed a stone next to his cenotaph that reads, "The Hon. John Collins, June 8, 1717–March 8, 1795, was elected to the Continental Congress and Served His Country in that Capacity from 1778–1783. He was Then

The grave of John Collins at the Collins Burial Ground, Newport, Rhode Island (photo by Lawrence Knorr).

JOHN COLLINS (1717–1795)

Elected Rhode Island's 3rd Governor, Further Serving His State and Country in that Capacity from 1786 to 1790. Gov. Collins Cast the Deciding Vote Calling for an Assembly, Which When Convened Voted for Rhode Island to Enter the Union of States."

Abigail Collins, the daughter of John and Mary, married John Warren, a surgeon in the Continental Army and founder of Harvard Medical School. Warren was the younger brother of Dr. Joseph Warren. Collins' grandson, John Collins Covell (1823–1887) was a principal of the Virginia and West Virginia schools for the deaf and blind. Collins' great-great-grandson, Collins Lawton Balch (1834–1910) was a successful businessman and merchant in Rhode Island.

The Rhode Island Society of the Sons of the American Revolution holds an annual observance of Rhode Island Independence Day every May 4th at Collins' grave.

Samuel Holten
(1738 – 1816)

Physician Continental Congressman

Buried at Holton Cemetery,
Danvers, Massachusetts.

Continental Congress • Articles of Confederation • U.S. Congress

Samuel Holten was a physician from Salem Village (now Danvers), Massachusetts, who became a long-serving Continental Congressman who signed the Articles of Confederation. He also served in several state positions, including nearly twenty years as a local judge. He was briefly a member of the US House of Representatives in the early republic.

Holten was born on June 9, 1738, in Salem Village, Massachusetts, the son of Samuel Holten, Sr., and Hannah (née Gardner) Holten, who was a member of the famous Gardner family of the colony. Holten was descended from his great-grandfather, Joseph Houlton, from Bedfordshire, England, who came to the colonies with his wife, Sarah Ingersoll, of the Connecticut Ingersolls.

Holten attended local grammar schools and then studied medicine under Dr. Jonathan Prince. Upon his certification as a physician, Holten opened a practice in Gloucester, Massachusetts. In 1758, he married Mary Warner with whom he had two daughters.

The young doctor and his family soon returned to Salem Village, where he continued his practice and became very popular. In 1768, he was appointed to the General Court.

As tensions began to mount with England, Holten was elected to the Massachusetts Provincial Congress from 1774 to 1775. He was next a member of the Massachusetts Committee of Safety.

SAMUEL HOLTEN (1738–1816)

Judge Samuel Holten

Holten was appointed to the Continental Congress on February 10, 1778, to replace John Adams, who had been sent to France. He arrived in York, Pennsylvania, in time to sign the Articles of Confederation on behalf of Massachusetts on March 10, 1778. He was then reelected on October 15, 1778, serving with Samuel Adams, John Hancock, Elbridge Gerry, Francis Dana, James Lovell, and Timothy Edwards through 1779.

In the 1840s, historian Mellen Chamberlain had the opportunity to make notes from Dr. Holten's diary used during the Continental Congress. Some of the entries follow:

> 1778, June 23. Attended in Congress, and the chief of the day was taken up in disputes on the articles of confederation [sic].
>
> 1778, July 11. This day was the first time that I took any part in the debates in Congress. We have accounts of the arrival of a French Fleet in the Delaware. 12 Ships of the line & 4 Frigates.
>
> 1778, July 14. I let the Hon. Samuel Adams Esqr. have 400.00, of which he is to pay to James Otis (a minor) being my part of what the delegates of our state have agreed to advance to sd [said] minr. & Mr. Adams is to write to his friends & procure the money, & account with me for the same.
>
> 1778, Oct. 7. Met a committee on this evening on General [Benedict] Arnold's accounts.
>
> 1778, Oct. 15. A manifesto or Proclamation from Commr. of the British king appeared in the papers of the day, offering a Gen. Pardon, but I believe there is but few people here want their pardon.

> 1778, Dec. 14. Monday. There was a grand ball at the City Tavern this evening, given by a number of French gentlemen of distinction. I had a card sent me, but declined attending. I think it is not a proper time to attend balls when the country is in such great distress.

Holten was again appointed to the Continental Congress on November 18, 1779, continuing his service until he resigned on July 29, 1780, when he began two years of service in the Massachusetts Senate and the Massachusetts Governor's Council, a role he held off and on for fourteen years. He was again appointed to the Continental Congress on October 4, 1780, but did not attend any sessions in 1781.

On October 4, 1782, Holten was again appointed to the Continental Congress. He served through November 1, 1783. The following year, in addition to his state senate seat, he returned for another term, serving through October 1785. On August 17, 1785, Holten was elected the president pro tempore of the Continental Congress, when President Richard Henry Lee was unable to preside. Holten ran the Congress until the new president, John Hancock was able to attend. During this time, he, Elbridge Gerry, and Rufus King blocked the call for a convention to reform the Articles of Confederation, believing not enough time had passed to judge the effectiveness of it.

In 1786, Holton continued in his state senate seat and was again elected to the Continental Congress, serving until August 9, 1787. Holten changed his mind about the Articles and participated in the Constitutional Convention in Philadelphia in 1787. However, he did not approve of its final form, with a strong central government and lacking a Bill of Rights. He opposed ratification of the Constitution. Meanwhile, he also served in the state House of Representatives and was in attendance at the Massachusetts ratifying convention in 1788. There, he allied himself with the anti-Federalists and opposed ratification. Unfortunately, Holten became ill at this time and was unable to have the desired impact.

As the Federalists took control of the Federal Government, Holten seemed finished with national politics. He sat in the state Senate in 1789 and 1790 and on the Governor's Council. He twice failed to be elected to the US House of Representatives in 1788 and 1790. He also lost a bid to be appointed to the US Senate in 1790.

In 1792, Holten finally won his seat in the US House of Representatives, serving in the Third Congress, from 1793 to 1795, representing Massachusetts' First District.

SAMUEL HOLTEN (1738-1816)

Following his single term, Holten returned to Danvers and served as a judge on the Essex County Probate Court for nearly twenty years, from 1796 to 1815.

In his 77th year, with his health failing, Holten resigned his judgeship in 1815. He died soon after on January 2, 1816. He was buried in the Holten Family Cemetery in Danvers, Massachusetts. His large tombstone reads:

> Erected to the Memory of the Hon. Samuel Holten, Who Died Jan. 2, 1716, aged 78 years. He Sustained Various Offices of Trust, Under the State Government, and That of the Union, With Ability and Integrity, to the Almost Unanimous Acceptance of His Constituents.

The Judge Samuel Holten House remains a historic site in Danvers, Massachusetts.

The grave of Samuel Holten

Titus Hosmer
(1736–1780)

Connecticut Lawyer

Buried at Mortimer Cemetery,
Middletown, Connecticut.

Articles of Confederation

Titus Hosmer was a lawyer and leading politician from Connecticut who was thrice elected to the Continental Congress but only attended briefly for one of his terms. He signed the Articles of Confederation.

Titus Hosmer was born in West Hartford, Connecticut, in either 1736 or 1737, the son of Captain Stephen Hosmer and his wife, Deliverance (née Graves) Hosmer. Titus was the third son among eight children. The Hosmer family originated in Kent, England. An ancestor emigrated to Newtown, Massachusetts, in the early 1600s.

Young Titus was educated in local schools as a youth. He then attended Yale College in New Haven. In a speech in 1850, scholar David Dudley said of Hosmer, "While at Yale College, he was distinguished for the acquisition of sciences, excelled in the languages and fine writing. Being graduated in 1757, [he] settled in Middletown about 1760."

Shortly after graduation, Hosmer was admitted to the Connecticut colonial bar and began practicing law in Middletown. The following year, he married Lydia Lord, and the two began a family. Throughout the 1760s, Hosmer gradually increased in stature as a lawyer, working on important estates and dealing with the disposition of debts and creditors. Meanwhile, seven children were born during these years, including Stephen Titus Hosmer, who would later

TITUS HOSMER (1736–1780)

Titus Hosmer

become chief justice of the Connecticut Supreme Court, and Hezekiah Lord Hosmer, who became a U. S. representative for the state of New York.

As Hosmer became better known, he entered politics, first in local offices such as justice of the peace. Following the collapse of royal rule in Connecticut, Hosmer was elected to the Connecticut General Assembly in October 1773, holding this seat until 1778. A strong advocate for independence, Hosmer was elected speaker of the state House of Representatives in 1777. He also served as a member of the local Committee of Safety.

As an emerging leader in the Connecticut assembly, Hosmer was elected to the Continental Congress three times: first on November 3, 1774; next on October 12, 1775; and again, on October 11, 1777. However, he only attended in 1778, including when the Congress was in York, Pennsylvania. There is no record as to why he did not attend but a few months, but some have speculated he may have been in poor health. Another possibility is the size of his family and the need to be close to home. Yet another is his attention to duty in the Connecticut Assembly, where he was the speaker and then a state senator beginning in May 1778. Regardless, records show he did attend sessions from June 23 to September 10, 1778, when he returned home.

Hosmer could have been a signer of the Continental Association, and the Declaration of Independence had he been in Philadelphia to fulfill his elected duties. However, it seems he had competing duties and opted to lead locally until the opportunity arose to sign the first constitution for the nation, the Articles of Confederation. The document had been negotiated the preceding two years and was reviewed by Congress during Hosmer's tenure. Starting on July 9, 1778, in Philadelphia, the delegates began to sign the document, after which it went to the states for ratification. Hosmer was one of five Connecticut delegates to sign. The others included Roger Sherman, Samuel Huntington, Oliver Wolcott, and Andrew Adams.

According to two letters written to Connecticut governor Johnathan Trumbull following the signing of the Articles, there was not much to do in Congress. Hosmer complained of the lack of progress with settling the debts of the army. He suggested the idleness was depressing him, and he worried about the continuing disagreements with the Southern States, suggesting the union might not hold together. He also reported on the behavior of some in Congress. Wrote Hosmer,

> ... When we are assembled, several gentlemen have such a knack at starting questions of order, raising debates upon critical, captious, and trifling amendments, protracting them by long speeches, by postponing, calling for the previous question, and other arts, that it is almost impossible to get an important question decided at one sitting; and if it is put over to another day, the field is open to be gone over again, precious time is lost, and the public business left undone ...

Upon returning to Connecticut, Hosmer continued as a state senator and was then elected as a judge on the maritime Court of Appeals in January 1780. Unfortunately, Hosmer was not able to take the seat. He died suddenly on August 4, 1780. Obituaries did not mention a cause of death despite his young age of only 43 or 44. He was laid to rest in Mortimer Cemetery in Middletown, Connecticut. Diplomat and poet Joel Barlow wrote a moving tribute to Hosmer entitled "An Elegy." Wrote Barlow:

> Come to my soul, O shade of Hosmer, come Tho' doubting senates ask thy aid in vain; Attend the drooping virtues round thy tomb, And hear a while the orphan'd Muse complain.

TITUS HOSMER (1736–1780)

Lydia followed Titus to the grave in 1798 and is buried next to him. Besides the sons mentioned previously, a grandson, also named Hezekiah Lord Hosmer, was an accomplished author and the first Chief Justice of the Montana Territory.

Titus Hosmer's grave.

Appendix A
List of Delegates to York

Delegate/Officer	Role	State	Lancaster?	York Arrival	Signed Articles?
Laurens, Henry	President	SC	Yes	9/30/1777	Yes
Thomson, Charles	Secretary	PA	Yes	9/30/1777	
Dyer, Eliphalet	Delegate	CT	Yes	9/30/1777	
Williams, William	Delegate	CT	Yes	9/30/1777	
Brownson, Nathan	Delegate	GA	Yes	9/30/1777	
Walton, George	Delegate	GA	Yes	9/30/1777	Yes
Carroll, Charles	Delegate	MD	Yes	9/30/1777	
Adams, John	Delegate	MA	Yes	9/30/1777	
Adams, Samuel	Delegate	MA	Yes	9/30/1777	Yes
Gerry, Elbridge	Delegate	MA	Yes	9/30/1777	Yes
Folsom, Nathaniel	Delegate	NH	Yes	9/30/1777	
Witherspoon, John	Delegate	NJ		9/30/1777	Yes
Duane, James	Delegate	NY	Yes	9/30/1777	Yes
Duer, William	Delegate	NY	Yes	9/30/1777	Yes
Harnett, Cornelius	Delegate	NC	Yes	9/30/1777	Yes
Penn, John	Delegate	NC	Yes	9/30/1777	Yes
Morris, Robert	Delegate	PA	Yes	9/30/1777	Yes
Roberdeau, Daniel	Delegate	PA	Yes	9/30/1777	Yes
Heyward, Thomas Jr.	Delegate	SC	Yes	9/30/1777	Yes
Middleton, Arthur	Delegate	SC	Yes	9/30/1777	
Harrison, Benjamin	Delegate	VA	Yes	9/30/1777	
Jones, Joseph	Delegate	VA	Yes	9/30/1777	
Lee, Francis Lightfoot	Delegate	VA	Yes	9/30/1777	Yes
Lee, Richard Henry	Delegate	VA	Yes	9/30/1777	Yes
Hancock, John	President	MA	Yes	10/1/1777	Yes
Law, Richard	Delegate	CT	Yes	10/1/1777	
Chase, Samuel	Delegate	MD	Yes	10/1/1777	
Lovell, James	Delegate	MA	Yes	10/1/1777	Yes
Burke, Thoms	Delegate	NC	Yes	10/1/1777	
Marchant, Henry	Delegate	RI	Yes	10/1/1777	Yes
Smith, William	Delegate	MD		10/4/1777	

Appendix A: List of Delegates to York

Delegate/Officer	Role	State	Lancaster?	York Arrival	Signed Articles?
Elmer, Jonathan	Delegate	NJ		10/14/1777	
Harvie, John	Delegate	VA		10/16/1777	Yes
Rumsey, Benjamin	Delegate	MD		11/1/1777	
Clingan, William	Delegate	PA		11/1/1777	Yes
Ellery, William	Delegate	RI		11/7/1777	Yes
Langworthy, Edward	Delegate	GA		11/17/1777	Yes
Wood, Joseph	Delegate	GA		11/17/1777	
Lewis, Francis	Delegate	NY		12/5/1777	Yes
Frost, George	Delegate	NH		12/8/1777	
Clark, Abraham	Delegate	NJ		12/11/1777	
Smith, James	Delegate	PA		12/16/1777	
Smith, Jonathan Bayard	Delegate	PA		12/18/1777	Yes
Dana, Francis	Delegate	MA		1/1/1778	Yes
McKean, Thomas	Delegate	DE		1/10/1778	Yes
Morris, Gouverneur	Delegate	NY		1/20/1778	Yes
Forbes, James	Delegate	MD		2/1/1778	
Henry, John Jr.	Delegate	MD		2/1/1778	
Scudder, Nathaniel	Delegate	NJ		2/9/1778	Yes
Huntington, Samuel	Delegate	CT		2/16/1778	Yes
Wolcott, Oliver	Delegate	CT		2/16/1778	Yes
Drayton, William Henry	Delegate	SC		3/30/1778	Yes
Reed, Joseph	Delegate	PA		4/6/1778	Yes
Adams, Thomas	Delegate	VA		4/16/1778	Yes
Banister, John	Delegate	VA		4/16/1778	Yes
Plater, George	Delegate	MD		4/18/1778	
Mathews, John	Delegate	SC		4/22/1778	Yes
Sherman, Roger	Delegate	CT		4/25/1778	Yes
Livingston, Philip	Delegate	NY		5/5/1778	
Hutson, Richard	Delegate	SC		5/13/1778	Yes
Bartlett, Josiah	Delegate	NH		5/21/1778	Yes
Wentworth, John	Delegate	NH		5/21/1778	Yes
Collins, John	Delegate	RI		6/20/1778	Yes
Holten, Samuel	Delegate	MA		6/22/1778	Yes
Hosmer, Titus	Delegate	CT		6/23/1778	Yes

Appendix B
The Articles of Confederation

To all to whom these Presents shall come, we, the undersigned Delegates of the States affixed to our Names send greeting. Whereas the Delegates of the United States of America in Congress assembled did on the fifteenth day of November in the year of our Lord One Thousand Seven Hundred and Seventy seven, and in the Second Year of the Independence of America agree to certain articles of Confederation and perpetual Union between the States of Newhampshire, Massachusetts-bay, Rhodeisland and Providence Plantations, Connecticut, New York, New Jersey, Pennsylvania, Delaware, Maryland, Virginia, North Carolina, South Carolina, and Georgia in the Words following, viz. "Articles of Confederation and perpetual Union between the States of Newhampshire, Massachusetts-bay, Rhodeisland and Providence Plantations, Connecticut, New York, New Jersey, Pennsylvania, Delaware, Maryland, Virginia, North Carolina, South Carolina, and Georgia.

Article I. The Stile of this confederacy shall be, "The United States of America."

Article II. Each state retains its sovereignty, freedom and independence, and every Power, Jurisdiction and right, which is not by this confederation expressly delegated to the United States, in Congress assembled.

Article III. The said states hereby severally enter into a firm league of friendship with each other, for their common defence, the security of their Liberties, and their mutual and general welfare, binding themselves to assist each other, against all force offered to, or attacks made upon them, or any of them, on account of religion, sovereignty, trade, or any other pretence whatever.

Article IV. The better to secure and perpetuate mutual friendship and intercourse among the people of the different states in this union, the free inhabitants of each of these states, paupers, vagabonds and fugitives from Justice excepted, shall be entitled to all privileges and immunities of free citizens in the several states; and the people of each state shall have free ingress and regress to and from any other state, and shall enjoy therein all the privileges of trade and commerce, subject to the same duties, impositions and restrictions as the inhabitants thereof respectively, provided that such restrictions shall not extend so far as to prevent the removal of property imported into any state, to any other State of which the Owner is an inhabitant; provided also that no imposition, duties or restriction shall be laid by any state, on the property of the united states, or either of them.

If any Person guilty of, or charged with, treason, felony, or other high misdemeanor in any state, shall flee from Justice, and be found in any of the united states, he shall upon demand of the Governor or executive power of the state from which he fled, be delivered up, and removed to the state having jurisdiction of his offence.

Full faith and credit shall be given in each of these states to the records, acts and judicial proceedings of the courts and magistrates of every other state.

Article V. For the more convenient management of the general interests of the united states, delegates shall be annually appointed in such manner as the legislature of each state shall direct, to meet in Congress on the first Monday in November, in every year, with a power reserved to each state to recall its delegates, or any of them, at any time within the year, and to send others in their stead, for the remainder of the Year.

No State shall be represented in Congress by less than two, nor by more than seven Members; and no person shall be capable of being delegate for more than three years, in any term of six years; nor shall any person, being a delegate, be capable of holding any office under the united states, for which he, or another for his benefit receives any salary, fees or emolument of any kind.

Each State shall maintain its own delegates in a meeting of the states, and while they act as members of the committee of the states.

In determining questions in the united states, in Congress assembled, each state shall have one vote.

Freedom of speech and debate in Congress shall not be impeached or questioned in any Court, or place out of Congress, and the members of congress shall be protected in their persons from arrests and imprisonments, during the time of their going to and from, and attendance on congress, except for treason, felony, or breach of the peace.

Article VI. No State, without the Consent of the united States, in congress assembled, shall send any embassy to, or receive any embassy from, or enter into any conferrence, agreement, alliance, or treaty, with any King prince or state; nor shall any person holding any office of profit or trust under the united states, or any of them, accept of any present, emolument, office, or title of any kind whatever, from any king, prince, or foreign state; nor shall the united states, in congress assembled, or any of them, grant any title of nobility.

No two or more states shall enter into any treaty, confederation, or alliance whatever between them, without the consent of the united states, in congress assembled, specifying accurately the purposes for which the same is to be entered into, and how long it shall continue.

No State shall lay any imposts or duties, which may interfere with any stipulations in treaties, entered into by the united States in congress assembled, with any king, prince, or State, in pursuance of any treaties already proposed by congress, to the courts of France and Spain.

No vessels of war shall be kept up in time of peace, by any state, except such number only, as shall be deemed necessary by the united states, in congress assembled, for the defence of such state, or its trade; nor shall any body of forces be kept up, by any state, in time of peace, except such number only as, in the judgment of the united states, in congress assembled, shall be deemed requisite to garrison the forts necessary for the defence of such state; but every state shall always keep up a well regulated and disciplined militia, sufficiently armed and accoutred, and shall provide and constantly have ready for use, in public stores, a due number of field pieces and tents, and a proper quantity of arms, ammunition, and camp equipage.

No State shall engage in any war without the consent of the united States in congress assembled, unless such State be actually invaded by enemies, or shall have received certain advice of a resolution being formed by some nation of Indians to invade such State, and the danger is so imminent as not to admit of a delay till the united states in congress assembled, can be consulted: nor shall any state grant commissions to any ships or vessels of war, nor letters of marque or reprisal, except it be after a declaration of war by the united states in congress assembled, and then only against the kingdom or State, and the subjects thereof, against which war has been so declared, and under such regulations as shall be established by the united states in congress assembled, unless such state be infested by pirates, in which case vessels of war may be fitted out for that occasion, and kept so long as the danger shall continue, or until the united states in congress assembled shall determine otherwise.

Article VII. When land forces are raised by any state, for the common defence, all officers of or under the rank of colonel, shall be appointed by the legislature of each state respectively by whom such forces shall be raised, or in such manner as such state shall direct, and all vacancies shall be filled up by the state which first made appointment.

Article VIII. All charges of war, and all other expenses that shall be incurred for the common defence or general welfare, and allowed by the united states in congress assembled, shall be defrayed out of a common treasury, which shall be supplied by the several states, in proportion to the value of all land within each state, granted to or surveyed for any Person, as such land and the buildings and improvements thereon shall be estimated, according to such mode as the united states, in congress assembled, shall, from time to time, direct and appoint. The taxes for paying that proportion shall be laid and levied by the authority and direction of the legislatures of the several states within the time agreed upon by the united states in congress assembled.

Article IX. The united states, in congress assembled, shall have the sole and exclusive right and power of determining on peace and war, except in the cases mentioned in the sixth article - of sending and receiving ambassadors - entering into treaties and alliances, provided that no treaty of commerce shall be made, whereby the legislative power of the respective states shall be restrained from imposing such imposts and duties on foreigners, as their own people are subjected to, or from prohibiting the exportation or importation of any species of goods or commodities whatsoever - of establishing rules for deciding, in all cases, what captures on land or water shall be legal, and in what manner prizes taken by land or naval forces in the service of the united States, shall be divided or appropriated - of granting letters of marque and reprisal in times of peace - appointing courts for the trial of piracies and felonies committed on the high seas; and establishing courts; for receiving and determining finally appeals in all cases of captures; provided that no member of congress shall be appointed a judge of any of the said courts.

The united states, in congress assembled, shall also be the last resort on appeal, in all disputes and differences now subsisting, or that hereafter may arise between two or more states concerning boundary, jurisdiction, or any other cause whatever; which authority shall always be exercised in the manner following. Whenever the legislative or executive authority, or lawful agent of any state in controversy with another, shall present a petition to congress, stating the matter in question, and praying for a hearing, notice thereof shall be given, by order of congress, to the legislative or executive authority of the other state in controversy, and a day assigned for the appearance of the parties by their lawful agents, who shall then be directed to appoint, by joint consent, commissioners or judges to constitute a court for hearing and determining the matter in question: but if they cannot agree, congress shall name three persons out of each of the united states, and from the list of such persons each party shall alternately strike out one, the petitioners beginning, until the number shall be reduced to thirteen; and from that number not less than seven, nor more than nine names, as congress shall direct, shall, in the presence of congress, be drawn out by lot, and the persons whose names shall be so drawn, or any five of them, shall be commissioners or judges, to hear and finally determine the controversy, so always as a major part of the judges, who shall hear the cause, shall agree in the determination: and if either party shall neglect to attend at the day appointed, without showing reasons which congress shall judge sufficient, or being present, shall refuse to strike, the congress shall proceed to nominate three persons out of each State, and the secretary of congress shall strike in behalf of such party absent or refusing; and the judgment and sentence of the court, to be appointed in the manner before prescribed, shall be final and conclusive; and if any of the parties shall refuse to submit to the authority of such court, or to appear or defend their claim or cause, the court shall nevertheless proceed to pronounce sentence, or judgment, which shall in like manner be final and decisive; the judgment or sentence and other proceedings being in either case transmitted to congress, and lodged among the acts of congress, for the security of the parties concerned: provided that every commissioner, before he sits in judgment, shall take an oath to be administered by one of the judges of the supreme or superior court of the State where the cause shall be tried, "well and truly to hear and determine the matter in question, according to the best of his judgment, without favour, affection, or hope of reward: "provided, also, that no State shall be deprived of territory for the benefit of the united states.

All controversies concerning the private right of soil claimed under different grants of two or more states, whose jurisdictions as they may respect such lands, and the states which passed such grants are adjusted, the said grants or either of them being at the same time claimed to have originated antecedent to such settlement of jurisdiction, shall, on the petition of either party to the congress of the united states, be finally determined, as near as may be, in the same manner as is before prescribed for deciding disputes respecting territorial jurisdiction between different states.

The united states, in congress assembled, shall also have the sole and exclusive right and power of regulating the alloy and value of coin struck by their own authority, or by that of the respective states - fixing the standard of weights and measures throughout the united states - regulating the trade and managing all affairs with the Indians, not members of any of the states; provided that the legislative right of any state, within its own limits, be not infringed or violated - establishing and regulating post-offices from one state to another, throughout all the united states, and exacting such postage on the papers passing through the same, as may be requisite to defray the expenses of the said office - appointing all officers of the land forces in the service of the united States, excepting regimental officers - appointing all the officers of the naval forces, and commissioning all officers whatever in the service of the united states; making rules for the government and regulation of the said land and naval forces, and directing their operations.

The united States, in congress assembled, shall have authority to appoint a committee, to sit in the recess of congress, to be denominated, "A Committee of the States," and to consist of one delegate from each State; and to appoint such other committees and civil officers as may be necessary for managing the general affairs of the united states under their direction - to appoint one of their number to preside; provided that no person be allowed to serve in the office of president more than one year in any term of three years; to ascertain the necessary sums of money to be raised for the service of the united states, and to appropriate and apply the same for defraying the public expenses; to borrow money or emit bills on the credit of the united states, transmitting every half year to the respective states an account of the sums of money so borrowed or emitted, - to build and equip a navy - to agree upon the number of land forces, and to make requisitions from each state for its quota, in proportion to the number of white inhabitants in such state, which requisition shall be binding; and thereupon the legislature of each state shall appoint the regimental officers, raise the men, and clothe, arm, and equip them, in a soldier-like manner, at the expense of the united states; and the officers and men so clothed, armed, and equipped, shall march to the place appointed, and within the time agreed on by the united states, in congress assembled; but if the united states, in congress assembled, shall, on consideration of circumstances, judge proper that any state should not raise men, or should raise a smaller number than its quota, and that any other state should raise a greater number of men than the quota thereof, such extra number shall be raised, officered, clothed, armed, and equipped in the same manner as the quota of such state, unless the legislature of such state shall judge that such extra number cannot be safely spared out of the same, in which case they shall raise, officer, clothe, arm, and equip, as many of such extra number as they judge can be safely spared. And the officers and men so clothed, armed, and equipped, shall march to the place appointed, and within the time agreed on by the united states in congress assembled.

The united states, in congress assembled, shall never engage in a war, nor grant letters of marque and reprisal in time of peace, nor enter into any treaties or alliances, nor coin money, nor regulate the value thereof nor ascertain the sums and expenses necessary for the defence and welfare of the united states, or any of them, nor emit bills, nor borrow money on the credit of the united states, nor appropriate money, nor agree upon the number of vessels of war to be built or purchased, or the number of land or sea forces to be raised, nor appoint a commander in chief of the army or navy, unless nine states assent to the same, nor shall a question on any other point, except for adjourning from day to day, be determined, unless by the votes of a majority of the united states in congress assembled.

The congress of the united states shall have power to adjourn to any time within the year, and to any place within the united states, so that no period of adjournment be for a longer duration than the space of six Months, and shall publish the Journal of their proceedings monthly, except such parts thereof relating to treaties, alliances, or military operations, as in their judgment require secrecy; and the yeas and nays of the delegates of each State, on any question, shall be entered on the Journal, when it is desired by any delegate; and the delegates of a

State, or any of them, at his or their request, shall be furnished with a transcript of the said Journal, except such parts as are above excepted, to lay before the legislatures of the several states.

Article X. The committee of the states, or any nine of them, shall be authorized to execute, in the recess of congress, such of the powers of congress as the united states, in congress assembled, by the consent of nine states, shall, from time to time, think expedient to vest them with; provided that no power be delegated to the said committee, for the exercise of which, by the articles of confederation, the voice of nine states, in the congress of the united states assembled, is requisite.

Article XI. Canada acceding to this confederation, and joining in the measures of the united states, shall be admitted into, and entitled to all the advantages of this union: but no other colony shall be admitted into the same, unless such admission be agreed to by nine states.

Article XII. All bills of credit emitted, monies borrowed, and debts contracted by or under the authority of congress, before the assembling of the united states, in pursuance of the present confederation, shall be deemed and considered as a charge against the united States, for payment and satisfaction whereof the said united states and the public faith are hereby solemnly pledged.

Article XIII. Every State shall abide by the determinations of the united states, in congress assembled, on all questions which by this confederation are submitted to them. And the Articles of this confederation shall be inviolably observed by every state, and the union shall be perpetual; nor shall any alteration at any time hereafter be made in any of them, unless such alteration be agreed to in a congress of the united states, and be afterwards con-firmed by the legislatures of every state.

And Whereas it hath pleased the Great Governor of the World to incline the hearts of the legislatures we respectively represent in congress, to approve of, and to authorize us to ratify the said articles of confederation and perpetual union, Know Ye, that we, the undersigned delegates, by virtue of the power and authority to us given for that purpose, do, by these presents, in the name and in behalf of our respective constituents, fully and entirely ratify and confirm each and every of the said articles of confederation and perpetual union, and all and singular the matters and things therein contained. And we do further solemnly plight and engage the faith of our respective constituents, that they shall abide by the determinations of the united states in congress assembled, on all questions, which by the said confederation are submitted to them. And that the articles thereof shall be inviolably observed by the states we respectively represent, and that the union shall be perpetual. In Witness whereof, we have hereunto set our hands, in Congress. Done at Philadelphia, in the State of Pennsylvania, the ninth Day of July, in the Year of our Lord one Thousand seven Hundred and Seventy eight, and in the third year of the Independence of America.

Sources

Books, Magazines, Journals, Files:

Alexander, Edward P. *Revolutionary Conservative: James Duane of New York*. New York: Ams Press, 1978.

Anthony, Katharine Susan. *First Lady of the Revolution; The Life of Mercy Otis Warren*. Port Washington, N.Y.: Kennikat Press, 1972.

Appleby, Joyce. *Inheriting the Revolution: The First Generation of Americans*. Cambridge, Massachusetts: Harvard University Press, 2000.

Atkinson, Rick. *The British Are Coming: The War for America, Lexington to Princeton, 1775–1777*. New York: Henry Holt & Co. 2019.

Bordewich, Fergus M. *The First Congress: How James Madison, George Washington, and a Group of Extraordinary Men Invented the Government*. New York: Simon and Schuster Paperbacks, 2016.

Boudreau, George W. *Independence: A Guide to Historic Philadelphia*. Yardley, Pennsylvania: Westholme Publishing, LLC. 2012.

Bowen, Catherine Drinker. *Miracle at Philadelphia: The Story of the Constitutional Convention May to September 1787*. Boston, Massachusetts: Little, Brown & Company, 1966.

Breen, T.H, *George Washington's Journey: The President Forges a New Nation*. New York: Simon & Schuster. 2016.

Brookhiser, Richard. *Gentleman Revolutionary: Gouverneur Morris The Rake Who Wrote the Constitution*. New York: Free Press, 2003.

———. *John Marshall: The Man Who Made the Supreme Court*. New York: Basic Books. 2018.

Brush, Edward Hale. *Rufus King and His Times*. New York: N.L. Brown, 1926.

Chadwick, Bruce. I Am Murdered: *George Wythe, Thomas Jefferson, and the Killing That Shocked a New Nation*. Hoboken, New Jersey: John Wiley & Sons, 2009.

Chambers, II, John Whiteclay. *The Oxford Companion to American Military History*. Oxford: Oxford University Press, 1999.

Commager, Henry Steele & Richard B. Morris. *The Spirit of 'Seventy-Six: The Story of the American Revolution as Told by Participants*. New York: Harper & Rowe, 1967.

Cole, Ryan. *Light-Horse Harry Lee: The Rise and Fall of a Revolutionary Hero*. Washington, D.C.: Regnery History. 2019.

Conlin, Joseph R. *The Morrow Book of Quotations in American History*. New York: William Morrow and Company, Inc., 1984.

Daniels, Jonathan. *Ordeal of Ambition*. Garden City, New York: Doubleday & Company, Inc., 1970.

Dann, John C. *The Revolution Remembered: Eyewitness Accounts of the War for Independence*. Chicago: University of Chicago Press, 1980.

DeRose, Chris. *Founding Rivals: Madison vs. Monroe: The Bill of Rights and the Election that Saved a Nation*. New York: MJF Books, 2011.

Drury, Bob & Tom Clavin. *Valley Forge*. New York: Simon & Schuster. 2018.

Ellis, Joseph J. *Revolutionary Summer: The Birth of American Independence*. New York: Alfred A. Knopf, 2013.

———. *The Quartet: Orchestrating the Second American Revolution, 1783–1789*. New York: Alfred A. Knopf, 2015.

———. *His Excellency: George Washington*. New York: Alfred A. Knopf, 2004.

Flexner, James Thomas. *George Washington in the American Revolution, 1775–1783*. Boston: Little, Brown & Company, 1967.

Flower, Lenore Embick. "Visit of President George Washington to Carlisle, 1794." Carlisle, Pennsylvania: The Hamilton Library and Cumberland County Historical Society, 1932.

Gerlach, Don R. *Proud Patriot: Philip Schuyler and the War of Independence, 1775–1783*. Syracuse, N.Y.: Syracuse University Press, 1987.

Goodrich, Charles A. *Lives of the Signers of the Declaration of Independence*. Charlotteville, N.Y.: SamHar Press, 1976.

Griffith, IV, William R. *The Battle of Lake George: England's First Triumph in the French and Indian War*. Charleston, South Carolina: The History Press, 2016.

Grossman, Mark. *Encyclopedia of the Continental Congress*. Armenia, New York: Grey House Publishing, 2015.

Hamilton, Edward P. *Fort Ticonderoga: Key to a Continent*. Boston: Little, Brown & Company, 1964.

Isenberg, Nancy. *Fallen Founder: The Life of Aaron Burr*. New York: Penguin Group, 2007.

Kennedy, Roger G. *Burr, Hamilton, and Jefferson: A Study in Character*. New York: Oxford University Press, 1999.

Kiernan, Denise & Joseph D'Agnese. *Signing Their Lives Away: The Fame and Misfortune of the Men Who Signed the Declaration of Independence*. Philadelphia: Quirk Books, 2008.

———. *Signing Their Rights Away: The Fame and Misfortune of the Men Who Signed the United States Constitution*. Philadelphia: Quirk Books, 2011.

Klarman, Michael J. *The Framers' Coup: The Making of the United States Constitution*. New York: Oxford University Press, 2016.

Langguth, A. J. *Patriots*. New York: Simon and Schuster, 1988.

Larson, Edward J. *A Magnificent Catastrophe*. New York: Free Press, 2007.

Lee, Mike. Written *Out of History: The Forgotten Founders Who Fought Big Government*. New York: Penguin Books, 2017.

Lewis, James E., Jr., *The Burr Conspiracy: Uncovering the Story of an Early American Crisis*, Princeton: Princeton University Press, 2017.

Lockridge, Ross Franklin. *The Harrisons*. 1941.

Lomask, Milton. *Aaron Burr: The Years from Princeton to Vice President, 1756–1805*. New York: Farrar Straus Giroux, 1979.

Lossing, Benson J. *Pictorial Field Book of the Revolution*. New York: Harper Brothers. 1851.

Maier, Pauline. *American Scripture: Making the Declaration of Independence*. New York: Alfred A. Knopf, Inc., 1997.
McCullough, David. *John Adams*. New York: Simon & Schuster, 2002.
Meltzer, Brad & Josh Mensch. *The First Conspiracy: The Secret Plot to Kill George Washington*. New York: Flat Iron Books. 2018.
Middlekauff, Robert. *The Glorious Cause: The American Revolution, 1763–1789*. Oxford: Oxford University Press, 2005.
Miller, Jr., Arthur P. & Marjorie L. Miller. *Pennsylvania Battlefields and Military Landmarks*. Mechanicsburg, Pennsylvania: Stackpole Books, 2000.
Millett, Allan R. & Peter Maslowski. *For the Common Defense: A Military History of the United States of America*. New York: The Free Press, 1984.
Moore, Charles. *The Family Life of George Washington*. New York: Houghton Mifflin, 1926.
Nagel, Paul C. *The Lees of Virginia: Seven Generations of an American Family*. Oxford: Oxford University Press, 1990.
O'Connell, Robert L. *Revolutionary: George Washington at War*. New York: Random House. 2019.
Racove, Jack N. *Revolutionaries: A New History of the Invention of America*. New York: Houghton Mifflin Harcourt, 2011.
Raphael, Ray. *Founding Myths: Stories That Hide Our Patriotic Past*. New York: MJF Books, 2004.
Rossiter, Clinton. *1787 The Grand Convention*. New York: The Macmillan Company, 1966.
Seymour, Joseph. *The Pennsylvania Associators, 1747–1777*. Yardley, Pennsylvania: Westholme Publishing, LLC. 2012.
Schweikart, Larry & Michael Allen. *A Patriot's History of the United States from Columbus's Great Discovery to the War on Terror*. New York: Penguin, 2004.
Sharp, Arthur G. *Not Your Father's Founders*. Avon, Massachusetts: Adams Media, 2012.
Stahr, Walter. *John Jay: Founding Father*. New York: Diversion Books, 2017.
Taafee, Stephen R. *The Philadelphia Campaign, 1777–1778*. Lawrence, Kansas: University of Kansas Press, 2003.
Tinkcom, Harry Marlin, *The Republicans and the Federalists in Pennsylvania, 1790–1801*. Harrisburg, Pennsylvania: Pennsylvania Historical and Museum Commission. 1950.
Ward, Matthew C. *Breaking the Backcountry: The Seven Years' War in Virginia and Pennsylvania, 1754–1765*. Pittsburgh, Pennsylvania: University of Pittsburgh Press, 2003.
Weisberger, Bernard A. *America Afire: Jefferson, Adams, and the Revolutionary Election of 1800*. New York: HarperCollins, 2000.
Wood, Gordon S. *The Radicalism of the American Revolution*. New York: Vintage Books, 1993.
———. *Empire of Liberty: A History of the Early Republic, 1789–1815*. New York: Penguin Books, 2004.
———. *Revolutionary Characters: What Made the Founders Different*. New York: Penguin Books, 2006.

———. *The Americanization of Benjamin Franklin.* Oxford: Oxford University Press, 2009.
Wright, Benjamin F. *The Federalist: The Famous Papers on the Principles of American Government: Alexander Hamilton, James Madison, John Jay.* New York: Metro Books, 2002.
Zobel, Hiller B. *The Boston Massacre.* New York: W. W. Norton & Company, 1970.

Video Resources:
Guelzo, Allen C. The Great Courses: *America's Founding Fathers* (Course N. 8525). Chantilly, Virginia: The Teaching Company, 2017.

Online Resources:
Archives.gov – for information on the Constitutional Convention.
CauseofLiberty.blogspot.com – for information on Daniel Carroll.
ColonialHall.com – for information about the signers of the Declaration of Independence.
DSDI1776.com – for information on many Founders.
FamousAmericans.net – for information on many Founders.
FindaGrave.com – for burial information, vital statistics and obituaries.
FirstLadies.org – for information on Abigail Adams.
Newspapers.com – Hundreds of newspaper articles were accessed—too numerous to mention here.
NPS.gov – for information on various park sites.
TeachingAmericanHistory.com – for information on Charles Pinckney and George Wythe.
TheHistoryJunkie.com – for information on multiple Founders.
USHistory.org – for information on multiple Founders.
Wikipedia.com – for general historical information.

Index

Adams, John, viii, 4–5, 19, 27, 47–53, 63, 76, 81, 96, 114–15, 120, 128, 139, 141, 197, 201, 203, 225, 250, 252, 275, 282
Adams, Samuel, 5–6, 8, 19, 53–59, 113, 128, 138–39, 141, 258, 275, 282
Adams, Thomas, 233–35, 283
Articles of Confederation, ix-x, 3, 6, 9, 11, 27, 53, 57, 59–60, 64, 67, 69, 71, 73–74, 76, 79, 81, 84, 86–88, 90, 93, 95, 97, 100–102, 116, 119, 121, 123, 125, 128, 138, 141, 143, 146, 149, 155, 158–59, 161, 164–65, 168, 171–73, 177, 180, 184, 187, 193, 196–97, 199, 203–4, 212, 214-215, 217-218, 220, 222, 224, 226, 228-229, 231, 233–234, 236, 238, 242, 244, 246, 248, 250, 256, 258-260, 263, 266–67, 270, 274–76, 278, 280, 282–83 (signers), 284–92 (text)
Banister, John, 236–39, 283
Bartlett, Josiah, 260–65, 267–69, 283
Brandywine, Battle of, viii, 143, 166, 187, 231
Brownson, Nathan, 35–37, 282
Burke, Thoms, 142–45, 282
Carroll of Carrollton, Charles, 42–47, 136, 212, 282
Chase, Samuel, 44–45, 134–37, 210, 282
Clark, Abraham, 185–88, 215, 283
Clingan, William, 164–67, 283
Collins, John, 270–73, 283
Conway Cabal, ix, 46, 119, 138, 141, 180, 205
Dana, Francis, 141, 196–98, 258, 275, 283
Drayton, William Henry, 106, 226–28, 246, 257–58, 283
Duane, James, 74–78, 114, 282
Duer, William, 79–83, 282
Dyer, Eliphalet, 25–28, 250, 282
Ellery, William, 148–49, 168–71, 283
Elmer, Jonathan, 154–57, 215, 283
Folsom, Nathaniel, 65–68, 184, 282
Forbes, James, 209–10, 283
Frost, George, 183–84, 283
Gates, Horatio, ix, 141, 151, 210
Germantown, Battle of, ix, 72, 166, 187, 231, 241
Gerry, Elbridge, viii, 59–64, 115, 141, 198, 258, 275–76, 282
Hancock, John, ix, 3–8, 11, 46, 56–59, 88, 115, 119, 128–29, 138, 141, 260, 263, 275–76, 282
Harnett, Cornelius, 84–86, 143, 282
Harrison, Benjamin V, viii, 19, 111–17, 127, 282
Harvie, John, 158–61, 283

Henry, John Jr., 211–13, 283
Heyward, Thomas Jr., 100–104, 107, 245–46, 258, 282
Holten, Samuel, 274–77, 283
Hosmer, Titus, 275–78, 283
Huntington, Samuel, 32, 218–21, 225, 280, 283
Hutson, Richard, 246–47, 256–59, 283
Jones, Joseph, 118–20, 282
Lancaster, Pennsylvania, viii–ix, 36, 97, 116, 119, 132, 143, 151, 155, 164–65, 189, 282
Langworthy, Edward, 172–74, 283
Laurens, Henry, x, 9–15, 88–89, 128, 246–47, 257–58, 282
Law, Richard, 131–33, 282
Lee, Francis Lightfoot, 121–25, 282
Lee, Richard Henry, 46, 113–15, 121, 123–30, 148, 276, 282
Lewis, Francis, 177–82, 283
Livingston, Philip, 179, 200, 252–55, 283
Lovell, James, viii, 138–41, 275, 282
Marchant, Henry, viii, 146–50, 282
Mathews, John, 101, 244–47, 258, 283
McKean, Thomas, 199–203, 283
Middleton, Arthur, 105–10, 114, 247, 257, 282
Morris, Gouverneur, 204–8, 258, 283
Morris, Robert, 81–82, 90–94, 128, 152, 165, 210, 282
Paoli, Battle of, viii
Penn, John, 87–89, 282
Philadelphia, Pennsylvania, vii-x, 6, 11, 14, 17–19, 21, 26–27, 32, 36, 39, 45–47, 56–57, 60, 66–67, 70, 76, 86, 90–97, 102, 109, 113–16, 119, 122, 132, 143, 146–47, 151, 154–55, 163–64, 173, 176–77, 180, 184, 186, 189–90, 192–95, 199, 201, 203, 206, 209–10, 212, 215–16, 223–32, 242, 246–47, 250, 252, 255, 258, 262–63, 271, 276, 280, 292
Plater, George, 240–43, 283
Reading, Pennsylvania, viii-ix
Reed, Joseph, 165, 229–32, 283
Roberdeau, Daniel, 95–99, 165, 282
Rumsey, Benjamin, 162–63, 283
Saratoga, Battle of, ix, 80, 224
Scudder, Nathaniel, 214–17, 283
Sherman, Roger, 50, 128, 219, 248–51, 258, 280, 283
Smith, James, 189–92, 283
Smith, Jonathan Bayard, 165, 193–95, 283

Smith, William, 151–53, 204–5, 245, 282
Thomson, Charles, x, 17–23, 169, 282
Treaty of Alliance (with France), ix, 50, 72, 119
Valley Forge, Pennsylvania, ix, 46, 68, 97, 159, 180, 196–97, 205
Walton, George, 38–41, 282
Washington, George, vii-ix, 6, 20–21, 46, 50, 52, 56, 59, 64, 78, 83, 90, 92–93, 97, 110, 115–16, 118–20, 123, 128, 131, 133, 136, 138, 140–41, 148, 150, 159, 171, 180–81, 187, 197, 201, 205–6, 220, 224–25, 229–31, 238, 241

Wentworth, John, 67, 262, 266–69, 283
Williams, William, 29–34, 282
Witherspoon, John, viii-ix, 69–73, 81, 181, 186, 215, 217, 282
Wolcott, Oliver, 32, 222–25, 280, 283
Wood, Joseph, 175–76, 283
York, Pennsylvania, ix-x, 11, 14, 27, 36, 67, 101, 116, 119, 132, 143, 149, 151, 155, 159, 163–65, 173, 176, 180, 184, 189–90, 192, 209–11, 214, 224, 238, 242, 246, 252, 254–55, 258, 267, 275, 279, 282–83

www.ingramcontent.com/pod-product-compliance
Lightning Source LLC
Chambersburg PA
CBHW010929180426
43194CB00045B/2837